D0552693

The Good Guide to the Lakes

Hunter Davies

Updated by Tom Holman

F

FRANCES LINCOLN LIMITED

PUBLISHERS

www.franceslincoln.com

Frances Lincoln Limited
4 Torriano Mews
Torriano Avenue
London NW5 2RZ
www.franceslincoln.com

The Good Guide to the Lakes
Copyright © Hunter Davies and Tom Holman 2008

British Library Cataloguing in Publication Data
A catalogue record for this book is available from the British
Library

ISBN 978-0-7112-2861-0

Designed by Ian Hunt

Printed in China

9 8 7 6 5 4 3 2 1

Contents

About our star ratings

Throughout this book we have used star ratings for almost everything, from mountains to restaurants, as a way of indicating places or services that we think are worth experiencing. Listings that have no stars are not meant to be avoided altogether, but they are there mainly for reference. All listings are arranged by star rating downwards and then alphabetically.

★★★ Not to be missed
★★ Highly recommended
★ Interesting

Introduction

This is the seventh brand-new, updated, totally excellent edition of *The Good Guide to the Lakes*, and the last one for which I will have the pleasure of writing the Introduction. But we'll come to that in a moment.

It all began 25 years ago when we were at our cottage near Caldbeck. Another rainy day and we'd done all the local hills, examined all the gifts in Caldbeck's only gift shop, and now our younger daughter Flora, then aged eight, and her two cousins, were moaning on: what are we going to do *now*? I was supposed to be the local expert, written books about Lakeland – surely I had lots of suggestions. I searched around for a guidebook that would give me not just ideas, but opinions about whether places would be worth seeing if and when we got there. But I could find nothing suitable.

So I decided to do it myself. Research and write and publish my own personalised Lakeland guidebook. I feared an ordinary publisher would want to restrain my opinions and be unamused by what I thought were my amusing remarks. They'd also leave empty pages and blanks all over the place. That's what publishers do, if you don't watch them. I'd recently done a children's book in which there were eight empty pages. Such a waste. I wanted every inch of space in my book to be filled up.

I thought I knew northern Lakeland well enough, but not the rest, so I hired Colin Shelbourn, fresh out of York University and then living in Grange-over-Sands, to cover the south. He also did some funny drawings, which we used as chapter headings.

I decided the book would be printed in Cumbria – why give work to outsiders – and we would pay for everything, meals and hotels, and accept no advertisements, even hidden ones. So many guidebooks do this, behind the scenes, charging hotels and such like a fee to appear in their listings.

A.J.P. Taylor, the famous historian, wrote from London and said it was a book 'of a thousand delights', though he didn't think we'd given enough prominence to the delights of Pillar. We had some complaints, of course. The Town Clerk of Barrow didn't like what we said about Barrow. The Lodore Swiss Hotel refused to stock copies because we had classed it as an 'Executive' hotel, as opposed to Classy or De Luxe, my other categories. A timeshare complex threatened to sue because they were not in the book.

1034. A CORNER OF LAKE SIDE TEA GARDENS. DERWENTWATER.

The Earl of Lonsdale wrote and said he was upset that we had recommended Askham as a village to visit. Absolute strangers were now knocking on his door, which was clearly marked Private. I read on quickly, fearing legal trouble, but he went on to say he was enclosing the money for six more copies. (And at full price. Toffs usually try for discount.)

As a marketing device – not that I knew anything about marketing – I got 1,000 free bars of Kendal mint cake from Romneys, which were given away to the first 1,000 purchasers of the book. (I didn't know anything about publishing either, or I would have been aware that this was illegal under the then Net Book Agreement whereby publishers didn't give inducements for sales.) There was a minor scene in a bookshop in Kendal when a customer, having been handed his free bar of mint cake along with my book, threw it back at the assistant in disgust. He turned out to be a dentist.

The first print, in April 1984, was 11,000 – and sold out at once. I went mad and ordered a reprint of 15,000, and then another. In all, that first edition – 226 pages, price £2.95 – sold 31,000 copies. I've had to look up those facts. And I still can't believe the ridiculously titchy price.

I was so carried away with the success of my little venture that I gave £1,000 from the profits to the Cumbria Tourist Board to set up and run an annual Lakeland Book of the Year Award. It's still going strong and is now a big event in Cumbria's literary and social calendar as the prize-giving takes place at a charity lunch at a different Lakeland hotel each year. I then said that completely new editions of the Good Guide would come out at regular intervals, for ever and ever. This has also come to pass.

For those collecting previous editions – surely there must be some by now – the colours of the six editions so far, in order, have been white, blue, red, green, yellow and brown. I was recently asked for a copy of the second edition by an American academic who was doing a book about indices. In the index of that second edition, under D, we had included 'Dump – see Barrow-in-Furness'. A pretty pathetic joke, which, of course, I now regret, as Barrow is a truly wonderful place. The academic wanted to include it in his book as, apparently, it was the only example he could find of humour, or at least childish abuse, in an index.

The gap, alas, between new editions, then tended to get longer. Not quite sure why. Life, I suppose, other projects, family affairs, Foot and Mouth – I remember blaming that one year for putting publication back. It's now five years since the sixth edition came out in 2003. So it's long overdue. Sorry about the wait. But it's been well worth it, as I hope you'll agree.

Miss Potter

Since the last edition, Lakeland has had a huge boost to its national and worldwide exposure thanks to the wonders of film and TV. *Miss Potter*, a very nice film, as everyone agreed, starring Renee Zellweger and Ewan McGregor, introduced many new readers to Beatrix Potter's books but also to the beauties of Lakeland. It did take a few liberties with her life and the scenery, which gave added interest to clever clogs trying to work out – as I did – how a shot of Loweswater turns into a view of Derwentwater. But of course we all loved it, especially the Cumbria Tourist Board. Lakeland did look awfully pretty.

In the film Beatrix Potter appeared surprised by her own success and innocent of things like royalties, but in reality she was pushing her own products from the beginning. As early as 1903 she registered a Peter Rabbit doll at the Patent Office and had hawked it round the big shops, such as Harrods. She also created Peter Rabbit wallpaper, which was taken by Sanderson.

In real life, Norman Warne, her publisher with whom she fell in love, proposed to her by letter, not in her bedroom as it was touchingly portrayed in the film. They were never ever alone with each other – always with a chaperone. The man she eventually married, William Heelis, a local solicitor, was five years younger, but in the film he is made older to accommodate a childhood meeting, which never actually happened.

None of these changes, or simplifications, was major, and they didn't worry me as the film was basically true to her life and character, as we think we know it.

It's been a huge success in Japan, which is not surprising as they adore Beatrix Potter and her books. There is now a Beatrix Potter museum in Japan, which is an exact reproduction of Hill Top. Except for one thing. It's twice as big.

It will be interesting in 2013 to see what happens with her books. It will then be 70 years since she died, and in theory her stuff will be out of copyright. Since 1901, when Peter Rabbit first appeared, 300 million of her books have been sold. The annual proceeds, from her works and associated merchandising, now reaches £225 million. Penguin own the copyright, having bought Warne, her publisher, for a reported £6 million in 1984. So they have done very well out of her – though they have handled her name and estate very tastefully. But will other, rougher, pushier publishers try to barge in? Or can Penguin somehow protect Miss Potter – for ever and ever? We shall see.

Wainwright

It was the centenary of the birth of the Blessed Wainwright in 2007, and BBC TV did him proud with an excellent hour-long documentary on his life. There were also two series of films about his walks – with possibly more to come. If you watched the documentary, and had your best specs on and concentrated really hard when they whizzed through all those credits at the end – so unfair how they do it – you might have spotted the name of the producer. Flora Davies. Yes, my little girl.

All the AW programmes were highly successful and got repeated several times, bringing millions of new people to the genius of AW and the delights of Lakeland. The result has been a huge increase in sales of Wainwright's *Pictorial Guides* and also in membership of the Wainwright Society. This is a fairly recent society, set up in 2003, which every Lakeland lover should join.

So what's the next Lakeland-ish subject for our film and TV makers? There has been talk for years of the novels of Hugh Walpole, especially Rogue Herries, being turned into films, but it never seems to happen. Coleridge and Wordsworth have appeared in films and TV dramas from time to time, but not yet on a Hollywood scale, like Miss Potter. I think Southey has been long overlooked. He married Coleridge's sister and got left with two families to look after when Coleridge did a runner, which resulted in lots of tears and drama.

Or how about Eddie Stobart, one of Cumbria's all-time greats? His rise from rural Hesket Newmarket into a national – nay, a European cult – is a story of our times. Don't you think those handsome lorries with pretty feminine names and lovely livery would make a perfect road movie?

Toys and bombers

Since the last edition there have, of course, been lots of changes, with quite a few restaurants and other attractions packing up. I was personally upset by the closure of the Toy Museum in Cockermouth, a museum that had been going for many years. This sort of dotty, one-man operation finds it harder to keep going now that museum authorities seem convinced that what the public needs is audio-visual fripperies, full of light and sound, buttons and projections, but very little real and original content. But I was pleased to see a new mining museum opening in Keswick and doing so well.

I'll have to stop talking about the Cumbria Tourist Board. That changed its name in 2006. We now have to call it Cumbria Tourism. It's also moved offices, from Windermere to Staveley. Carlisle Airport, as ever, is promising to tool up and have regular flights all over the place, but I'll believe that when I see it. The threat of mass unemployment, speed

The Royal Oak Hotel, Keswick

boat owners committing suicide, Windermere being a waste land, didn't quite happen. It was in 2005 that at long last the 10mph (16kph) speed limit came in on Windermere. Obviously some businesses have been badly affected, but the overall results have been good for the environment and for most visitors.

Recent visitors to Lakeland, attracted no doubt by the beauty and peace and quiet, a chance to get away from it all, have included some terrorist bombers. That's according to a recent court case, when it came out that a group of them had gone on an outdoor training camp in the Langdale Valley. Had they read this book? Anyway it must have cheered up Cumbria Tourism after all the stick they had received for appealing only to the white, middle-aged middle classes.

Future treats

By the next edition the Lake District could be designated a World Heritage Site. An all-party parliamentary group has been pushing for it. I'm sure the Cumbria Tourist Board, sorry Cumbria Tourism, will be pleased, but I can't see that it

BASSENTHWAITE LAKE AND SKIDDAW
LAKE DISTRICT NATIONAL PARK
CUMBERLAND

will make much difference. There's no development money or special grants, just extra status. And we have lashings of that already. Everyone now knows it's a World Heritage Training Site.

By the edition after next, something much more exciting might have happened – Chateau Lakeland. Lots of vines have been planted at Holehird, the Lakeland Horticultural Society gardens near Windermere. Thanks to global warming, it's thought that grapes grown outside in Lakeland will now mature and be suitable for

wine making. Tests will show the best varieties for our climate, and about the year 2012 we might even get some bottles. Let's hope they can produce something suitable to be drunk with tatie pot.

Stock Exchange alert, mega take-over ...

Yes, there will be another edition, and another, for ever, because Forster Davies, the little publishing company that has been producing the *Good Guide* since 1984, has been taken over. Not by Rupert Murdoch, though obviously he is spitting to have missed it, but by Frances Lincoln, a very distinguished publishing company, which do a lot of outdoor books. A large three figure sum has changed hands (nineteen shillings, eleven pence ha'penny). The boss of the company is John Nicoll, who comes originally from Kendal. The late Frances Lincoln was his wife, who began the company thirty

years ago. They are now the publishers of all the Wainwright books, and making a brilliant job of it. It's a perfect home for *The Good Guide to the Lakes*.

At the same time, I'm also handing over the editorship of the guide to Tom Holman. He has been responsible for the research and all the new ideas and topics in this edition. By coincidence, he is a graduate of York University and lives near Grange-over-Sands – just like Colin Shelbourn, all those years ago. Colin, by the way, is now a full-time Lakeland author and cartoonist for the *Westmorland Gazette*. Pam Williamson, who took over from Colin as chief researcher, is now a well-known Lakeland artist.

Forster Davies was just me, of course, though I tried to pretend it was a proper company. The Forster part came from my dear wife, a real Cumbrian, born in Carlisle, whereas I didn't come over the border from Scotland till I was aged four.

During these last few years it has become harder to fit in the organising and research, printing and distribution, along with my other projects, especially having to get to grips with all these boring websites, whatever they are, and this internet nonsense, which a modern guidebook publisher and author should be able to use.

It needs a proper, efficient, well-run company to do it justice, which Frances Lincoln certainly is, to expand and develop and take it forward. On my own, though, working with pigeons and a quill pen, plus my trusty Amstrad, I did manage to shift 100,000 copies, making it the bestselling Lakeland guidebook in modern history.

Thanks to everyone who helped me, to the friends and experts who gave advice and, of course, to all readers. I know that Tom Holman and Frances Lincoln will take it on to even greater glories. I wish them success. And most of all, fun.

Hunter Davies
Loweswater, 2008

11

CHAPTER ONE

Planning

*Things to know before leaving home
or when you arrive*

What is it?

Is that all it is, that little hilly region up in the top left-hand corner of the map of England? How can so much fuss have been made for the last 200 years over such a small area? Ah, but in that pocket handkerchief area are all of nature's delights, plus a few manmade wonders, as you will quickly discover.

The Lake District is all in the county of Cumbria, formerly Cumberland, Westmorland and a bit of Lancashire until the boundaries were redrawn in 1974. It is now England's second largest county in terms of area at 2,630 square miles (6,811 sq km), though one of its emptiest in terms of people (just under half a million at the last count). There is a large circle inside the county called the Lake District National Park, which was established in 1951. Its boundary line can seem perverse, cutting out some parts of Cumbria that are equally beautiful, but it does contain the jewels in the Lake District's crown.

The National Park measures only 30 miles (48 km) across, making it not much bigger than Greater London. It stretches west as far as the coast in some places, and is bordered on its east side by the M6 motorway. If you were driving fast you could pass the Lake District in half an hour and never know it was there. What a tragedy that would be.

The Lake District National Park covers an area of 885 square miles (2,292 sq km) and among other things contains England's highest mountain and deepest lake. There are four mountains over 3,000 feet (914 m), and the lakes are up to 10 miles (16 km) long. As far as the world's highest mountains and largest lakes are concerned they are mere pimples, but they are big in British terms, and the biggest in English terms.

This place has been called lots of things over the years. Cumbria Tourism billed it for years as 'English Lakeland – the Most Beautiful Corner of England', then changed it to 'Lakeland – the Roots of Heaven' and then, rather more modestly, 'Cumbria – The Lake District'. Some people know it as the Lakes, the English Lakes or Lakeland. When we refer to these places in this book, we mean that part of Cumbria designated as the Lake District National Park.

How to get there

Road

Most visitors zoom up the M6 by car from the south. As motorways go, it can be surprisingly attractive, far less crowded than stretches around Manchester and Birmingham, and once beyond Lancaster the Lake District's scenery and mountains come into view. Watch out for the police: empty stretches of the M6 in Cumbria can make the mind wander, the heart soar and the speedometer rise above 70mph (110kph).

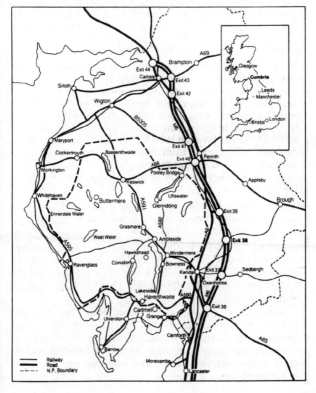

From London it's about 260 miles (418 km) to Kendal, the southern gateway of the Lake District. Turn left at junctions 36 or 37 for southern parts like Kendal and Coniston, and at junction 40 for the northern or western Lakes and Keswick and Ullswater. With clear traffic it's four or five hours to the Lake District from London or three from Birmingham. The M6 proper peters out just north of Carlisle, but those coming down from Scotland – from Glasgow or Edinburgh – do have reasonably good dual carriageways most of the way to the motorway.

It's less easy coming to the Lake District from the east. The roads over the Pennines are pretty, and the one over Hartside Pass, via Alston, is sensational, but they are narrow and twisty and can take forever. Don't try a short cut or attempt a minor road if you're coming for the first time. You might never be seen again.

Rail

There are no direct trains into the Lake District. The main rail gateway is Oxenholme, where you can change and travel as far as Windermere on the only railway line inside the National Park. There were others, many of them set up to serve the mining industries, but they have now all gone. It means that Oxenholme, a toy town station just outside Kendal, has become a meeting place for what seems in the summer to be all the rucksacks in the Western world. But it is handily placed on the west coast main line from London to Scotland, and – Virgin Trains willing – you can get there from most British cities far quicker than by road. The fastest train times are:

London	3 hours
Birmingham	2 hours
Manchester	1 hour 15 minutes
Liverpool	1 hour 30 minutes
Glasgow	1 hour 45 minutes
Edinburgh	2 hours

An alternative station gateway for the north Lakes is further up the London to Oxenholme line at Penrith, though you have to transfer by bus or taxi to your destination. Carlisle is another stop on the line, and it connects with the amazing Cumbrian coastal line – how did Beeching never kill it? This is very handy for exploring the western Lakes and the Furness peninsula, though it never actually touches any of the Lakes proper.

Wherever you come in, National Rail Enquiries can help you plan your journey (tel. 08457 48 49 50 or visit *www.nationalrail.co.uk*). Virgin Trains can book your tickets to Oxenholme, Penrith or Carlisle (tel. 08457 222 333 or visit *www.virgintrains.co.uk*). For more on rail transport within Cumbria see Chapter 3.

Bus

National Express have good connections into the Lake District. There's at least one bus a day from London Victoria, Manchester's Chorlton Street station and Birmingham's coach station to Windermere, Ambleside, Grasmere and Keswick. Fares are generally much lower than train tickets (tel. 08705 808080 or visit *www.nationalexpress.com*).

Air

There is no large Lakeland airport, though Carlisle has a little one and is trying to market itself as a gateway to the Lakes. If you happen to own a private plane this is the handiest place to land it.

Useful resources

If you're coming to Britain from abroad it's possible to get information and advice about a holiday in the Lake District from the nearest office of Visit Britain. Most major cities in the US and most capital cities elsewhere have a Visit Britain office (start at *www.visitbritain.com*).

Within Britain Cumbria Tourism can provide a wealth of information about the Lakes (tel. 015398 22222 or visit *www.golakes.co.uk*). Copies of Cumbria Tourism's official annual brochure guide, which includes comprehensive details of accommodation, can be ordered from the website or by calling the brochure line, 0870 067 2904. Its Booking Hotline, 0845 450 1199, is a useful service for all the accommodation needed for late bookings, short breaks or special offers on holidays in Cumbria, though they do levy a £3.00 service fee. For all advance travel queries contact the Traveline (tel. 0871 200 2233 or visit *www.traveline.info*).

Websites offering information about the Lake District are springing up all the time. Ten of the most useful for planning a trip are:

www.lake-district.gov.uk
The site of the Lake District National Park, with information about its work and events as well as some of the best things to see and do within the park.

www.lakedistrictoutdoors.co.uk
Cumbria Tourism's online guide to the great outdoors of the Lake District. Contains walking and cycling routes around the region, as well as public transport and tourist information, weather details and some ideas for high-adrenaline thrills.

www.cumbria.gov.uk
Cumbria County Council site. Boring stuff about bin collections and so on, but some useful information for trip planning too.

www.thecumbriadirectory.com
Searchable database that takes in tourist resources, accommodation and businesses, divided by area.

www.visitcumbria.com
Comprehensive guide to Lakeland attractions, with excellent aerial photos.

www.lakesnet.co.uk
Searchable listings of events, businesses and places.

www.lakelandwebs.co.uk
Gateway to some useful sites for regions of the Lake District: Buttermere, Wasdale, Gosforth, Eskdale, Langdale and Coniston. Good, solid local info.

www.lakelandgateway.info
Council-backed guide to the southern half of the Lakes.

www.western-lakedistrict.co.uk
What's best in the west, run by the area's tourism partnership.

www.lakelandcam.co.uk
New pictures are uploaded every day of one man's walks around the Lakes. Good for seeing what the weather's like or if you're pining for the Lake District from afar.

The Lake District Visitor Centre

Once you've arrived in the Lake District there are plenty of places and people to help you plan your time. The main resource is the Lake District National Park Authority's Lake District Visitor Centre at Brockhole near Windermere. It's open daily from 10.00am to 5.00pm from April to October inclusive (tel. 015394 46601 or visit *www.lake-district.gov.uk*). The grounds are open every day of the year from dawn to 6.00pm.

The LDNPA's aim is to get you to start your holiday here, stock up on information and then sally forth among the lakes and fells, a better informed person. There are also things to amuse and entertain, especially aimed at family groups. If you want to spend some time wandering about, try a sunny day in the middle of the week, because it gets very busy on wet weekends.

The building is easy to miss, despite its size. From the name 'Visitor Centre' you might expect something modern, but Brockhole is, in fact, a stately home, a large, detached building in its own grounds on the shores of Windermere, about 2 miles (3.2 km) south of Ambleside on the A591. Keep an eye out for the signs. Even when you're inside the car park it is still confusing because you can't tell the way to the house. Go through a little house, which leads on to the Big House.

In the 19th century Brockhole was the country home of a Lancashire cotton magnate, one of the many who built imposing residences along the shores of Windermere. It was converted in 1969 to its present use. In 1996 they did another internal re-vamp, adding a new exhibition about the Lakes. It's hard to understand why they bothered, because you can see plastic notices, plastic walls and plastic trees in any motorway service station. Most visitors probably aren't even aware of it as they traipse through into what is now a mega-shop. But they have made much more of an effort to attract and entertain families with new walking trails, an adventure playground and audio-visual presentations. The best things are often the special events and talks by local experts. Check beforehand to see what's on.

Brockhole has excellent grounds of some 30 acres (over 12 ha), landscaped by Thomas Mawson and all open to the public, with picnic spots and play areas. Don't miss the fine vegetable garden, which looks as if it's private but isn't, or the Orangery (no oranges, but grapes if you're lucky). You can catch Windermere Lake Cruises' boats to and from Brockhole every day from Easter to September (tel. 015394 43360 or visit *www.windermere-lakecruises.co.uk* for times).

Brockhole has wisely made admission free to help bring back the crowds, though there is a catch: parking has to be paid for and isn't cheap, even if you're only visiting briefly. It's best to arrive by bus – no. 555 and no. 599 will drop you at the entrance – which allows you a totally free day at one of the best access points to Windermere's eastern shore.

Brockhole currently gets about 100,000 visitors a year, but numbers have been dropping lately, and it runs at a loss. At the time of writing the Lake District National Park Authority was drawing up new plans for the house, which may or may not include knocking it down to create a brand-new whizz-bang visitor experience. It says the old house isn't very practical and is eating up money, but the plans have already caused a lot of fuss among locals.

Other Tourist Information Centres

There are plenty of Tourist Information Centres (TICs) dotted around the Lake District, despite recent funding cut-backs that have led to some branches being closed by the Lake District National Park Authority. The branches are now run variously by the LDNPA, Cumbria Tourism, local councils and volunteers who got fed up with the cutbacks and decided they could do a better job for the area themselves.

These TICs provide information on what to see and do as well as advice on transport. They should all have lists of local accommodation, and most provide a booking service for personal callers. Opening hours vary, but most major centres will be open daily from 10.00am to 6.00pm in summer, per-haps closing earlier in winter. They are open all year round unless otherwise stated:

Town Hall, Front Street, **Alston** (tel. 01434 382244)

Market Cross, **Ambleside** (tel. 015394 32582)

Moot Hall, Boroughgate, **Appleby** (tel. 017683 51177)

Forum 28, Duke Street, **Barrow-in-Furness** (tel. 01229 894784)

Bowness Bay, **Bowness-on-Windermere** (tel. 015394 42895)

Moot Hall, Market Place, **Brampton** (tel. 01697 73433);
open Easter to October

Town Hall, The Square, **Broughton-in-Furness**
(tel. 01229 716115)

Old Town Hall, Greenmarket, **Carlisle** (tel. 01228 625600)

Town Hall, Market Street, **Cockermouth** (tel. 01900 822634)

Ruskin Avenue, **Coniston** (tel. 015394 41533)

Main Street, **Egremont** (tel. 01946 820693)

Main car park, **Glenridding** (tel. 017684 82414)

Victoria Hall, Main Street, **Grange-over-Sands**
(tel. 015395 34026)

Town Hall, Highgate, **Kendal** (tel. 015397 25758)

Moot Hall, Market Square, **Keswick** (tel. 017687 72645)

Main Street, **Kirkby Lonsdale** (tel. 015242 71437)

Market Street, **Kirkby Stephen** (tel. 017683 71199)

Maritime Museum, Senhouse Street, **Maryport**
(tel. 01900 702840)

Station Building, **Millom** (tel. 012297 71762)

Robinson's School, Middlegate, **Penrith** (tel. 017688 67466)

Rheged (tel. 017688 60034)

Main Street, **Sedbergh** (tel. 015396 20125)

Visitors Centre, **Sellafield** (tel. 019467 76510)

Criffel Street, **Silloth-on-Solway** (tel. 06973 31944)

M6 service station, **Southwaite** (tel. 016974 73445)

Coronation Hall, County Square, **Ulverston**
(tel. 01229 587120)

Market Hall, Market Place, **Whitehaven** (tel. 01946 598914)

Victoria Street, **Windermere** (tel. 015394 46499)

Finkle Street, **Workington** (tel. 01900 606699)

Since the funding cutbacks, several tourist hotspots have had
to make do with **Visitor Information Points**, places offering a
more limited range of information about what to see and do.
They can be found at:

Market Street, **Dalton-in-Furness**

Dale Lodge Hotel, Red Bank Road, **Grasmere**

Summittreks, The Square, **Hawkshead**

Finkle Street, **Pooley Bridge**

Seatoller Barn, **Seatoller**

Waterhead (promenade in summer, pier in winter)

Guidebooks

Since Thomas West wrote the first proper guide to the Lake District in 1778, well over 50,000 books have been published about the Lake District, more than on any similar sized region in the UK. The choice is enormous and still growing.

Beware the over-glossy booklets with chocolate box covers and unbelievably blue skies and lakes. They have probably put their money and energy into colour reproduction at the expense of the words and new information. Also be wary of publications taking advertisements. How can they possibly give real opinions?

William Wordsworth's ★★ *Guide to the Lakes* was first published in 1835 but is now available from Frances Lincoln in a facsimile edition. Don't try to plan anything from it, but it still makes fascinating reading while you're on holiday or afterwards, and some of Wordsworth's thoughts on the weather, walking and tourism are still spot on today. Notice how many subsequent writers have pinched ideas and phrases from Wordsworth when they're trying to capture the essence of Lakeland scenery.

Walking books

★★★ *The Pictorial Guide to the Lakeland Fells*
By Alfred Wainwright; published in seven volumes and a box set by Frances Lincoln. Essential for all walkers. Wainwright divided the Lake District into seven areas, so buy the one you will be visiting most or buy them all to take home and wonder at. In his own words and with his own pen (for there is not an ounce of printer's type in any of his books), he draws and describes exactly every walk up every fell you could ever possibly make. He spent 13 years on his walks, and though the first volume came out in 1955, they reprint endlessly and are still hugely popular.

Frances Lincoln is now reissuing the books in alternative editions, updated to make sure that all the paths and directions are correct. And you can even now get a Wainwright podcast, downloadable to your MP3 player, to accompany you up Helm Crag (the words from his book are spoken by a very convincing actor; get it from *www.golakes.co.uk/wainwrightpodcast*). Flat cap nav, not sat nav. But more than 50 years on, the original books still fly off the shelves, each of them a work of art and full of wit, wisdom and love of the Lakes. The first editions are collectors' pieces. Buy them now as they keep going up in price. They will be a joy for ever. *Wainwright: The Biography* by Hunter Davies is meanwhile available in paperback from Orion. Don't say you haven't read it.

★★ *Best Walks in the Lake District*
By Frank Duerden (Frances Lincoln). A collection of 40 fine walks for all abilities, ranging from short strolls on the flat to day-long horseshoe hikes.

★★ *Complete Lakeland Fells*
By Bill Birkett (Collins). Probably the closest a modern walker has got to Wainwright in chronicling all the fells. An encyclopedic book of fells and all the ascents of them. Birkett is also the author of several other books on the Lakes, including some fine collections of photographs.

★★ *Pathfinder Lake District Walks* and *More Lake District Walks*
These are good slim volumes of various routes, with Ordnance Survey 1:25,000 maps to go with them (Jarrold Publishing).

★★ *Rocky Rambler's Wild Walks*
By Colin Shelbourn (Cicerone Press). A great guide to ten short walks for children. They'll love being put in charge of directions (and they'll probably spend less time working out maps and getting lost).

★ *The Lakeland Peaks*
By W.A. Poucher (Frances Lincoln). An alternative or more likely companion to Wainwright. Dozens of routes up the fells, nicely illustrated by tracks superimposed on photographs.

★ *On High Lakeland Fells* and *On Low Lakeland Fells*
By Bob Allen (Frances Lincoln). Real walkers' stuff. Be wary of his estimates of time and exertion level – he must be very fit.

There are plenty of specialist walking books catering for the quick and slow, those looking for a nice church or a nice pub. Good ones include *Lakeland Church Walks* by Peter Donaghy and John Laidler, *Walks in Ancient Lakeland* by Robert Harris (both Sigma) and *Short Walks in North Lakeland* and *South Lakeland* and *West Lakeland* (Cicerone Press). If you're after an epic walking tour of the Lakes, try Jim Reid's *Tour of the Lake District* (Cicerone Press). Cyclists have *Cycle Tours of Cumbria and the Lakes* (Philip's).

General Lakeland books

Some more good books about the Lake District or set there. This doesn't include the usual suspects – William Wordsworth, Beatrix Potter, Arthur Ransome *et al.* – because you'll find them everywhere you go in any case.

★★ *Portrait of the Lakes*
By Norman Nicholson (Hale). The late Norman Nicholson has been our most recent poet of the Lakes, born and bred in Millom. Good on history and geology. Perhaps the best-written modern book on Lakeland. Now sadly out of print, so look in second-hand bookshops.

★ *Feet in the Clouds*
By Richard Askwith (Aurum Press). A brilliant portrait of the lunatic sport of fell-running and its hardy legends. It's as much about the Lake District as it is about the running.

★ *The Grasmere Journals*
By Dorothy Wordsworth (OUP). A facsimile of the diaries
that William's sister kept of their life together at Dove Cottage
in the early 1800s. Knowing something of Wordsworth's life
beforehand will help you understand what is going on,
because it is very confused in parts. But there are charming
and illuminating descriptions of day-to-day life with her
Beloved Brother, either helping him with his muse or making
his pies.

★ *Haweswater*
By Sarah Hall (Faber). A vivid novel set in the Mardale Valley
in the 1930s as they flooded it to make the Haweswater
reservoir. Hall is Cumbrian born and bred.

★ *Life and Traditions of the Lake District*
By William Rollinson (Weidenfeld & Nicolson). An original
work of non-fiction describing and illustrating the vanishing
or vanished folk culture of Lakeland, from dry stone walls,
sports and dialect to diet and folk medicine.

★ *A Lifetime of Mountains*
By A. Harry Griffin (Aurum Press). A collection of the late
journalist's 'Country Diary' pieces for the *Guardian*, which
he wrote for more than 50 years. Griffin has also written a
handful of other good books on the Lakes and its people,
including a memoir of rock climbing heroics, *The Coniston
Tigers* (Sigma).

★ *A Literary Guide to the Lake District*
By Grevel Lindop (Sigma). The best guide by far to the dozens
of literary places and people of the Lakes.

★ *The Maid of Buttermere*
By Melvyn Bragg (Sceptre). Just one of Bragg's many
Lakeland novels – the romantic and tragic story of Lakeland's
renowned beauty.

★ *Recollections of the Lakes and Lake Poets*
By Thomas De Quincey (various editions). Wonderfully
indiscreet memoir of The Big Three – Wordsworth,
Coleridge, Southey – and some nice glimpses of their
Lakeland life.

★ *The Shining Levels*
By John Wyatt (Penguin). The story of one man's return to
nature among the Lakeland fells. A nice book to take home
and read once the holiday is over.

A Walk Around the Lakes
By Hunter Davies (Orion). Dreadfully out of date; why
do they keep buying it in their millions? But a joy to read,
the most loved general book on the Lakes ever written.
Unquote.

An American President's Love Affair with the English Lake District
By Andrew Wilson (Lakeland Press Agency). Charming brief account of how the US president fell in love with the Lakes (his mum was born in Carlisle).

The Silent Traveller in Lakeland
By Chiang Lee (Mercat Press). A Chinese artist explores the Lakes – an interesting perspective.

Maps

The ordinary Ordnance Survey Landranger Maps (1:50,000 scale or 2 cm to 1 km) are detailed enough for walking, but you have to buy seven to cover Cumbria and you could go mad trying to work out the overlaps. Better to buy …

★★★ *Ordnance Survey Explorer Maps*
1:25,000 or 4 cm to 1 km. These divide the Lake District neatly into four: northeast, northwest, southeast and southwest. Worth investing in all four, whether for walking or driving. Look out for the plastic-covered versions, which are more expensive but invaluable for walkers in the rain.

★★ *Ordnance Survey Lake District and Cumbria Touring Map*
1:100,000 or 1 cm to 1 km. This does at least give you the whole of the Lakes in one map. (Well, almost. They have cut a nasty slice off the top of Caldbeck.) Good detail, but a bit cumbersome to use for those who are only exploring one area of the Lakes.

★★ Lake District Lap Map
Published by Cardtoons. A small, easy-to-use road, cycling or walking map, designed for those who don't want the fuss and expense of large-scale sheets. Loads of tourist info and suggested tours on the back. Very good value and a long-running bestseller. Also now available in jigsaw and tea towel form, though best not to trust to these on the fells. They do a Walker's Lap Map and Cyclist's Lap Map too.

★★ Lake District National Park
A CD Rom, produced by Anquet Technology, which is crammed full of Ordnance Survey 1:25,000 maps and aerial photography for your computer. You can plot routes, create tailored maps and all sorts of other clever things. Great fun to have on your PC, though less useful when you're lost in the mist, of course.

Cumbria Tourism publishes various maps, including interactive versions at *www.golakes.co.uk*.

Newspapers

The Lake District's newspapers are good places to go for the latest information, news and events. Many now have good websites, updated daily as a useful addition to the weekly paper.

Cumberland News
Weekly (Friday) broadsheet on Carlisle and the north Lakes (*www.cumberland-news.co.uk*).

Cumberland and Westmorland Herald
Weekly (Saturday) broadsheet for Penrith and east Cumbria (*www.cwherald.com*).

Evening News and Star
Nightly for northern Cumbria (*www.newsandstar.co.uk*).

Keswick Reminder
Independent weekly (Friday) covering Keswick and the north Lakes. Worth it just to admire the prehistoric layout (*www.keswickreminder.co.uk*).

North West Evening Mail
Nightly on the Barrow and Furness areas (*www.nwemail.co.uk*).

Westmorland Gazette
Weekly (Friday). Covers Kendal and the south Lakes (*www.thisisthelakedistrict.co.uk*).

Whitehaven News
Weekly (Thursday). Covers Whitehaven and the west Lakes (*www.whitehaven-news.co.uk*).

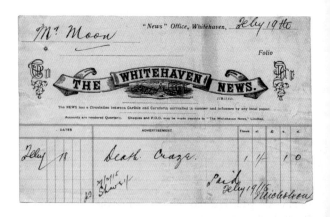

Workington Times and Star
West Cumbria's weekly (Friday) (*www.timesandstar.co.uk*).

Magazines

Lakeland magazines come and go and tend to be short on opinions but long on useful listings.

Cumbria
A popular small-format, glossy monthly magazine (*www.dalesman.co.uk*).

Cumbria Life
A substantial bi-monthly magazine with lots of glossy photos and supplements. Some good reading (*www.cumbrialife.co.uk*).

Lake District Life
Big monthly glossy carrying a good balance between information for tourists and locals (*www.lakedistrict-life.co.uk*).

Lakeland Walker
Magazine with walking routes and news. Every two months (*www.outandaboutlive.co.uk*).

Out and About
A free annual magazine from the Lake District National Park Authority, with a useful diary of events over the year (*www.lake-district.gov.uk*).

When to come

If you have school-age children you are lumbered with coming in the school holidays. August has recently been the hottest month and the busiest. For pretty scenery, May and June, then September and October, are the best months.

May and June are usually the driest months, while September and October are the most colourful, with the bracken and trees turning from green to brown to gold.

The Lake District never closes, and the last decade or so has seen a steady rise in off-season tourism. Lake steamers have expanded their winter services, cultural places now offer winter programmes, and many attractions are open all year round. Lakeland is lovely in frost and snow, and the hotels do have central heating. With people taking more holidays in general, the numbers visiting between January and March are double what they were in the past.

The weather

Fascinating. Yes, that's what I think. There are few places in the world where you can get such variations from place to place, from day to day or even from hour to hour in such a short distance. If you don't like the weather where you are, move on a few miles or come down a few thousand feet. Naturally, it could be *worse*, but at least it is unlikely to be the same.

Now for some hard facts about Lakeland weather. South Devon gets more rain than Carlisle. Honestly. It's the high bits at the head of the valleys that give the Lake District a bad name for rainfall. Elsewhere in Lakeland, the rainfall is normal-to-dry for Britain.

Seathwaite, at the head of Borrowdale, is admittedly the wettest place in England, with about 10 feet (3 m) a year. And nearby Sprinkling Tarn holds the record for the most rain ever recorded in the country – about 21 feet 4 inches (6.5 m) in 1954. But if you travel just 8 miles (13 km) over to Keswick, the rainfall average drops dramatically to about 50 inches (127 cm) a year. Move on another 20 miles (32 km), into the Solway Plain at Carlisle, and the figure is only 30 inches (76 cm) a year. Positively arid.

Keswick has milder winters than London, and it's sweltering in the winter compared with really cold places like New York or Berlin. Though there is a great variation from day

THE HUNTSMAN

to day in Lakeland villages or valleys, there are not enormous seasonal extremes. Average temperatures are 41°F (5°C) in winter, rising to 68°F (20°C) in summer. Shepherds and farmers tend to wear the same clothes all the year round – usually a jacket and trousers that don't match and old boots that sometimes don't match either. Inside their cottages, the fire is often lit all year round.

The summer can be hot, but don't bank on it. A nice bonus is that you get three-quarters of an hour more daylight every summer's evening compared with the south of England, and the weather often gets better as the day wears on. With luck, you can have two days in one and organise two separate expeditions. Many climbers set out at six in the evening and get in a day's worth of climbing before dark.

Weather forecasts are available from the National Park's Weatherline 24 hours a day (tel. 0870 055 0575 or online at *www.lake-district.gov.uk/weatherline*). These are usually reliable (they're taken from the Met Office) and essential if you are planning a day's walking. An outlook for the following day is usually given after 4.00pm, and there's an update at around 7.00am each morning. During the winter the same number gives vital information about walking conditions on the fell tops, assessed by one of two men whose job it is to climb Helvellyn and see what the weather's doing. Nice work if you can get it.

What to wear

Clothes. They don't like you going naked in the Lakes. It frightens the sheep.

Experts would have you dressed for a simple fell walk as if you were going up Everest, with oxygen masks and ice picks and very bright colours. But the most important rule for walkers (and I stress walkers not climbers) is 'Comfort is All'. The second most important rule is 'It Won't Last'. So even if it's warm when you set off, take a pullover and some sort of raincoat or waterproof anorak. It's always colder on the tops. In winter, or in obvious bad weather, I take leggings as well. The third rule is always to tell someone exactly where you are going and when you plan to return. The fourth rule is to take a map, compass and whistle.

As for footwear, I walked happily for 20 years on the fells with plimsolls in summer and wellingtons in winter. Now, for walking in winter and bad weather I have to admit that I've changed to lightweight boots. After two cartilage operations, caused by football not walking, I found that wellingtons hurt my calves. I now love my boots, but there is no need for you to buy them if you don't want to. The same goes for fancy climbing socks or natty plus fours in thick hairy tweed. I once got a pair as a present, and I looked terrific in them, but they itched like hell and I now never wear them. Have a look at the next shepherd you see working on the fells. How many are wearing climbing boots or plus fours and carrying ropes? Well then.

Hospitals

Just in case you should need one, here's a list of hospitals in Cumbria. Be aware that some of these hospitals are small and might not be able to help you in an emergency 24 hours a day. Those marked with an asterisk have doctors available round the clock and can cope with major accidents; the others all call on local GPs or refer patients to the nearest large hospital. Hopefully you'll never need them, but see Chapter 9 for some guidance on what to do if you have an accident while out walking.

South Cumbria

Furness General Hospital ★, Dalton Lane, Barrow-in-Furness (tel. 01229 870870)

Westmorland General Hospital, Burton Road, Kendal (tel. 015397 32288)

West Cumbria

West Cumberland Hospital ★, Hensingham, Whitehaven (tel. 01946 693181)

Cockermouth Community Hospital, Isel Road, Cockermouth (tel. 01900 822226)

Victoria Cottage Hospital, Ewanrigg Road, Maryport (tel. 01900 812634)

Workington Community Hospital, Park Lane, Workington (tel. 01900 602244)

North and East Cumbria

Cumberland Infirmary ★, Newtown Road, Carlisle (tel. 01228 523444)

Keswick Cottage Hospital, Crosthwaite Road, Keswick (tel. 017687 67000)

Penrith Hospital, Bridge Lane, Penrith (tel. 01768 245300)

Calendar of events

The Lake District has dozens of big annual events, some of which have been running for centuries. They are worth bearing in mind when you're planning a holiday, and August is by far the busiest month. Don't worry if you can't understand some of the words at this stage. Egremont Crab Fair has nothing to do with fish, for instance. We'll come to fuller descriptions of the major events and activities later in the book. Most events are held on the same day year in year out, but check with local newspapers, TICs or the organisers direct for the precise dates if you're particularly keen to get along.

February

Word Market Literary Festival, Ulverston – first and second week (*www.word-market.co.uk*)

Keswick Film Festival – third week (*www.keswickfilmfestival.org*)

March

Words by the Water Literary Festival – second week (*www.wayswithwords.co.uk*)

Daffodil and Spring Flower Show, Ambleside – third or fourth weekend (*www.ambleside-show.org.uk*)

April

Ulverston Walking Festival – first week

May

Ullswater Walking Festival – second week (*www.ullswater.com*)

Keswick Jazz Festival – second week

Keswick Mountain Festival – third week (*www.keswick-mountainfestival.co.uk*)

Women's Arts International Festival, Kendal – last two weeks (*www.womensartsinternational.co.uk*)

Cartmel Races – second bank holiday weekend (*www.cart-mel-steeplechases.co.uk*)

June

Cockermouth Summer Festival – all month

Holker Festival – first weekend (*www.holker-hall.co.uk*)

Appleby Horse Fair – runs until the second Wednesday in June, usually from the preceding weekend

Ullswater Country Fair, Patterdale – last Sunday (*www.ullswater.com*)

Warcop Rushbearing – St Peter's Day, 29 June, or the preceding Saturday if the 29th is a Sunday

July

Coniston Water Festival – first weekend (*www.conistonwater-festival.org.uk*)

Ambleside Rushbearing – first Saturday

Great Musgrave Rushbearing – first Saturday

Ulverston Carnival – first Saturday

Furness Tradition Folk Festival – second week (*www.furnesstradition.org.uk*)

Lakeland Rose Show, Crooklands – second weekend (*www.lakelandroseshow.co.uk*)

Cumberland County Show, Carlisle – third Saturday (*www.cumberlandshow.co.uk*)

Coniston Country Fair – penultimate Sunday (*www.conistoncountryfair.com*)

Penrith Show – fourth Saturday (*www.penrithshow.co.uk*)

Ambleside Sports – last Thursday

August

Lake District Summer Music Festival, various venues – first two weeks (*www.ldsm.org.uk*)

Cartmel Agricultural Show – first Wednesday (*www.cartmelshow.co.uk*)

Lake District Sheep Dog Trials, Staveley – first Thursday

Cockermouth Agricultural Show – first Saturday (*www.cockermouthshow.org.uk*)

Grasmere Rushbearing – Saturday nearest to St Oswald's Day (5 August)

Lowther Horse Trials and Country Fair, Askham – first or second weekend (*www.lowther.co.uk*)

Rydal Sheep Dog Trials – second Thursday after first Monday in August

Gosforth Agricultural Show – third Wednesday

Threlkeld Sheepdog Trials – third Wednesday

Skelton Horticultural and Agricultural Show, Penrith – third Saturday (*www.skeltonshow.com*)

Langdale Country Fair – third Sunday

Grasmere Sports and Show – third or fourth Sunday (*www.grasmeresportsand-show.co.uk*)

Hawkshead Show – penultimate Tuesday (*www.hawksheadshow.co.uk*)

Cartmel Races – bank holiday weekend (*www.cartmel-steeplechases.co.uk*)

Millom and Broughton Agricultural Show – bank holiday Saturday (*www.millomandbroughtonshow.co.uk*)

Patterdale Dog Day – bank holiday Saturday (*www.patterdaledogday.co.uk*)

Keswick Agricultural Show – bank holiday Monday

Ennerdale Show – last Wednesday

Ambleside Summer Flower Show – last weekend (*www.ambleside-show.org.uk*).

September

Ulverston Charter Festival – first two weeks; lantern procession on second Saturday (*www.ulverston.net*)

Loweswater and Brackenthwaite Agricultural Show – first Sunday

Westmorland County Show, Kendal – second Thursday (*www.westmorland-county-show.co.uk*)

Kendal Torchlight Carnival – second Friday (*www.kendal-torchlightcarnival.co.uk*)

Egremont Crab Fair – third Saturday (*www.egremontcrabfair.org.uk*)

Borrowdale Shepherds' Meet and Show, Rosthwaite – third Sunday (*www.borrowdaleshow.org.uk*)

Eskdale Show – last Saturday (*www.eskdale.info*)

Urswick Rushbearing – Sunday nearest St Michael's Day (29 September)

October

Wasdale Head Shepherds' Meet and Show – second Saturday

Buttermere Shepherds' Meet and Show – third Saturday

November

Coniston Power Boat Records Week – second week (*www.conistonpowerboatrecords.co.uk*)

Kendal Mountain Film Festival – second week (*www.mountainfilm.co.uk*)

Biggest Liar in the World Competition, Santon Bridge – third Thursday (*www.santonbridgeinn.com/liar*)

CHAPTER TWO

Background Briefing

*All you need to know about Lakeland
past and present*

The Promenade, Bowness.

Getting your bearings

Having arrived in the Lakes, the first thing is to try to get
your bearings. Not just working out how to get out of the
bedroom or undo the tent flap, but to work out the shape
of things to come, as well as the history, background and
organisation of the area you will shortly be exploring.

It was William Wordsworth who first likened the shape
of the Lake District to a wheel, with the lakes and dales radiating from the centre like spokes. It's a good description.
Things do radiate from a centre, and it is hard to jump from
one spoke to another. Even though transport links are much
better than in Wordsworth's day, you still have to make
some tortuous journeys to get to some of the outer spokes,
especially in the west.

But a handier image to keep in your head is of the Lakes
as two wheels, one in the north radiating from Keswick and
one in the south, radiating from Ambleside. Though the
two towns are only 15 miles (24 km) apart, separated by the
Dunmail Raise, they often seem to be in different countries.
They even talk differently, with the folks round Windermere
and Coniston sounding almost Lancastrian, while the rougher
folks up north appear to have a Scottish influence in their
dialect, at least to southern ears.

The natives hardly move between the two divisions, but
then Cumbrian natives have traditionally hardly moved
anywhere. They often consider the folks in the next dale as
foreigners. Most visitors who stay in the northern Lakes, with
Keswick as the nearest town, tend to stick there, exploring the
lakes and mountains nearby. In the south they look towards
Ambleside and Windermere. Crossing the Dunmail Raise can
begin to seem like a major expedition, which it often is.

Start by acquiring a general feeling of Lakeland as a whole, then concentrate on the names and places and character of the area where you are based. In a week's holiday, you will probably hardly venture into the other section. That will be for your next visit.

Geology

It's a tough subject to take in for absolute beginners. But come on, we can zip through it quickly. It's well worth it.

Roughly speaking, there are three major rock bands running across the Lake District, and they have created three different types of scenery and buildings.

In the north there are the **Skiddaw Slates**, which give rounded, smooth hills, gentle horizons and not a great deal of colour. One result is that Skiddaw is relatively safe to climb, with smooth slopes and no dangerous crags. Skiddaw Slates were formed under the sea about 500 million years ago from shales and mudstones and are inherently weak. Skiddaw is considered to be the oldest mountain in Europe, and the Lakeland hills as a whole are among the oldest in the world, more ancient even than the Alps or Himalayas.

The central zone of the Lake District is dominated by a band of **Borrowdale Volcanic** rocks, which arrived just as the Skiddaw Slates had been laid down. Violent volcanic explosions threw up a much harder, more jagged rock and created dramatic, angular sky lines like Scafell and the Langdales. They're perfect for rock climbers, providing something to get hold of yet not fall off. They hope. The rocks and resultant vegetation are colourful, rich in reds, pinks and greens, and creating technicolour autumn views for the photographers.

Next came the Silurian period, about 300 million years ago, resulting in a band across the south of the Lake District known as the **Silurian Slates**. Like the Skiddaw Slates, these have left more rounded hills. The distinctive green slate of the Coniston area, which you see in walls and roofs, are from this period.

Running around the edge of the Lake District are two more distinctive rock formations that should be mentioned: **sandstone** on the west coast and in the Carlisle and Eden Valley areas, which can clearly be seen in the local buildings; and **limestone** in the south and towards the Pennines.

Just to mess up these rather neat divisions, along came the Ice Age. It was quite recent really, under 2 million years ago, and it put everything into the melting pot – or in this case the freezing pot – and the final shape of the Lakes eventually emerged. The effects of glaciation are easy to spot and much loved by teachers on field courses. The valley floors were swept clean, tarns and lakes scooped out, valley heads built up, debris dumped, deltas formed and all those cwms and corries created. The variety is incredible for such a small area. Little wonder that for the last 200 years the Lake District has been an adventure playground for geologists.

History

If there were inhabitants before the Ice Age they left no clues about their presence. Not even an ancient Kendal Mint Cake wrapper. The earliest evidence possibly suggests some sort of primitive Stone Age settlements on the west coast, round about 4000 BC.

There are quite a few definite Bronze and Iron Age remains scattered across the Lakes, such as stone circles and burial areas. Though none of them are as dramatic as elsewhere in England, several, like Castlerigg near Keswick and Long Meg and Her Daughters near Penrith, have become popular tourist attractions.

The **Romans** came, saw and conquered. They were led by Agricola, who marched north to Carlisle but stuck mainly to the plain. You will see on the Ordnance Survey maps of Lakeland numerous references to Roman remains, mostly small but quite interesting. By far the best Roman site – in the country as well as the Lake District – is Hadrian's Wall, which enters Cumbria north of Carlisle and ends at Bowness-on-Solway on the west coast.

After the Romans departed around AD 400, the natives were left to their own devices, till the hordes of invaders from the coasts of western Europe started arriving. The ancient **Celts** clung on to their old ways for a long time in central Lakeland, just as they did in Wales. There are strong connections between them: they each called themselves Cymry, or Cymri, hence Cumbria, and there are many Celtic place-names to this day that sound Welsh. Examples include those beginning with *pen*, meaning head or hill, as in Penrith or Penruddock; or *blaen*, meaning summit, as in Blencathra. Helvellyn sounds decidedly Welsh, though so far the experts haven't been able to agree about its derivation.

Next came the **invaders**. The Anglo-Saxons mostly invaded the softer and easier eastern coasts of England, though they did reach some of the fertile plains on the western slopes of the Lakes. Their characteristic Anglian name endings of *-ham* or *-ton* can be seen in places like Brigham and Dearham, Dalton and Alston.

A Lakeland Cottage

It was the Norse, rather than the Danes or Saxons, who colonised Cumbria as they came down the west coast of Scotland to Ireland and the Isle of Man. Some of the most typical Lakeland words have Norse origins: dales come from *dalr*, fells from *fjall*, becks from *bekkr*, tarns from *tjorns* and force (meaning waterfall) from *foss*. The ending -*thwaite*, which you see in place-names everywhere, is also Norse, meaning a clearing in the forest.

The northern half of present-day Cumbria – the old Cumberland – has had its history and personality fashioned by the very fact of being on the **border** between England and Scotland. For several centuries there was constant conflict, looting and pillaging. Families and villages would swap loyalties, depending on who they thought would win. Much of Cumberland was, in fact, part of Scotland for many years. The strife has been romanticised by the novels of Walter Scott, but until as recently as the 18th century it was a dangerous place to live. Even today many isolated north Cumbrians can be suspicious folk, preferring to winter you, then summer you and winter you again. Then if you're lucky, they might say hello.

The legacy of all this border conflict is a large number of castles, fortified houses and pele towers, not beside the lakes or mountains themselves but well away in the surrounding towns and plains, such as Carlisle, Penrith, Cockermouth and Kendal. This was where the nobs lived, and they were very keen on protecting themselves. Up on the fells there was really not much worth stealing. Life, such as it was, went on, whether it was Agricola, William the Conqueror, Bonnie Prince Charlie or Henry VIII who was out there causing all that nuisance, starting wars, leading rebellions or pinching land. The people who lived in the Lakes were 'statesmen', small-time farmers with small estates and small farmhouses, much as they are today.

Trades and industries

You'll see an awful lot of sheep in the Lakes, and not all of them are wearing orange anoraks. The four-footed versions might well be Herdwicks, the native Cumbrian breed, which is supposed to have originally come from Spain some 400 years ago, when an Armada galleon was wrecked on the Cumbrian coast. Another theory has it that they were here in Roman times. They have white faces, and only the males have horns. They have black wool, which gets greyer with age. They never get fat and no wonder, living the lives they lead out on the most barren of fells in the most barren of winters. They are reputed to be the hardiest breed of all sheep, and when they're really hungry they will eat their own wool to stay alive. (Well, they suck out the oils, just to keep themselves going.) They were great favourites of Beatrix Potter, who bought dozens of flocks and farms with the money from her books. For a while Herdwicks were in

danger of becoming a rare breed, but they have come back into fashion a bit lately. Another common breed are the Swaledales, which are dark faced with a light nose, and both sexes have horns.

It must have taken ages to count them all, but the Department for Farming and Rural Affairs reckoned there were 2,049,539 sheep in Cumbria at its last census in 2005. With those sort of numbers the wool industry has always been strong in Cumbria. Kendal was the heart of it for six centuries, and local cloths were known throughout the land. In *Henry IV* (*c*.1597) Shakespeare refers to a material as Kendal Green. It was a cottage industry in those days, with endless strings of packhorses carrying the raw and finished goods in and out of the town.

With the industrial revolution Carlisle became a busy manufacturing centre for the cotton industry, until the main mass trade eventually moved to Lancashire and Yorkshire. But Carlisle today still has some high-quality mills. Mining in the Lake District is equally ancient, and the Romans exploited the lead mines round Alston. There are old mines all over the northern fells and around Coniston, as well as extensive quarrying.

Heavy industry in Cumbria has always been restricted to the west, around Barrow and Millom, or up the coast around Maryport, Workington and Whitehaven, an important centre for many years for the coal and iron industries as well as for shipping. At one time, around 1780, Whitehaven was the second port in the land after London, ahead of Liverpool and Bristol. It was one of the earliest planned towns in Europe. The west coast is now much lighter on heavy industry, though some success has been made with new chemical and lighter industries, and the nuclear plant at Sellafield has been a huge financial boost to the area.

Farming has always been an important industry, but pressure on prices and the foot and mouth crisis of 2001 mean that it has been harder than ever for farmers to make a decent living lately. Whatever they might have you believe, tourism is now the main industry of the Lake District.

A brief history of Lakeland tourism

It's hard to believe there were Lake District guidebooks before this one, but it's true. The first dedicated one, published in 1778, was Thomas West's *Guide to the Lakes in Cumberland, Westmorland and Lancashire*. There had been visitors to the Lakes before then, of course, but this book brought a new wave of people who came to enjoy the views and the fresh air. More guides sprang up, including William Wordsworth's *Guide to the Lakes* (1810).

Wordsworth worried even back then about tourists spoiling the Lakes, so goodness knows what he would make of the 15 million people who now visit each year. The poet inspired in particular a breed of cultural tourist, and other writers and artists flocked to find the same sort of inspiration as he did. The irony that his book was encouraging tourism while he simultaneously complained that the Lakes were being overrun was probably not lost on him.

As visitors flocked in, the tourist industry began to take shape, but at that time it wasn't fish and chip shops that were springing up to cater for visitors. Instead, people flocked to various 'stations' from which West and the like prescribed the best view. Facilities sprang up around them (a good example can still be seen on Claife near Windermere), and windows were sometimes tinted to enhance the scene. Tourists would stand here with their backs to the views, observing them through a hand-held Claude-glass, framing it to its best advantage. Not dissimilar to modern-day tourists with their cameras and camcorders, only they usually face the right direction.

These days Keswick, Ambleside and Windermere are largely tourist towns, full to bursting in the summer months. Yet surprisingly the towns just a few miles away are still *real* towns. Places like Penrith, Cockermouth and Kendal are all market towns with old industries, hardly ruffled by slate lamps and signs boasting B&B in every second window.

Cumbria today

Cumbria now has a population of a little under half a million and an area of 2,630 square miles (6,811 sq km). The county is divided into six district councils, four of which – Copeland, Allerdale, Eden and South Lakeland – share the Lake District National Park among them.

Cumbria County Council
The Courts, Carlisle
Tel. 01228 606060 or visit *www.cumbria.gov.uk*

Allerdale Borough Council
Allerdale House, Workington
Tel. 01900 702702 or visit *www.allerdale.gov.uk*

Barrow-in-Furness Borough Council
Town Hall, Duke Street, Barrow
Tel. 01228 894900 or visit *www.barrowbc.gov.uk*

Carlisle City Council
Civic Centre, Carlisle
Tel. 01228 817000 or visit *www.carlisle.gov.uk*

Copeland Borough Council
Catherine Street, Whitehaven
Tel. 0845 054 8600 or visit *www.copeland.gov.uk*

Eden District Council
Town Hall, Penrith
Tel. 017688 17817 or visit *www.eden.gov.uk*

South Lakeland District Council
Lowther Street, Kendal
Tel. 015397 33333 or visit *www.southlakeland.gov.uk*

The Lake District National Park

The National Park is that nice bit right in the middle of
Cumbria – but what *is* a National Park? Visitors are always
asking that. Read on.

There are now 14 National Parks in England, Scotland
and Wales (the South Downs is trying to become the 15th).
The Lake District National Park, set up in 1951, was the
second one to be designated, and it's also the second biggest,
covering 885 square miles (2,214 sq km), which is some way
short of the Cairngorms at 1,467 square miles (3,800 sq km).
It covers all the hilly, watery and touristy bits of the Lake
District, but doesn't include Carlisle, Cumbria's biggest
town, or Penrith, Cockermouth, Kendal or the west coast.

The National Park is looked after by the Lake District
National Park Authority, which protects the area for both
residents and visitors. It doesn't actually own the land, but
it does have control over planning and development. It is
very strict about all new buildings and is trying to restrict
the number of second homes, timeshares and leisure centres
in the area. People feel quite proud to be residents of the
National Park, as if they were living in one of nature's listed
buildings – until, that is, they want to add a new window or
put a bed in the barn and they come up against the battle
to get planning permission, when they suddenly wish they
were a few feet outside the boundary. But the LDNPA does

a worthwhile job in protecting the Lake District for us all, keeping an eye on developments and protecting footpaths and open land. Once you get above the field line you can walk almost anywhere in the Lake District. The open fell is common land, still owned by someone but where the freedom to walk unhindered has been enjoyed for generations. There is no need to ask permission.

The National Park gets most of its money from the government but makes about a third from commercial activities. It provides about 15 full-time Rangers to patrol the park, giving help and advice to visitors, working on properties, policing by-laws, leading parties on walks or doing jobs from litter-sweeps to repairing footpaths or dry stone walls. As well as administrative staff at its headquarters in Kendal, it also employs forestry teams, ecologists, archaeologists and information centre people. More information about the work of the LDNPA can be found at *www.lake-district.gov.uk* or tel. 015397 24555.

Some National Park statistics

Area of the National Park: 885 square miles (2,214 sq km)

Area covered by lakes or reservoirs: 25 square miles (65 sq km)

Area under crops: 15 square miles (39 sq km)

Area under grass: 295 square miles (764 sq km)

Area of common land: 236 square miles (611 sq km)

Area of woodland: 95 square miles (246 sq km)

Length from north to south: 40 miles (64.4 km)

Length from east to west: 33 miles (53 km)

Residents: 41,831

Household spaces: 17,937

Miles of footpaths and bridleways: 2,225 miles (3,580 km)

Listed buildings and churches: 1,744

Scheduled monuments: 275

Sites of Special Scientific Interest (SSSIs): 132

Proportion owned by the National Trust: 24.8 per cent

Owned by United Utilities: 6.8 per cent

Owned by the Forestry Commission: 5.6 per cent

Owned by the LDNPA: 3.8 per cent

Owned privately: 58.8 per cent

Owned by the Ministry of Defence: 0.2 per cent

Transport

Getting around the Lake District

Traffic in all major tourist areas has increased tremendously, and transport infrastructures haven't always been able to keep up. At least in Lakeland, with its 15 million or so visitors a year, the problem is beginning to be recognised and some alternative strategies developed.

Public transport – finding it, catching it and paying for it – can still be a hassle, but Cumbria County Council has cut out a lot of the hard work with its 'Getting Around Cumbria and Lake District', a twice yearly round-up of train, bus, coach and ferry information for the whole of Cumbria. Along with a handy 'Cumbria Public Transport' map, it's free from TICs and the Lake District National Park Visitor Centre. The Lake District National Park Authority publishes a series of leaflets called 'Give the Driver a Break', which offer tips on getting about without a car and are available from the same places. Or, for a useful service offering advice for any journey in, to or from Cumbria, contact Traveline (tel. 0871 200 2233, lines open 7.00am to 8.00pm every day, or visit *www.traveline.info*).

Trains

The main railway routes in Cumbria skirt the National Park (see Chapter 1). Since privatisation the routes are under different and confusing names, though it's still just about possible to book tickets and get information from stations if you visit in person. Otherwise, all information about train times and fares has been centralised on 08457 48 49 50 or at *www.nationalrail.co.uk*. If you're planning to do a lot of train travel, you can buy a Cumbria and Lake District Rail Rover or Lakes Day Ranger ticket, which will allow you to roam across the area and can save families in particular a lot of money. Fares and participating rail operators change all the time, so it's worth contacting National Rail Enquiries (above) for help in planning and buying the right ticket.

Cumbria once had a decent network of rail lines, many of them set up to serve the mining industries. The decline of those industries and the Beeching Report of 1963 put paid to many of them, but some lines have since been revived by enthusiasts. Here are some of the most useful and interesting lines in the Lakes.

★★★ The Ravenglass and Eskdale Railway

Built to link with the Furness Railway at Ravenglass on the west coast. Opened in 1875 to carry iron ore and granite out of Eskdale, it fell into decline on several occasions but was rescued and revitalised by steam enthusiasts in the 1970s. It still runs on narrow gauge track and is a brilliant way to travel the 7 miles (11.3 km) into spectacular scenery at the head of the valley. It takes 40 minutes for the full journey, calling at four little stations along the way. Also known locally as La'al Ratty, local dialect for 'little narrow way'. Tel. 01229 717171 or visit *www.ravenglass-railway.co.uk* for timetables.

★★★ Settle to Carlisle Railway

A Victorian development running the length of the Pennines and up to Carlisle. Built by Midland Railways in the 1870s, through seemingly impossible terrain and with much loss of life, all because the London and North West Railway Company refused to share its line further west. With 19 viaducts (including the famous Ribblehead with 24 arches) and 13 tunnels to maintain, the line has faced recurring threats of closure, but fierce campaigning by several support and pressure groups and local financial input have saved it. The route is now run by Northern Rail and has been belatedly recognised as a national treasure, usually billed as the most scenic line in the country. It's also a good way of exploring villages in the area. The support groups share a good website with lots of information about the railway at *www.settle-carlisle.co.uk*.

★★ The Cumbrian Coast line

This is a wonderful and much forgotten gem, skirting the entire length of the west Cumbrian coast from Arnside in the south to Carlisle in the north, taking in five major aqueducts and 18 miles (29 km) of sea wall along the way. It began as transport for iron ore in 1846, and the southern section up to Whitehaven is still known as the Furness Railway after the original company. Trains will stop at all stations, although few are now manned, and rather confusingly it's run by two companies: Northern Rail north of Barrow and TransPennine Express south of it. Grange-over-Sands station is a good link for buses into the central Lakes, and Ravenglass connects you with the Ravenglass and Eskdale railway.

★★ The Lakeside and Haverthwaite Railway

Originally an offshoot of the Furness Line, connecting Ulverston to Lake Windermere. Like many branch lines it was closed by British Rail in the 1960s, but it was reopened by a private company ten years later. It uses steam trains to travel the 3½ miles (5.6 km) of track that still exist. There is good car parking at Haverthwaite, and you can buy combined tickets with the steamers at Lakeside, which makes it a clever way of getting up into the Lakes without taking a car north of Newby Bridge. Tel. 015395 31594 or visit *www.lakesiderailway.co.uk* for timetables.

★ The Lakes Line

The only line left that connects the National Park with the rest of the country. From Oxenholme the train goes through Kendal, Burneside and Staveley to Windermere, a dinky little station whose existence is fiercely guarded by the Lakes Line Rail User Group. It takes about 20 minutes in all, but be warned that the train dashes out of Oxenholme to meet its punctuality targets, regardless of delays to the west coast main line train that is meant to connect with it. Trans-Pennine Express also runs trains between Windermere and Manchester, including the airport.

★ South Tynedale Railway

In the extreme northeast of the county is another of Cumbria's little oddities. It is a relic of the Newcastle Carlisle Railway Company, opened in 1852, closed in the 1970s by British

BURNESIDE

Rail and then resurrected as a tourist attraction by volunteer rail enthusiasts. Trains run on narrow gauge track between Alston and Kirkhaugh, over the border in Northumberland. There's only 2¼ miles (3.6 km) or 30 minutes' worth of track, but plans are afoot to extend the line on to Slaggyford, and they do sometimes use steam trains; check the timetables if you're especially keen to catch one. Trains run from April to October and on a few days in December. The station at Alston has a café and railway shop. Tel. 01434 381696 or visit *www.strps.org.uk* for timetables.

The west coast main line

Run by Virgin from London Euston to Glasgow, this passes the Lake District on the east. You can get off at Lancaster in the south to connect with the West Cumbrian line; Oxenholme, just outside Kendal, to connect with the Lakes line; Penrith to connect with buses; or Carlisle to connect with the other end of the West Cumbrian line.

Buses

Stagecoach, which gobbled up most of the small Cumbrian bus companies after deregulation, covers most of the bus routes. Some of its routes are subsidised to make sure that buses continue to serve routes that otherwise wouldn't be profitable, and, given the wide area it has to cover, connections are generally pretty good.

Stagecoach has forged good links with rail and ferry companies to provide 'all in' days out, and if you're planning a day or a whole holiday around bus routes it's worth buying an Explorer ticket, valid on the whole network. You can buy a ticket from the driver, and it costs £9 for a day or £28 for a week.

There are several other multi-journey tickets, including a Lakes Day Rider, which offers unlimited travel in the central region between Bowness and Grasmere. All details can be found in a very good brochure, *The Cumbria and Lakesrider*. It also has timetables for all services and some tips on walks and pubs near bus routes. It's published twice a year and available free on buses or from TICs, as are a handful of leaflets called *From A to B to See*, outlining some good walks around Stagecoach's routes. For more information about Stagecoach services, contact Traveline (tel. 0871 200 2233 or visit *www.traveline.info*).

The **Youth Hostel Association** runs another route that's worth remembering if you're staying with them. The YHA Shuttle Bus picks up from Windermere station and connects the Windermere, Ambleside, Hawkshead, Coniston, Elterwater, Langdale and Grasmere hostels between Easter and October. It can also transfer your bags ahead of you if you want to walk between hostels. Tel. the Ambleside hostel for details on 0870 770 5672.

Another handy service is the Royal Mail's **Post Buses**, which deliver and collect mail in larger than usual minibuses, complete with seats, so that passengers can be transported along with the post. It's a brilliant idea as the buses trundle round places that would be uneconomic for a private company. There are scheduled services between, among others, Ulpha and Duddon Bridge, Grisebeck and Broughton Beck and Wreaks End and Foxfield. For times contact the Royal Mail's consumer service centre (tel. 08457 740 740).

Minibus tours

Astute little bus companies, knowing the strain of private motoring on unfamiliar narrow roads, have developed a good alternative: minibus tours. They usually have a guide or knowledgeable driver on hand to point out things of interest along the way. ('That's where Hunter Davies lives, but don't gape, he'll go potty.') Prices for an adult are usually from around £20 for a half-day tour to £35 for a full day out. They go all over the place, some doing request tours tailored to your interests. You could try:

Mountain Goat
A wide variety of daily routes, from half-day trips to week-long holidays. Pick-ups from Windermere, Ambleside, Grasmere and Keswick (tel. 015394 45161 or visit *www.mountain-goat.com*).

Lakes Supertours
Based in Windermere, they do a good mix of routes, some linking with steamer trips or visits to tourist attractions. Offer plenty of stops for short strolls or to take photos (tel. 015394 42751 or visit *www.lakes-supertours.com*).

Fellrunner
Based in the north of the county, this is unusual in that it's run as a charity; the money raised supports scheduled bus services driven by volunteers from the Eden Valley to Penrith and Carlisle. Cheap and fun, but tours run in the main tourist season only (tel. 01768 88232 or visit *www.fellrunnerbus.co.uk*).

Touchstone Tours
Themed trips, many of them clustered around local history or literary connections, run from Keswick (tel. 017687 79599 or visit *www.touchstonetours.co.uk*).

Taxis

There are lots of these around, and fares are surprisingly competitive – they're usually based on miles, not time taken. TICs have lists of local companies, and hotels, restaurants, etc. are good at finding available taxis for you.

Ferries

Four of the lakes have public transport – Windermere, Coniston, Ullswater and Derwentwater (see Chapter 7 for more details) – but only Windermere has a car ferry. It's run by Cumbria County Council and operates every day except Christmas Day and Boxing Day between Ferry Nab, south of Bowness, to Ferry House at Far Sawrey. It costs £3 one way for a car and all passengers. It generally runs from 7.00am until 9.00pm from Mondays to Saturdays and from 9.00am to 9.00pm on Sundays. It's a splendid way to travel, but beware in summer – the traffic queues build up horrendously, with waits of up to an hour. It can close in bad weather – signs on the roads will warn you if this is the case. A smug way to cross is by foot or bike, which lets you straight on, and you only pay 50p. Which brings us to …

Cycling

Of course, you could cycle all the way to the Lake District or bring your machine on the train. Unfortunately, the new rail providers are distinctly bike-unfriendly. Ring 08457 48 49 50 with copious details of your route to find out if they'll let you on board. Alternatively, there are now dozens of bike hire outlets in the National Park, so there's plenty of scope once you arrive. Most towns and larger villages have hire shops. Prices are around the £20 mark for a full day, or £80 for a week, including helmets, locks and so on. There are bike lock-ups and racks in many of the larger car parks and town and village centres.

Off-road cycling is becoming very popular, much to the displeasure of some walkers. If you want to explore by bike there are some excellent long routes set up, including the **Cumbria Cycleway**, a 260 mile (418 km) circular tour round the Furness Peninsula, up the west coast, to Carlisle, then through the Eden Valley, Appleby and on to Kirkby Lonsdale. Uses mainly quiet minor roads and goes through some brilliant and peaceful scenery, though not actually in the National Park itself. There's a guide to the route, published by Cicerone Press.

The **Sea to Sea Cycle Route** was developed by Sustrans, the national network of traffic-free routes. It's an excellent idea, using a mix of redundant railway tracks, bridleways and minor roads suitable for bikers. The Cumbrian section crosses the Lake District in the north, beginning in either Whitehaven, following the reclaimed mineral railway track, or Workington through Cockermouth. The routes converge in Whinlatter Forest, then continue through Keswick, Penrith and out of Cumbria beyond Alston. It's a 140 mile (225 km) trip from the west coast to Newcastle or Sunderland in the east, and about 15,000 people complete it every year. More information, plus advice about breaking the journey into manageable chunks, can be found at *www.c2c-guide.co.uk*.

Other bike trails passing through Cumbria include the **Hadrian's Cycleway**, starting in Ravenglass and passing through Whitehaven, Maryport and Carlisle, and the **Reivers Cycle Route**, which kicks off in Whitehaven and ends in Tynemouth, via Cockermouth and Caldbeck among other places. Both are around the 170 mile (274 km) mark. Sustrans looks after the National Cycle Network and can provide more information and maps (tel. 08451 130065 or visit *www.sustrans.org.uk*). There are shorter cycle routes in the Cumbria forests managed by the Forestry Commission, and these actively encourage mountain bikers. Try Ennerdale, Whinlatter or Grisedale, which have excellent marked routes varying in length or difficulty. You can hire bikes at Grisedale (tel. 01229 860369 or visit *www.grisedalemountainbikes. co.uk*).

As it tries to get people out of cars and on to bikes, the Lake District National Park Authority has compiled some leaflets on good cycle routes across the area; you can pick them up from TICs or download them from *www.lake-district.gov.uk*.

If you want to bike elsewhere, check before you pedal off – access is not always straightforward. Bridleways and byways are generally open to cyclists – although feet and hooves have priority – and footpaths are not.

Motoring

First a word of warning: in the middle of the season it can take an age to get through Bowness and Ambleside on the A592 and A591, which regularly feature on the AA's 'summer jam' maps. If you have to get through them, set off early. Keswick is easier than it once was thanks to new roads and flyovers round the town, but if you *have* to get through the town to Borrowdale then that too can be hell. Similarly, in July and August don't expect to get along the A592 from Bowness to Newby Bridge in a hurry. You *always* end up behind someone travelling at 19 miles an hour looking at the view. (This is a good road for spotting locals – they are the ones with steam coming from their ears.) If you can travel

without the car in the main summer months, you'll save yourself a lot of aggravation.

And if you have not already secreted a spare key on your car, do it now, before you hit the Lakes. All TICs moan that one of the most common enquiries is from people who have locked themselves out of their own car. Also beware of theft from cars in isolated car parks. Always hide or remove valuables. Finally, be cunning with your time of arrival and departure and plan to avoid the back-up of traffic that occurs every Saturday morning heading into the Lakes, and every Sunday late afternoon heading out. From the central Lakes it's worth heading north to the dual carriageway at the Penrith end of the A66 that sweeps you to the M6 at junction 40, and avoid struggling south on the congested A591.

Motoring organisations

AA – 24-hour breakdown 0800 887766;
traffic and weather information 09003 401100

Green Flag – 24-hour breakdown 0800 0510636;
traffic information 60010 from mobiles

RAC – 24-hour breakdown 0800 828282;
traffic information 0906 4701740

Other 24-hour recovery companies

Ambleside – Young Motors (tel. 015394 32322)

Carlisle – Auto Recoveries (tel. 01228 534121)

Kendal – Ullswater Road Garage (tel. 015397 30730)

Milnthorpe – Atkinson (tel. 015395 67401)

Penrith – Davidsons (tel. 01768 867101)

Workington – Peel & Son (tel. 01900 605267)

Car parks

In the summer season all the Lakeland towns are murder for parking, and even popular villages get quickly overrun. The car parks are generally pay and display, so bring a pile of change. They are fairly pricey – £6 for a full day is about average in popular places.

Ambleside
Parking on Ambleside's streets is limited to 30 minutes or an hour during the day, depending on where you pull up, and it's regulated by a disc system. You can pick up a disc from any shop or hotel and place it on your dashboard to display your arrival time. There is a car park in the centre, by the library, but this is usually full and transforms itself into a market on Wednesdays. If you're coming from the north, use the big car park opposite St Martin's College – it's handy for the town

and it's a nice walk alongside the river past the Bridge House. (Caution: do not be tempted at weekends by the College's invitingly empty, free car park because they threaten clamps.) From the south, use the car park just past Hayes Garden World. Waterhead has two good car parks and the walk into town is pleasant.

Bowness
This is *the* place to avoid with a car in the busy months. There is limited street parking in Lake Road, coming down from Windermere, but you won't get in. (You will, however, get stuck behind someone else who is trying to get in and blocking the traffic.) There is a small car park next to the cinema, invariably full. The large car park in Rayrigg Road is good if you're early, but after 11.00am there are usually queues to get in. Far better are the car parks down by the Bay. Or, if you're feeling like a nice stroll, use the car park at Ferry Nab and walk back into town along the lake shore and through Cockshott Point. Nearby Braithwaite Fold becomes a car park in summer, opening up 900 more spaces. Don't risk any kerbside parking – Bowness has very efficient traffic wardens.

Carlisle
Like Ambleside, Carlisle has some disc parking if you're visiting briefly. It's free, but for one hour maximum. Look out for the signs. Otherwise use one of the several big car parks. The Viaduct one is usually busy, so try the one beside the Castle or West Walls, which has a short cut to the city centre.

Coniston
Use the main car park in the centre of the village. You have to pay, but it's by far the easiest.

Grasmere
The traffic police in Grasmere are very keen, so be warned. A few summers ago one policeman even booked his own wife for parking on a yellow line. There is a car park in Stock Lane, just as you enter the village from the south, and it's handy for Dove Cottage. If it's full, try the one behind the garden centre, opposite the church. Beware parking in the garden centre car park by mistake, because their charges are huge unless you go in and buy something. They're not very keen on giving change for the ticket machine in the other car park. Also try Broadgate Meadow at the northern end of the village – there's a nice riverside path from it which emerges by St Oswald's Church and misses the crowds.

Hawkshead
Hawkshead is rapidly becoming one large car park with a small village adjacent. The village itself is nearly all pedestrians only, so use one of the main car parks on both sides of the road as you enter from the B5285, and saunter about Hawkshead without fear of being run over.

Kendal

Another horrid place to park. You always end up finding no spaces and having to go all round the one-way system to get back to the first car park you saw but decided to ignore in order to get closer to the shops. There is a good car park by Abbot Hall in Kirkland, and a bigger one on Blackhall Road, behind the shopping centre. There's a free car park by the river, but it's always full by mid-morning.

Keswick

Terrible for parking. There are plenty of options, but they're all tiny and full. The central one off Victoria Street often has queues to get into, so try the one off Heads Road. It's always best to get into Keswick as early as you can to beat the crowds. Another possibility is the car park on Lake Road, from where you can walk back into town, or Booths on Tithebarne Street. Disc zones in town offer an hour or two's free parking if you can ever find a space. Very cheeky visitors have been known to use the Pencil Museum's car park.

Windermere

Windermere has limited street parking, if you're very lucky. Use the car park behind the library. You can also use the vast car park at Booths supermarket if you can combine a trip with your shopping.

Recommended excursions

Two by public transport

If all those warnings about traffic jams and parking have put you off driving, here are a couple of ideas for days out without the car.

A good road for this is the A591, especially between Ambleside and Keswick. It has excellent public transport, with buses (no. 555) every hour. It's also the only route in central Lakeland where you'll see a double-decker. Set off early from Ambleside (the buses leave from the car park opposite the library) and get on the top deck – the view as you go over the Dunmail Raise on a good day is tremendous. Travel up to Keswick, and make two stops on the way, at Dove Cottage in Grasmere and Castlerigg Stone Circle just before Keswick. Time each visit so you don't have to wait too long for the next stage of your bus journey. Spend some time in Keswick, then catch the bus back to Ambleside, this time stopping off at Rydal Mount on the way. Coleridge and Wordsworth did this route all the time when visiting each other. On foot, of course. They were tough in those days.

Another good expedition taking in lots of water and scenery begins by parking at the railway station at Haverthwaite. Buy a combined train and steamer ticket through to Bowness – they usually connect quite well. Once off the boat, walk up Biskey Howe above the village, admiring the panorama as the Victorians did. Then around the Glebe right beside the lake to the Windermere ferry. Cross the lake to Sawrey, and walk up the footpath to Beatrix Potter's Hill Top house. The no. 525 bus runs hourly from here to take you to Hawkshead, where you can get some food and admire Potter's watercolours in the Gallery (see Chapter 10 for opening hours), before catching the no. 505 bus to Ambleside, the steamer the length of the lake down to Lakeside and the train back to Haverthwaite. Allow plenty of time towards the end of the day for delays and missed connections, and plan your schedule carefully to minimise time spent hanging around. Excellent views all the way.

An excursion by car

Start early to enjoy fully, or go in the middle of the week when it's quieter. Leave Bowness via the A592. Go up the Kirkstone Pass to Ullswater, and enjoy the wonderful views over the lake as you come down the other side. After a few miles driving alongside the lake, turn left on to the A5091 through Dockray to join the A66 at Troutbeck. Turn left and blast along to Keswick. Near the town, follow the signs for the Borrowdale Valley on the B5289, stopping at the Bowder Stone. Continue on over the Honister Pass. Park up at Buttermere and stretch your legs by walking round the lake. Then continue on the same road to Lorton, before turning right on to the B5292, which takes you back over the Whinlatter Pass to Keswick. Leave Keswick via the A591 and stop off just outside the town at Castlerigg Stone Circle. Turn off at the southern end of Thirlmere to go round the west side of the lake; it's quiet and pretty with places to park and explore the shore. Then back on to the A591 through Grasmere and Rydal (where you can take your pick of two Wordsworth homes) and back to Bowness via Ambleside.

CHAPTER FOUR

Accommodation

Where to stay – hotels, guesthouses, farmhouses, caravans, camping and renting

The choice is enormous, so all we intend to offer is a personal selection of the best places to stay, plus some broad general advice.

At the last count there were more than a thousand hotels and guesthouses in the Lakes, plus 4,000 cottages, houses, flats and chalets for hire and 8,000 or so camping and caravan pitches. In all, in serviced and non-serviced accommodation, there are more than 60,000 beds to choose from – and more than 100,000 across the whole of Cumbria. So where do you start? Well, it's relatively easy to get a list of the local beds available, and most of the TICs will help – just turn up and ask – but no official is going to tell you what they're really like.

General hints

The official guide to accommodation is published each year by Cumbria Tourism, and you can get copies sent to you to help plan a visit. They'll be in most TICs too. Cumbria Tourism also runs a Booking Hotline (tel. 0845 450 1199) and a website that lets you search through all the places on offer (*www.golakes.co.uk*). It's worth pointing out that the guide only lists Cumbria Tourism members and that entries in the guide are paid for.

Annual accommodation registers are also produced by local councils and tourism partnerships, each covering a specific area and giving the majority – though not all – of the accommodation available. They're available from TICs or direct from the councils. South Lakeland District Council produces *Where to Stay in South Lakeland* (tel. 05397 33333 or visit *www.lakelandgateway.info*). The Keswick Tourism Association produces *Keswick on Derwentwater and the North Lakes* (tel. 017687 72645 or visit *www.keswick*.org). Eden District Council produces *Where to Stay in Eden* (tel. 017688 67466 or visit *www.visiteden.co.uk*). Allerdale and Copeland District Councils produce the *Western Lake District Visitor Guide* (tel. 01900 818741 or visit *www.western-lakedistrict.co.uk*). *Where to Stay in South Lakeland* also covers the Furness region, known rather grandly these days as the Lake District Peninsulas.

In the summer and school holidays, anything in a town like Bowness, Windermere, Ambleside and Keswick is bound to be busy, noisy and hectic. Unless you love that sort of thing, try a rural spot or head for the fringes, such as Furness, Cockermouth or the Eden Valley. In those places, you will at least be able to park your car outside your digs. At most of the hotels and larger guesthouses it is worth asking about winter prices and bargain breaks – there are all sorts of price incentives to get people into the area out of season.

Even with money to burn, I would not spend the whole of a week's holiday at one of the posh hotels featured in this chapter. You can have too much of a good thing. So even if you have the money, save these places to the end of the hols as a treat, perhaps booking in for one or two nights – with dinner, of course, as that's the highlight. Before that, book into a cheap inn or guesthouse in a completely different part of the Lakes for the first part of the week, and have some active days and simple, hearty meals.

Prices

We don't give exact hotel prices. We did so in the first edition, and oh the moans and groans from proprietors when they put their charges up and expected us to reprint immediately. Just think of our extra printing costs every time they muck around with their details. So we are lumping them all into five price bands, where A is cheap and cheerful and E is posh and expensive.

The grades need to be treated with a bit of caution. Few hotels have flat rates across the year; instead they tend to operate a sliding scale according to demand. So you'll pay much more for a weekend in August than you would for a midweek break in February. Many places vary their rates according to the size and quality of the room and whether it's got a good view. A lot of places impose a minimum two-night stay at weekends, and may expect you to have dinner there too. Some places don't offer a price for singles; others do but put on such a heavy penalty that the price approaches that of a double.

Our price bands are per person per night, for bed and breakfast, based on sharing a double or twin room.

A	£40 or less
B	£41–£70
C	£71–£100
D	£101–£130
E	£131 or more

The top hotels

Accommodation at the high end of the market is increasing all the time in the Lake District. There has been something of a revolution in the country house concept in particular, with several places smartening up their act, losing some of their stuffiness and formality, and creating luxurious, contemporary places to stay. In previous editions we set Sharrow Bay and Miller Howe apart from the rest, but while these two are still at the top of the pile in terms of comfort, places like Holbeck Ghyll, Gilpin Lodge and The Samling have upped their game to such an extent that they deserve to be bracketed with them. What's particularly pleasing is that these hotels are creating their individual personalities and not slavishly following the luxury formula.

You can eat extremely well in all these hotels too, the standard of cooking in general bearing no comparison to the dismal country house fare on offer in most places even ten years ago. All this means that they're very expensive, of course, and you will often have to book weeks in advance in the summer. But if you have the money, Sharrow Bay and the like are well worth it for one night, if only for the experience.

★★★ *Gilpin Lodge*
Crook Road, 2 miles (3.2 km) southeast of Bowness
Tel. 015394 88818 or visit *www.gilpin-lodge.co.uk*

Price E

Luxurious, relaxed hotel, pretty lounges and 20 acres (8 ha) of fine grounds. There are 14 bedrooms in the main bit, plus six more out in the grounds with their own gardens and hot tubs. Outstanding dinners and enormous breakfasts. Tasteful, charming and an unpretentious take on the country house concept.

★★★ *Holbeck Ghyll Country House Hotel*
Holbeck Lane off the A591 north of Windermere
Tel. 015394 32375 or visit *www.holbeckghyll.com*

Price E

Classy hotel, restaurant and spa in a 19th-century hunting lodge. There are 21 luxurious bedrooms, in either the main lodge or the 8 acres (3.2 ha) of grounds. Relaxing rooms and great views over Windermere. The restaurant has a Michelin star, and most room rates include dinner there.

★★★ Miller Howe
Rayrigg Road, 1 mile (1.6 km) north of Bowness
Tel. 015394 42536 or visit *www.millerhowe.com*

Price E

Standards at this Lakeland institution have been kept consistently high by recent new owners despite a few changes of hands in the last few years. It's a very English place, making good use of Cumbrian produce, materials and staff. The food is terrific and imaginative, served in the evenings with some theatre, and the views over the lake are sensational. It has a quiet but friendly atmosphere, with handsome drawing rooms and conservatory, filled with antiques and art and deep sofas. Downsides: while the hotel has fabulous lake views on one side, on the other it's on a busy, boring road, and some bedrooms might be thought more flash than tasteful. There are three self-contained cottage suites in the grounds if you want a bit more space, though, of course, you'll pay for the privilege. Great breakfasts.

★★★ Sharrow Bay Country House Hotel
2 miles (3.2 km) south of Pooley Bridge on the eastern shore of Ullswater
Tel. 017684 86301 or visit *www.sharrowbay.co.uk*

Price E

The original country house hotel, founded in 1948 and still one of the best in England, let alone the Lakes. Still wins accolades and awards from all the top guides, and attracts the quality, or at least the famous and well off. Has its own helipad if you happen to be arriving by helicopter. The food here is sensational – it's one of four places in the Lakes with a Michelin star and claims to have created the original sticky toffee pudding. The setting on the shore of Ullswater is equally wonderful. Each bedroom is a work of art, while the conservatory and drawing rooms are also very posh, stuffed with antiques and books to read. Always quiet and discreet, with staff who are always attentive without being intrusive. No bar – you have your drinks served in the drawing rooms as if in a private home. Occasionally people complain that the food and rooms are too fancy or that it's chintzy, dated or overly formal – and it's true that you can feel a bit on display – but if you have the money there's nowhere more luxurious, and so far corporate ownership hasn't diminished it. If you want to get a flavour of Sharrow Bay without spending a fortune, book in for the excellent afternoon tea.

★★ Armathwaite Hall
North end of Bassenthwaite Lake
Tel. 017687 76551 or visit *www.armathwaite-hall.com*

Price D

Magnificent 16th-century mansion in vast grounds with deer and woodland. Lots of oak and roaring fires in the lounges. Updated nicely, and the rooms are very comfortable. Outstanding views over Bassenthwaite Lake.

★★ The Drunken Duck
Barngates, 2 miles (3.2 km) north of Hawkshead
Tel. 015394 36347 or visit *www.drunkenduckinn.co.uk*

Price **D–E**

Still technically a pub, but one that's a good deal smarter than your average Lakeland boozer of years gone by. The 16 bedrooms are individually styled to great taste, and there are fine views of the valley. The food in the restaurant is very good, if expensive. Relaxed, friendly service and excellent own-brew beers.

★★ L'Enclume
Cavendish Street, Cartmel
Tel. 015395 36362 or visit *www.lenclume.co.uk*

Price **C**

More a restaurant with rooms than a hotel, but outstanding whatever it is. The bedrooms are all individually designed, and most people are staying to sleep off one of the long tasting menus in the Michelin-starred restaurant. Rooms aren't as expensive as you might think, especially if you come midweek.

★★ Moss Grove Organic Hotel
Grasmere
Tel. 015394 35251 or *www.mossgrove.com*

Price **B–D**

An amazing newcomer. Totally refurbished on organic principles – handmade beds from recycled timbers, duck down duvets, woollen carpets, clay paints. Organic and fair-trade food, of course. The 11 rooms have modern touches like hi-fis and internet access.

★★ The Punch Bowl
Crosthwaite
Tel. 015395 68237 or visit *www.the-punchbowl.co.uk*

Price **C**

A 300-year-old place in the pretty Lyth Valley, brought firmly up to date by the owners of the Drunken Duck in Hawkshead. The rooms are plush, and the restaurant serves refined food. Like the Drunken Duck, it's more of a hotel or restaurant with rooms than a traditional Lakeland pub, but the bar area is relaxed.

★★ Rothay Manor
Rothay Bridge, ½ mile (800 m) southwest of Ambleside
Tel. 015394 33605 or visit *www.rothaymanor.co.uk*

Price **D**

A fine Regency hotel, run by the same family for generations. It has featured in all 30 editions of the *Good Hotel Guide*. Fine food and grounds.

★★ *The Samling*
Ambleside Road, between Windermere and Ambleside
Tel. 015394 31922 or visit *www.thesamling.com*

Price **E**

An imaginative and luxurious country house hotel, popular with celebs (including Tom Cruise). Excellent food and a relaxed atmosphere. Set in 67 acres (27 ha) of gardens. Not cheap, but certainly classy. Wordsworth knew this place (though before it had hot tubs and DVD players in the rooms).

★★ *Swinside Lodge*
Newlands, 3 miles (4.8 km) south of Keswick
Tel. 017682 72948 or visit *www.swinsidelodge-hotel.co.uk*

Price **B–C**

A pretty setting under Cat Bells, near Derwentwater; it's great for walks and good for guzzling. Cumbria Tourism's small hotel of the year in 2007.

★★ *Underscar Manor*
Applethwaite, near Keswick
Tel. 017687 75000 or visit *www.underscarmanor.co.uk*

Price **D–E**

Magnificent setting under Skiddaw, set in 40 acres (16 ha) of gardens with deer and red squirrel, with marvellous conservatory–dining room, but it has suffered a little from endless changes. Comfortable bedrooms and good food.

★★ *White Moss House*
Rydal Water, Grasmere
Tel. 015394 35295 or visit *www.whitemoss.com*

Price **B–C**

A well-established, popular hotel with great views of Rydal Water and ideally situated for any number of walks. Cottage suites. Big country house style dinners and breakfasts include porridge cooked overnight in the Aga. Closed in December and January.

★ *Aynsome Manor*
½ mile (800 m) outside Cartmel
Tel. 015395 36653 or visit *www.aynsomemanorhotel.co.uk*

Price **C**

A comfortable, perennially popular country house hotel that has just emerged from a refurbishment. Dinner comes with the room rate and is a formal, single-sitting affair. Closed in January.

★ *Borrowdale Gates Country House Hotel*
Grange-in-Borrowdale
Tel. 017687 77204 or visit *www.borrowdale-gates.com*

Price **C**

A splendid situation in the Borrowdale Valley and a great base for walking. There are 29 bedrooms and a very good restaurant.

★ *Dale Head Hall*
Thirlmere, near Thirlspot
Tel. 017687 72478 or visit *www.daleheadhall.co.uk*

Price **B–C**

A marvellous setting on Thirlmere, once the summer retreat of the Lord Mayor of Manchester. The dining room dates back to 1577. Lovely gardens. Good value.

★ *Fayrer Garden House Hotel*
Lyth Valley Road, 1 mile (1.6 km) south of Bowness
Tel. 015394 88195 or visit *www.fayrergarden.com*

Price **C**

An elegant Victorian country house hotel overlooking Windermere with 24 en-suite bedrooms. Good dinners. Rooms vary from rather small and basic to large and luxurious, so choose carefully.

★ *Langdale Chase*
Off the A591, 3 miles (4.8 km) north of Windermere
Tel. 015394 32201 or visit *www.langdalechase.co.uk*

Price **D**

A terrific secluded lakeside setting, lots of carved oak and a traditional country house atmosphere. Various room categories, including some tucked away in the grounds. Well-regarded restaurant.

★ *Lindeth Fell Country House Hotel*
Lyth Valley Road, 1 mile (1.6 km) south of Bowness
Tel. 015394 43286 or visit *www.lindethfell.co.uk*

Price **B**

A small, friendly, high-class hotel set on the fells above the town. Brilliant views and well away from the hordes. Strong emphasis on fresh food and local specialities.

★ *Linthwaite House*
Crook Road, 1 mile (1.6 km) south of Bowness
Tel. 015394 88600 or visit *www.linthwaite.com*

Price **B–E**

An excellent, well-run hotel set in 14 acres (5.7 ha), including its own tarn, overlooking Windermere. Its country house style has been updated with modern luxuries like flat screen TVs in the bedrooms. Rates vary enormously according to room size, views, time of visit and whether you're staying for the very good dinner, but you can get some bargains at off-peak times.

★ *Lyzzick Hall*
Underskiddaw, 2 miles (3.2 km) northwest of Keswick
Tel. 017687 72277 or visit *www.lyzzickhall.co.uk*

Price **B**

A great setting on the sunny side of Skiddaw. Family-run with 31 bedrooms. Informal, relaxed but efficient. Nice gardens. Lyzzick meant 'light oak' in medieval times.

★ *Rampsbeck Country House*
Watermillock
Tel. 017684 86442 or visit *www.rampsbeck.fsnet.co.uk*

Price **C–D**

A fine 18th-century house with 18 acres (7.3 ha) of grounds on the shores of Ullswater. Very welcoming.

★ *Sawrey House*
Near Sawrey
Tel. 015394 36387 or visit *www.sawrey-house.com*

Price **B**

A Victorian country house in Beatrix Potter village, over-looking Esthwaite Water. Good food.

★ *Storrs Hall*
On the eastern shore of Windermere, just off the A592
Tel. 015394 47111 or visit *www.elh.co.uk*

Price **B–D**

This grand Georgian mansion has its own folly in the grounds. Rooms vary from plain to luxury. No children under 12. It's famous for its 'Ultimate Picnic Hamper' with lobster, caviar and gold leaf shavings instead of curled sand-wiches and packets of crisps. A snip at £1,566 for two.

★ *Uplands Hotel*
Haggs Lane, Cartmel
Tel. 015395 36248 or *www.uplands.uk.com*

Price **C**

Spawned by Miller Howe and run by two of former owner John Tovey's right-hand people. You get much of the quality and comfort you would expect there at around half the price. Only five bedrooms.

★ *Waterhead Hotel*
Waterhead, Ambleside
Tel. 015394 32566 or visit *www.elh.co.uk*

Price **B–D**

A new boutique hotel, billed as the Lake District's first town house hotel. Rooms are nicely designed and kitted out with natty things like flat screen TVs and DVDs. Swish bar and restaurant. Not yet quite found its character, but very smart nonetheless.

Executive hotels

This section is for those first-class hotels that have most of the accepted amenities but that are a bit lacking in individual character or atmosphere compared to the ones noted above. They are generally large, good for business people, large parties or, very important, good for children. (Some of the luxury-end places actively discourage children. And they might be wasted on them in any case, unless they're very discerning diners.) The following are not executive in the Hilton, monster new building sense – and luckily nothing in the Lake District is like that – but in being large and efficient. You might actually prefer them to some of the personal eccentricities and strange customs of the classier hotels.

★★ *Lodore Falls Hotel*
Borrowdale Valley, off the B5289
Tel. 017687 72285 or visit *www.lakedistricthotels.net*

Price **C–E**

The hotel used to complain that it wasn't classed as 'classy' in previous editions, but it's too big (71 rooms) and too functional to be hailed as an experience. But it's excellent at what it sets out to do and has a fine setting on Derwentwater in the lovely Borrowdale Valley. Not many hotels can say they have a waterfall in the grounds. A good restaurant and lots of facilities, including swimming pools (inside and out), tennis and squash courts, beauty salon and gym. Minimum stay including dinner at weekends. Now owned by a mini chain of Lake District hotels with places in Keswick, Penrith and Ullswater.

★★ *Wordsworth Hotel*
College Street, Grasmere
Tel. 015394 35592 or visit *www.thewordsworthhotel.co.uk*

Price **D**

A skilful conversion of an old building with lots of amenities like swimming pool and sauna. The decor is traditional but the rooms have been updated lately to include wireless internet and other gizmos. There's a bar-bistro, the Dove and Olive Branch, and restaurant, the Prelude. Relaxed and comfortable and a good location in the middle of Grasmere. All connections with Wordsworth are entirely in the hotel's imagination.

★ *Beech Hill Hotel*
Newby Bridge Road, 3 miles (4.8 km) south of Bowness
Tel. 015394 42137 or visit *www.beechhillhotel.co.uk*

Price **B–D**

A modern hotel with swimming pool, sauna and solarium. Terraced gardens drop down to the lake shore.

★ *Belsfield Hotel*
Kendal Road, Bowness
Tel. 0870 6096109 or visit *www.corushotels.com*

Price **B**

A large Victorian house with 64 bedrooms and 6 acres (2.4 ha) of gardens. Lots of family amenities, including swimming pool and sauna. Great views, perched on the hills above the ferry area. Now part of a chain, with some of the blandness that can bring.

★ *Burn How Garden House Hotel*
Black Belsfield Road, Bowness
Tel. 015394 46226 or visit *www.burnhow.co.uk*

Price **B**

An unusual combination of nice Victorian house with modern motel-style chalets. Peaceful location, yet among all the Bowness action. Good for families.

★ *The Inn on the Lake*
Glenridding
Tel. 017684 82444 or visit *www.lakedistricthotels.net*

Price **C–D**

Recently refurbished, with 46 bedrooms and grounds sloping down to Ullswater. Lots of leisure facilities and croquet on the lawns.

★ *Lakeside Hotel*
Newby Bridge
Tel. 015395 30001 or visit *www.lakesidehotel.co.uk*

Price **D–E**

An excellent situation by the Lakeside Pier on Windermere, yet somehow still looks more stunning outside than inside. Health and leisure spa and 77 en-suite rooms.

★ *Low Wood Hotel*
Ambleside Road, between Windermere and Ambleside
Tel. 08458 503502 or visit *www.elh.co.uk*

Price **B–C**

Lakeland's biggest hotel, with 110 bedrooms, has a magnificent lakeside setting, albeit with a busy road between the hotel and shore. Loads of facilities, including a leisure centre and several places to eat. It bills itself as a resort hotel and has always been popular with coach parties and business conferences. A rather soulless place, but good for keeping the kids entertained.

★ *North Lakes Hotel and Spa*
Ullswater Road, Penrith
Tel. 017688 68111 or visit *www.shirehotels.com*

Price **C**

Penrith's answer for all busy business people. There are 84 rooms and a leisure club.

★ *Old England Hotel*
Church Street, Bowness
Tel. 015394 42444 or visit *www.macdonald-hotels.co.uk*

Price **B–D**

An old established mansion hotel with all the usual amenities and 56 bedrooms. The grounds lead down to the shore of Windermere.

★ *The Regent by the Lake*
Waterhead Bay, Ambleside
Tel. 015394 32254 or visit *www.regentlakes.co.uk*

Price **C**

Formerly known as The Regent, so they obviously wanted to make the point about its location. It's a family-run place with 30 rooms and good food, including late breakfasts. They pick up from the train or bus stations.

★ *Swan Hotel*
Newby Bridge
Tel. 015395 31681 or visit *www.swanhotel.com*

Price **C–D**

This smart hotel in a good base for exploring the southern lakes. It has a swimming pool, good restaurant and nicely appointed rooms. Popular for weddings and conferences.

Small hotels and pubs

Here are the best of the many such places across the Lakes – the ones that might one day well jump up to be called 'classy'. Lakeland pubs have smartened up their act no end in the last few years and now offer some of the best and most reasonably priced accommodation. The pubs mentioned here are particularly good for accommodation, but see also the selection in Chapter 5.

★★ *Old Dungeon Ghyll Hotel*
Great Langdale
Tel. 015394 37372 or visit *www.odg.co.uk*

Price **B**

Hugely popular with walkers and climbers over three centuries. There are 13 simple but comfortable rooms in a stunning location down the Langdale Valley. Good beers and hearty bar meals after a day on the fells. The New Dungeon Ghyll 1 mile (1.6 km) down the road has nicer rooms but none of the character.

★★ *Wasdale Head Inn*
Wasdale Head
Tel. 019467 26229 or visit *www.wasdaleheadinn.co.uk*

Price **B**

A classic walkers' pub and hotel, this is the unofficial head-quarters of English rock climbing. Basic rooms but hearty meals and own-brew beers. Perhaps the best located hotel in Lakeland.

★★ *Wood House*
Just outside Buttermere and off Crummock Water
Tel. 017687 70208 or visit *www.wdhse.co.uk*

Price **A–B**

A beautifully situated 17th-century house, with its own gardens running down to a bay at the end of Crummock Water, just ½ mile (800 m) from Buttermere village. Only three bedrooms, plus a separate self-catering cottage, but what taste, what artistry, what comfort … They do great dinners and packed lunches and issue permits for the lakes. Look out for red squirrels in the grounds.

★ Boot Inn
Boot
Tel. 019467 23224 or visit *www.bootinn.co.uk*

Price **B**

A friendly pub and hotel for walkers. There are nine rooms, and meals come in ravenous walker-sized portions.

★ Coniston Lodge
Station Road, Coniston
Tel. 015394 41201 or visit *www.coniston-lodge.com*

Price **B**

Six rooms in an award-winning small hotel. It's handy for the village and the lake. Home cooking.

★ The Cottage in the Wood
Whinlatter Pass, 5 miles (8 km) northwest of Keswick
Tel. 017687 78409 or visit *www.thecottageinthewood.co.uk*

Price **A–B**

A welcoming 17th-century coaching inn. Good food using local produce.

★ Hazel Bank Country House
Rosthwaite, Borrowdale
Tel. 017687 77248 or visit *www.hazelbankhotel.co.uk*

Price **C**

A fine Victorian house and gardens. There are outstanding views from most of the eight rooms, and four-course dinner is included in the room rate.

★ Lancrigg Vegetarian Country House
Easedale Road, just northwest of Grasmere
Tel. 015394 35317 or visit *www.lancrigg.co.uk*

Price **C**

A wonderful setting, hidden away from the Grasmere crowds in Easedale. There are 13 rooms, some with four-poster beds and whirlpool baths (veggies have fun too, you know). Splendid unkempt gardens. Wordsworth was a regular visitor. Room rates include dinner. An ideal base for walkers.

★ Langstrath Country Inn
Stonethwaite
Tel. 017687 77239 or visit *www.thelangstrath.com*

Price **B**

A friendly, cosy pub in one of the Lakes' best valleys. Very popular with walkers. You have to book for dinner.

★ The Leathes Head Hotel
Borrowdale, 3 miles (4.8 km) south of Keswick
Tel. 017687 77247 or visit *www.leatheshead.co.uk*

Price **C**

An elegant Edwardian place with great views of the valley. It's getting a good reputation for food, with daily-changing menus.

★ The Mill Hotel
Mungrisdale
Tel. 017687 79659 or visit *www.themillhotel.com*

Price **C**

Not to be confused with the Mill pub next door, though you can stay there too. Excellent food and reasonable country house style accommodation. Closed from November to February.

★ Temple Sowerby House
6 miles (9.7 km) northwest of Penrith off the A66
Tel. 017683 61578 or visit *www.temple-sowerby.com*

Price **C**

Not in the Lake District proper, being 6 miles (9.7 km) the other side of Penrith, on a main road, but it's a handsome Georgian house with a good reputation for imaginative food.

★ Travellers Rest Inn
Just outside Grasmere on the A591
Tel. 015394 or visit *www.lakedistrictinns.co.uk*

Price **A–B**

Really hot on atmosphere, though it could just be the log fires. Good bar meals.

Bower House Inn
Eskdale Green, Eskdale
Tel. 019467 23244 or visit *www.bowerhouseinn.co.uk*

Price **A**

A pretty 17th-century inn in a pretty valley. The 29 bedrooms are all en suite.

Fleatham House
High House Road, St Bees
Tel. 01946 822341 or visit *www.fleathamhouse.com*

Price **A–B**

This Victorian house is in pretty grounds in the equally pretty small town of St Bees, a short walk from the beach. Ideal for coast to coast walkers starting off. As patronised by Tony Blair and family when he was told he ought to go on holiday in Britain. Six en-suite bedrooms. Relaxed and friendly.

Pheasant Inn
Near Dubwath, just off the A66 on the west side of
Bassenthwaite Lake
Tel. 017687 76234 or visit *www.the-pheasant.co.uk*

Price **C–D**

In summer this old-style inn can be a bit like a roadhouse
with passing tourists, but it's very attractive. Good food with
quite formal dinners.

Red Lion Hotel
Red Lion Square, Grasmere
Tel. 015394 35579 or visit *www.hotelslakedistrict.com*

Price **B–C**

An 18th-century inn on the outside; a 21st-century hotel with
jacuzzis and spas on the inside.

Three Shires Inn
Little Langdale
Tel. 015394 37215 or visit *www.threeshiresinn.co.uk*

Price **B**

A comfortable, simple, small hotel with ten bedrooms.
Friendly atmosphere and welcoming to walkers.

Guesthouses and farmhouses

There are hundreds of guesthouses in the Lake District, and
this is just a personal selection. The difference between a
guesthouse and a hotel is that hotels have to offer lunch or
dinner to non-residents. More and more farms are offering
accommodation as they try to diversify a bit, and they can be
a good option for families. They'll usually be glad to show
you round the farm, and breakfasts are invariably superb. For
more farms offering B&B, try Farm Stay (tel. 0247 669 6909
or visit *www.farmstay.co.uk*). Several farms are also part of
the 'Luxury in a Farm' scheme (*www.luxuryinafarm.co.uk*).

Ambleside

Compston House
Compston Road
Tel. 015394 32305

Price **A**

American motel chic comes to the Lakes.

High Wray Farm
High Wray, Ambleside
Tel. 015394 32280

Price **A**

Comfy rooms and self-catering cottage in a 17th-century farmhouse.

Lakes Lodge
Lake Road
Tel. 015394 33240

Price **A–B**

Very smart, contemporary B&B, all DVDs and lilac wallpaper.

Borrowdale

Ashness Farm
4 miles (6.4 km) south of Keswick off the B5289
Tel. 017687 77361

Price **A**

Five rooms in a lovely working farm; they'll show you round.

Coniston

Yew Tree Farm
Off the A593 just north of Coniston
Tel. 015394 41433

Price **A**

Doubled as Hill Top in the film *Miss Potter* and consequently very popular.

Grasmere

Banerigg Guesthouse
Lake Road
Tel. 015394 35204

Price **A**

Outstanding location on the lake and very friendly owners.

How Foot Lodge
Town End
Tel. 015394 35366

Price **B**

Six rooms very close to Dove Cottage.

Riversdale
White Bridge
Tel. 015394 35619

Price **A–B**

Three bedrooms. The winner of Cumbria Tourism's B&B of the year in 2006.

Great Langdale

Millbeck Farm
Off the B5343 by the New Dungeon Ghyll
Tel. 015394 37570

Price **A**

A 250 acre [100 ha] working farm owned by the National
Trust. A bargain for the location.

Hawkshead

Ann Tyson's Cottage
Wordsworth Street
Tel. 015394 36405

Price **A–B**

Stay where Wordsworth once lodged – a bit more comfy than
in his time, though.

Yewfield
Hawskhead Hill
Tel. 015394 36765

Price **B**

A charming guesthouse with famous vegetarian breakfasts.
Lovely grounds. Hosts occasional free classical concerts (they
have a grand piano). Closed December and January.

Ireby

Boltongate Old Rectory
Boltongate, 1 mile (1.6 km) north of Ireby
Tel. 016973 71647

Price **B**

One of the new breed of swish, plush guesthouses. Cumbria
Tourism's 2007 B&B of the year.

Keswick

Charnwood Guesthouse
Eskin Street
Tel. 017687 74111

Price **A**

Five rooms in a listed Victorian building.

Highside Farm
Near Bassenthwaite
Tel. 017687 76952

Price **A**

Upmarket accommodation in a working farmhouse dating
back to 1668.

Linnett Hill Hotel
Penrith Road
Tel. 017687 73109

Price **A**

A cheap and cheerful base for Keswick and the north Lakes.
Good veggie breakfasts.

Longtown

Bessiestown Farm
Catlowdy, Penton
Tel. 01228 577219

Price **A–B**

Not your actual Lakeland, though it's handy for the Borders,
but it's a proper farm with, you won't believe it, a heated
indoor swimming pool for guests. It's expanded to take in
self-catering accommodation too.

Lorton

New House Farm
2 miles (3.2 km) south of Lorton on the B5289
Tel. 01900 85404

Price **B**

A lovely 17th-century farmhouse and wide grounds. Hearty
dinners.

Rosthwaite

Yew Tree Farm
Up the lane opposite the shop
Tel. 017687 77675

Price **A**

Prince Charles's B&B of choice when he visits the Lakes.
Three en-suite bedrooms, traditionally chintzy. An excellent
tea room, the Flock-In, is attached.

Sawrey

Ees Wyke Country House
Near Sawrey
Tel. 015394 36393

Price **B**

A cosy Georgian house, sometime holiday home of Beatrix
Potter.

Seatoller

Seatoller House
Tel. 017687 77218

Price A–B

A characterful 17th-century farmhouse, popular with walkers. Honesty bar and communal dinners.

Torver

The Old Rectory
2 miles (3.2 km) south of Coniston
Tel. 015394 41353

Price A

A very welcoming little guesthouse with good homemade food. An excellent base for walking.

Windermere

Brendan Chase Guesthouse
College Road
Tel. 015394 45638

Price A

A popular place with eight rooms.

Glenburn Hotel
New Road
Tel. 015394 42649

Price A–B

Recently refurbished into a very smart little place, with rain showers, spa baths and the like.

Hawksmoor Guesthouse
Lake Road
Tel. 015394 42110

Price A–B

Ten bedrooms in a pleasant spot between Bowness and Windermere.

Meadfoot Guesthouse
New Road
Tel. 015394 42610

Price A–B

A comfortable, welcoming place with gardens.

Youth Hostels

There are 26 Youth Hostel Association hostels in Cumbria, 22 of them inside the Lake District proper. They vary in standard and scale, from bustling places like Ambleside, with all mod cons and a lake view, to small, remote mountain huts like Black Sail. In general, though, the standard of them is getting better all the time, and prices are still incredibly cheap, usually starting from £10 to £15 per person per night. They're great if you're on a tight budget.

You don't have to be a youth to join the YHA, and a neat way of using them, if the adults prefer more comfort in their old or middle age, is to book into a good hotel while putting the kids in the nearest youth hostel. You can join the YHA at any hostel or by tel. 0870 770 8868. Alternatively, visit *www.yha.org.uk* for details of all hostels and membership.

Which hostels are best can depend a lot on the warden, but four good ones in fantastic locations are:

★★★ Black Sail
Perfect for anyone wanting to get away from it all and do some serious walking – it's a remote former shepherd's bothy at the head of Ennerdale, reachable only by foot. Basic facilities but unparalleled location (tel. 07711 108450).

★★ Coniston Coppermines
A mile and a bit from Coniston and half of the way up to the fells, including the Old Man (tel. 0870 770 5772).

★★ Honister Hause.
Up the Honister Pass in former quarry workers' buildings (tel. 0870 770 5870).

★★ Skiddaw House
Not actually part of the YHA network any longer, this is now looked after by an enthusiastic charitable foundation. A dramatic remote location 3 miles (4.8 km) from the nearest road and with no mains electricity (tel. 07747 174293).

And the rest:

Ambleside	Tel. 0870 770 5672
Arnside	Tel. 0870 770 5674
Borrowdale	Tel. 0870 770 5706
Buttermere	Tel. 0870 770 5736
Carlisle	Tel. 0870 770 5752
Cockermouth	Tel. 0870 770 5768
Coniston Holly How	Tel. 0870 770 5770
Derwentwater	Tel. 0870 770 5792

Elterwater	Tel. 0870 770 5816
Ennerdale	Tel. 0870 770 5820
Eskdale	Tel. 0870 770 5824
Grasmere Butharlyp House and **Thorney How**	Tel. 0870 770 5836
Hawkshead	Tel. 0870 770 5856
Helvellyn	Tel. 0870 770 5862
Kendal	Tel. 0870 770 5892
Keswick	Tel. 0870 770 5894
Lakeside	Tel. 015395 39012
Langdale	Tel. 0870 770 5908
Patterdale	Tel. 0870 770 5986
Wasdale	Tel. 0870 770 6082
Windermere	Tel. 0870 770 6094

Holiday villages

These are another growth industry in the Lake District. Self-enclosed places with all the facilities you could want, they're great for families but not really the proper Lakeland. Here are a few of them.

Center Parcs Whinfell Forest Holiday Village
Tel. 08700 673030 or visit *www.centerparcs.co.uk/whinfell*

Good quality lodges in Whinlatter Forest, some 700 in total, with a vast range of facilities, including swimming pools, cinema and archery.

The Lakelands
Tel. 015394 33777 or visit *www.the-lakelands.com*

A complex of 11 luxury apartments with a leisure club near Ambleside.

The Langdale Estate
Tel. 015394 37302 or visit *www.langdale.co.uk*

There are timeshares as well as self-catering options, plus loads of leisure facilities.

Low Briery Riverside Holiday Village
Tel. 017687 72044 or visit *www.keswick.uk.com*

There are 50 cottages, chalets, apartments and caravans on the outskirts of Keswick.

Camping and caravanning

There are campsites and caravan parks across the lakes. Many are open only from March to October, although plenty of hardy campers pitch their tents all year round. The best guide to sites is Cumbria Tourism's annual *Caravan and Camping Guide*, which is available from TICs. Other useful resources are the Camping and Caravanning Club, which has several sites around the county (tel. 0845 130 7631 or visit *www.campingandcaravanningclub.co.uk*) or the web-only Lake District Camping guide (*www.lakedistrictcamping. co.uk*).

Campsites can get very busy in July and August, when it's worth booking a pitch if you can, and it's also worth noting that many have grown very wary of large groups. It's a cheap way of doing the Lakes – prices start at a couple of pounds a night for very basic facilities and won't rise much above £10 – and if the weather is good there's no better way to stay. Despite the opening up of access, campers are not encouraged to pitch tents wherever they fancy. Rangers have been known to come rattling on tent poles first thing in the morning to point out that you're illegally parked, which isn't conducive to sleep – or anything else. That said, if you're staying out of the way, leave no trace of your stay and pitch late and leave early, you're unlikely to get into trouble.

Three of the best located campsites in the Lakes are run by the National Trust. They are all among this pick of ten top sites.

Fisherground Farm
Eskdale
Tel. 019467 23349)

Quiet, good for families. Open March to October. No bookings.

Great Langdale
Tel. 015394 37668

A National Trust site. At the head of the valley, it's a perfect base for walking. Great pubs nearby. Open all year round.

Hollins Farm
Boot
Tel. 019467 23253

A friendly farm site. Open from March to October.

Low Wray
Ambleside
Tel. 015394 32810

A National Trust site on the western side of Windermere. Open Easter to October.

The Old Post Office Campsite
Santon Bridge
Tel. 01946 726286

A family-run riverside site. Open mid-March to November.

Side Farm
Patterdale
Tel. 017684 82337

Good for Ullswater and fells. Open Easter to October.

Stonethwaite
Borrowdale
Tel. 017687 77602

Very basic facilities but beautiful site by the river in Borrow-dale. Open all year.

Syke Farm
Buttermere
Tel. 017687 70222

Lovely spot just outside the village. Open all year.

Wasdale
Tel. 019467 26220

A National Trust site. Close to Scafell Pike and, more impor-tantly, the Wasdale Head Inn. Open all year.

Waterside House Campsite
Pooley Bridge
Tel. 017684 86332

Great quiet spot near Ullswater. Open mid-March to September.

Camping barns

These offer a Lakeland sleeping experience, unquote – that is, basic overnight accommodation. Also known as Stone Tents. Lakeland farmers can now get grants to tart up their unused barns and provide clean, dry shelter, aimed at walkers or cyclists who don't want the drag of carrying a tent. They're use-ful for families or parties, especially in winter or bad weather, and if there are enough of you, you can sometimes book sole use. Each barn offers a wooden sleeping platform, table, slate cooking bench, cold water tap and WC. There's no heating, so it can get cold, although some have log fires. Bring your own sleeping bag and stove. Unisex accommodation. Some farms also sell eggs and milk. The cost is usually £6 a night, making it the cheapest roof you'll ever have over your head in the Lakes.

There are now 13 barns scattered around the Lake District, and you could put together quite a good itinerary walking between several of them. There's a centralised booking service (tel. 019467 58198 or visit *www.lakelandcampingbarns.co.uk*).

Caravan parks

These are subject to a voluntary grading scheme, in which points are given for services, cleanliness and the like (visit *www.ukparks.com*). Well-regarded Cumbrian parks include these ten.

Castlerigg Hall Caravan Park
Keswick
Tel. 017687 74499 or visit *www.castlerigg.bigmag.co.uk*

Fallbarrow Park
Rayrigg Road, Windermere
Tel. 015394 44422 or visit *www.southlakelandparks.co.uk*

Greaves Farm Caravan Park
Barber Green, Cartmel
Tel. 015395 36329

Greenhowe Caravan Park
Great Langdale
Tel. 015394 37231 or visit *www.greenhowe.com*

Holgates Caravan Park
Silverdale
Tel. 015247 01508 or visit *www.holgates.co.uk*

Newby Bridge Country Caravan Park
Canny Hill, Newby Bridge
Tel. 015395 30105 or visit *www.cumbriancaravans.co.uk*

The Quiet Site
Watermillock
Tel. 017684 86337 or visit *www.thequietsite.co.uk*

Skelwith Fold Caravan Park
Ambleside
Tel. 015394 32277 or visit *www.skelwith.com*

Waterfoot Park
Pooley Bridge, Ullswater
Tel. 017684 or visit *www.waterfootpark.co.uk*

Wild Rose Park
Ormside, near Appleby
Tel. 017683 51077 or visit *www.wildrose.co.uk*

Self-catering

You'll never be short of options for self-catering accommodation in the Lakes. Prices can vary enormously between the central Lakes and the fringes and according to the time of year you book. Rates in the summer school holidays can often be well over double those in the depths of winter. You can often get some good bargains if you're booking late on, and it's worth shopping around the agencies. Local TICs will also have up-to-date availability.

The Cumbria and Lakeland Self Caterers Association (CaLSCA) seeks to provide minimum standards for properties and is a good place to start if you want to be sure of a good quality place. They have 110 or so properties on their books, all searchable at *www.lakesbreaks.co.uk*. In addition to the nationwide brokers, these are well worth trying.

The Coppermines and Lakes Cottages
There are 80 or so cottages, many in the Coniston area (tel. 015394 41765 or visit *www.coppermines.co.uk*).

Cumbrian Cottages
More than 700 cottages across the Lakes (tel. 01228 599950 or visit *www.cumbrian-cottages.co.uk*).

Heart of the Lakes
300 or so cottages in all parts (tel. 015394 32321 or visit *www.heartofthelakes.co.uk*).

The Lakeland Cottage Company
Southern Lakes specialist (tel. 015395 38180 or visit *www.lakeland-cottage-company.co.uk*).

Lakeland Cottage Holidays
Specialising in Keswick and Borrowdale (tel. 017687 76065 or visit *www.lakelandcottages.co.uk*).

Lakelovers
Hundreds of places, mostly in the south and west; free membership of a local leisure club with your booking (tel. 015394 88858 or visit *www.lakelovers.co.uk*).

Loweswater Holiday Cottages
(7 units) Scale Hill, Loweswater (tel. 01900 85232 or visit *www.loweswaterholidaycottages.co.uk*).

Monkhouse Hill Cottages
Nine cottages on a converted 17th-century farm near Caldbeck, aiming at the luxury end of the market; offer lots of extra services like meal deliveries and champagne breakfasts (tel. 016974 76254 or visit *www.monkhousehill.co.uk*).

National Trust
Only a handful of properties, but just about all special (tel. 0870 458 4422 or visit *www.nationaltrustcottages.co.uk*).

Wheelwright's
Good for the Langdales and Ambleside (tel. 015394 37635 or visit *www.wheelwrights.com*).

Accommodation for the disabled

This is now much better than it once was, and there is also much better listing of disabled-friendly places in mainstream brochures. Cumbria Tourism and TICs are usually very good at providing on-the-spot information about disabled loos, access and so on – they'll have lists of suitable accommodation and visitor attractions and ideas for walks on the flat. The Lake District National Park Authority publishes *Miles without Stiles*, which includes 21 good walks suitable for wheelchairs, and it has leaflets on countryside access for people with disabilities. Its Coniston Boating Centre has a wheelchair-accessible boat for hire. The National Trust has made a lot of improvements too, providing better disabled access to properties and trails and Braille guides at many properties.

Several trusts provide accommodation and activities in the Lake District for the disabled.

The Bendrigg Trust
Bendrigg Lodge, Old Hutton, near Kendal
Tel. 015397 23766 or visit *www.bendrigg.org.uk*

This residential centre caters for the disabled and runs lots of outdoor activities. Its main lodge provides accommodation for up to 40 people, and there's self-catering for 22 more.

The Calvert Trust Adventure Centre
Little Crosthwaite, Keswick
Tel. 017687 72255 (minicom) or visit
www.calvert-trust.org.uk

This has accommodation for 40 people, plus self-catering for 12, and the trust runs activities, including archery, abseiling, hill walking, rock climbing, canoeing, horse riding and sailing.

The Kepplewray Project
The Kepplewray Centre, Broughton-in-Furness
Tel. 01229 716936 or visit *www.kepplewray.org.uk*

Run by a Christian charity, which aims to bring disabled and non-disabled people together. Housed in a converted old mansion in Broughton-in-Furness.

Windermere Manor Hotel
Rayrigg Road, Windermere
Tel. 015394 45801 or visit
www.actionforblindpeople.org.uk

This not-for-profit hotel is run by Action for Blind People and caters for visually impaired people and their guide dogs. There are adapted rooms, station pick-ups and lots of treats for the dogs.

CHAPTER FIVE

Food and Drink

From Michelin-starred fine dining to humble tea rooms, plus the best of Lakeland drinking and a few recipes to try yourself

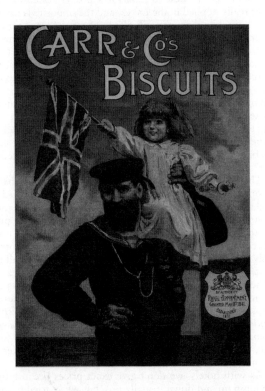

The Lake District's tourist industry has smartened up its act no end in the last few years, and hotels and tourist attractions are much more consistently professional than they once were (not to say more consistently expensive, too). But nowhere has the transformation been more startling than in food and drink. It's always been a good place for foodies, but there's been a true revolution in the restaurants, pubs and even humble cafés of Cumbria, leaving it with some of the best eating and drinking to be found anywhere in the country.

Part of this transformation is down to the general raising of standards in tourism and the wider British food revolution, but it's also thanks to a growth in the number of brilliant producers turning out fabulous food up and down the county. Plenty of people now come to the Lakes primarily to eat and drink, and they're certainly well served. Cumbria now has four Michelin-starred restaurants, dozens more outstanding eating places, more than 20 breweries, a dozen farmers' markets, great little artisan producers and even someone organising foodie tours around the best of them all. And then there's all the special food that the Lakes is famous for: Cumberland sausages, Herdwick lamb, sticky toffee pudding, Kendal mint cake and the rest.

The old general rule of the big cities that hotel meals are poor and that it's best to look for a proper restaurant has never really applied in the Lakes, and the opposite is usually true. But while there are still plenty of tourist traps turning out fry-ups and take-aways for visitors, wherever you are in the Lakes you won't have to travel too far to find places turning out imaginative cooking, many of them now using locally sourced produce and taking a lot of pride in the tradition of Lake District food and drink. There's a wide choice at the top end of the market, taking in the perennially popular country houses and some stand-alone newcomers, but you can also eat very well on a budget these days if you seek out the best of the Lakeland pubs or cafés. All places are no smoking since the ban on lighting up in public places was introduced in 2007. Hurrah. Unless you're a smoker.

This pick of the best Lakeland eating places is based on our own tastings and expert soundings. We've tried to single out the very best, then given a place-by-place guide to the rest. In this edition we've listed the best foodie pubs together with restaurants, as the distinction between them is becomingly increasingly blurred. Vegetarian places, previously listed separately, are incorporated too. Despite all the meat that's about there is a long tradition of veggie eating in the Lakes, and it has some of the best such places in the country; more details about vegetarian restaurants, hotels, shops and pub meals are in Viva's *Vegetarian Lake District Guide*, available for a pound from bookshops or *www.vegetarianguides.co.uk*. We've singled out the best hotels for food here, but see also Chapter 4 for a few more places offering decent food.

As with hotels, we don't give exact prices because they can jump up and down (usually up), but we've tried to indicate what you might expect to pay with the following bands, based on an average price for dinner for one, without drinks or service.

A	Under £15
B	£15–£30
C	£30 plus

The Big Four

First, those four Michelin-starred restaurants. A Michelin star doesn't always mean best, of course, and there's a very definite formula of cooking and service that impresses Michelin inspectors. And you pay a hefty premium for that star. But all these places have built excellent local reputations – two of them over decades, two of them in a much shorter time. You can stay over in all of them; see the accommodation listings in Chapter 4 for more. (Throughout this chapter, star ratings may not always be the same because they're rated here on food rather than accommodation.)

★★★ *Gilpin Lodge*
Crook Road, 2 miles (3.2 km) southeast of Bowness
Tel. 015394 88818 or visit *www.gilpin-lodge.co.uk*

Price C

Outstanding food in a wonderful setting. The menus are seasonal; dinners are multi-course affairs, and puddings and cheeses are excellent. As in many places like this, lunches are simpler, cheaper and offer a good taster of the full experience.

★★★ *Holbeck Ghyll Country House Hotel*
Holbeck Lane off the A591 north of Windermere
Tel. 015394 32375 or visit *www.holbeckghyll.com*

Price C

Refined, well-balanced British–French food. This place has turned itself into a very modern country house lately, and the restaurant isn't as intimidating as many Michelin-starred places.

★★★ *L'Enclume*
Cavendish Street, Cartmel
Tel. 015395 36362 or visit *www.lenclume.co.uk*

Price C

Amazingly inventive cooking, with vast tasting menus that read like cryptic crossword clues and ingredients you may well never have heard of. Chef Simon Rogan is rated as one of the rising stars of British cooking. Also offers cookery classes if you're feeling brave. Enclume is French for anvil, by the way.

★★★ *Sharrow Bay Country House Hotel*
2 miles (3.2 km) south of Pooley Bridge on the eastern shore of Ullswater
Tel. 017684 86301 or visit *www.sharrowbay.co.uk*

Price C

Outstanding, refined country house fare in this Lakeland institution. The emphasis has turned increasingly to Cumbrian ingredients. Dinners are multi-course, formal affairs, but you can get some (relative) bargains at lunch. It claims to be the birthplace of sticky toffee pudding and has been listed in the *Good Food Guide* for 47 years; only four places in the country can beat that.

More top Lakeland restaurants

Now the best of the rest. Again, some of these can be found in the accommodation listings too.

★★★ Miller Howe
Rayrigg Road, 1 mile (1.6 km) north of Bowness
Tel. 015394 42536 or visit *www.millerhowe.com*

Price C

An inventive twist on the country house formula, and standards are just about as high as they've ever been here. Good-value set menus at lunchtimes. There are fabulous views of Windermere from the dining room.

★★ The Drunken Duck
Barngates, 2 miles (3.2 km) north of Hawkshead
Tel. 015394 36347 or visit *www.thedrunkenduckinn.co.uk*

Price C

The archetypal gastropub, with more of the gastro than the pub these days. You can try their own-brew beers in the small bar area, but most of the space is given over to the smart restaurant, which serves ambitious, very good food that stays just the right side of pretentious. Book in advance. Cheaper, plainer lunches are often more fun.

★★ Linthwaite House
Crook Road, 1 mile (1.6 km) south of Bowness
Tel. 015394 88600 or visit *www.linthwaite.com*

Price C

Modern, unfussy and delicious food in this plush but relaxed country house. There are great views over Windermere and friendly service.

★★ Lucy's on a Plate
Church Street, Ambleside
Tel. 015394 31191 or visit *www.lucysofambleside.co.uk*

Price B

Imaginative food from top-notch ingredients and a mind-boggling range of homemade puddings. If you book in advance you'll find your name on the top of the daily menu. Garden at the rear and family friendly. Open from 10.00am every day. Lucy Nicholson has expanded her Ambleside empire to take in a very well-stocked delicatessen and a relaxed wine bar and bistro too, and she runs a cookery school at Staveley.

★★ Mason's Arms
Strawberry Bank, Cartmel Fell
Tel. 015395 68486 or visit *www.masonsarmsstrawberry-bank.co.uk*.

Price **B**

A fine country inn with food that's a cut above the average pub fare. There's also a wide variety of exotic beers. The lovely valley is off the tourist track, and there are great views from the outside tables.

★★ Quince and Medlar
Castlegate, Cockermouth
Tel. 01900 823579 or visit *www.quinceandmedlar.co.uk*

Price **B**

Colin le Voi, who cooks, and wife Louisa, who waits, are both ex-Sharrow Bay and have made this one of the best vegetarian restaurants in the country, with awards to prove it. Really, we should give them three stars, but as a dedicated meat eater I'm keeping them in their place. The ingenious menu uses vegetarian and ethnic dishes from all over the world. Excellent roulades and cheese beignet. Good wine list. It's a small place, so essential to book. Closed Mondays.

★★ Rothay Manor
Rothay Bridge, ½ mile (800 m) southwest of Ambleside
Tel. 015394 33605 or visit *www.rothaymanor.co.uk*

Price **C**

This Regency hotel offers four-course dinners and cheaper, simpler lunches. Renowned for its soups. Afternoon teas.

★★ Underscar Manor
Applethwaite, near Keswick
Tel. 017687 75000 or visit *www.underscarmanor.co.uk*

Price **C**

Chef Robert Thornton has managed to combine delicate, balanced, imaginative French cuisine with decent helpings. Taste thrills all the way. The service is rather formal, but the manor has a lovely location on the slopes of Skiddaw.

★★ White Moss House
Rydal Water, Grasmere
Tel. 015394 35295 or visit *www.whitemoss.com*

Price **C**

A friendly, relaxed place with long-time owners. Dinner is five courses and single sitting, often involving some Lakeland classics. It's had 35 years of continuous listings in the *Good Food Guide*.

★★ *Zest*
Low Road, Whitehaven
Tel. 01946 692848

Price **B–C**

Not in Lakeland, but definitely a top restaurant and well worth the excursion, even if the building looks boring from the outside. Inside it's all crisp, white decor, highly imaginative menus and excellent service. It's done a brilliant job of bringing high-class food to the west coast. Dinner only, from Wednesday to Saturday. They've opened a new spin-off, tapas-type place on the harbour that does simpler, lighter meals (tel. 01946 66981; price **B**).

★ *Aynsome Manor*
½ mile (800 m) outside Cartmel
Tel. 015395 36653 or visit *www.aynsomemanorhotel.co.uk*

Price **C**

This pleasant, welcoming manor house offers good set dinners. Men need to wear a tie. Closed January.

★ *The Bay Horse*
Canal Foot, Ulverston
Tel. 01229 583972 or visit *www.thebayhorse.co.uk*

Price **B**

Formerly a simple hostelry overlooking Morecambe Bay for cross-sands travellers; then a bistro with an accommodation extension; now a destination eating place. Don't be put off by the horrible road approach past the Glaxo works. The chef came from Miller Howe, but this is less theatrical and cheaper. Regularly changing menus and a bar with a proper pubby atmosphere.

★ *Déja Vu*
Stricklandgate, Kendal
Tel. 015397 24843 or visit *www.dejavukendal.co.uk*

Price **B**

A French bistro with a left-bank atmosphere, it's classier in the evenings. Good for tapas at lunchtimes.

★ *The Eagle and Child*
Kendal Road, Staveley
Tel. 015398 21320 or visit *www.eaglechildinn.co.uk*

Price **B**

A bustling foodie pub in a nice, quiet village. Home cooking with a Cumbrian emphasis. It was CAMRA's Westmorland pub of the year for 2007–8.

★ *Gate Inn*
Yanwath, near Penrith
Tel. 017688 62386 or visit *www.yanwathgate.com*

Price **B**

An excellent gastropub with the emphasis on local, organic ingredients. Retains its pubby atmosphere despite the firm emphasis on food.

★ *The Highwayman*
Burrow, Kirkby Lonsdale
Tel. 01524 273338 or visit *www.highwaymaninn.co.uk*

Price **B**

A newcomer to the ranks of Cumbria's gastropubs. Celebrated local chef Nigel Haworth sources everything from close by, and there are plenty of Cumbrian and Lancastrian favourites on the menu.

★ *Jericho's*
Birch Street, Windermere
Tel. 015394 42522 or visit *www.jerichos.co.uk*

Price **B–C**

The top choice in Windermere, with brasserie-style modern British food. Created by ex-Miller Howe staff. Dinner only and closed on Mondays.

★ *The Jumble Room*
Langdale Road, Grasmere
Tel. 015394 35188 or visit *www.thejumbleroom.co.uk*

Price **B**

This comfy, relaxed place has a burgeoning reputation, run by a friendly couple. Dishes from around the world. Closed Mondays and Tuesdays.

★ *Lancrigg Vegetarian Country House*
Easedale Road, just northwest of Grasmere
Tel. 015394 35317 or visit *www.lancrigg.co.uk*

Price **B**

A long-running veggie hotel and restaurant serving imaginative four-course dinners.

★ *Lucy 4 at the Porthole*
Ash Street, Bowness
Tel. 015394 42793 or visit *www.lucy4.co.uk*

Price **B**

Formerly the Porthole Eating House, now a franchise of Ambleside's 'Lucy 4' concept offering informal, tapas-style eating.

★ *The Punch Bowl*
Crosthwaite
Tel. 015395 68237 or visit *www.the-punchbowl.co.uk*

Price **B**

This country pub was made famous by local food hero Steve Doherty, then refurbished in 2005 by the owners of Hawkshead's Drunken Duck into a similarly upmarket country pub with rooms. Excellent cooking with a definite Cumbrian emphasis. Cheaper meals in the pub area.

★ *Queen's Head*
Troutbeck
Tel. 015394 32174 or visit *www.queensheadhotel.com*

Price **B**

Like many of its counterparts, it's officially a pub but winning lots of plaudits for its imaginative, freshly prepared food. One of the places where locals like to eat. Sit outside in summer.

★ *Rampsbeck Country House*
Watermillock
Tel. 017684 86442 or visit *www.rampsbeck.fsnet.co.uk*

Price **C**

Ambitious, inventive dinner menus and a good wine list, combined with a sensational situation right on the shore.

★ *The Samling*
Ambleside Road, between Windermere and Ambleside
Tel. 015394 31922 or visit *www.thesamling.com*

Price **C**

Small but ambitious restaurant in the boutique country house hotel. Suitably expensive. It held a Michelin star for a while, though that's now gone.

★ *The Strickland Arms*
Sizergh, near Kendal
Tel. 015395 61010

Price **B**

A grand, National Trust-owned Victorian coaching inn. Imaginative menu and good beers. Right by the gates of Sizergh Castle.

★ *Uplands Hotel*
Haggs Lane, Cartmel
Tel. 015395 36248 or visit *www.uplands.uk.com*

Price **C**

A Miller Howe offshoot, it's less formal but still offers excellent food. Lunch from Friday to Sunday, dinner nightly except Mondays.

★ *The Wheatsheaf*
Brigsteer, near Kendal
Tel. 015395 68254 or visit *www.brigsteer.gb.com*

Price **B**

A nice pub, recently refurbished and now with a growing reputation for high-quality but hearty food. Good set menus if you eat early in the evening.

★ *Zeffirelli's*
Compston Road, Ambleside
Tel. 015394 33845 or visit *www.zeffirellis.com*

Price **B**

There's an Italian restaurant downstairs and a snazzy jazz bar upstairs. Has expanded in size but is often full; book in advance for an evening meal. Famous for its wholemeal-base pizzas. You might not realise it's a vegetarian place until you've finished. Open all day. It's part of a cinema, and you can get a two-course meal and cinema ticket for £15.95.

Other recommendations: restaurants, pubs, cafés and tea rooms

This list includes some of the smaller – and often less pretentious – places that haven't made it into our list of top restaurants but that are probably no less worth visiting for all that. It includes more pubs that are particularly good for food (others are listed below), plus some examples of that famous Lakeland speciality – the tea room with home-baked cakes, sometimes, as with Brantwood and Dalemain, combined with other attractions. Prices where given are for dinner (see above); where there's no indication of price they offer teas or light lunches only.

Ambleside

Apple Pie
Rydal Road
Tel. 015394 33679

A busy, cheerful café and bakery, great for breakfasts and with homemade pies and soup for lunch.

★ *The Glass House*
Rydal Road
Tel. 015394 32137

Price **B**

An imaginative restoration of a 16th-century mill, next door to a glassmaking workshop. Good modern British food. Doesn't seem to have suffered from a mauling on Gordon Ramsay's *Kitchen Nightmares* TV programme; in fact, they say business has increased. Early evening offers.

Taste of Lakeland
Rydal Road
Tel. 015394 32636

Good tea rooms and shop selling some of the best of local produce. Daytime only.

Bowness

Hole in't Wall
Fallbarrow Road
Tel. 015394 43488

Price **A**

Bowness's oldest and best pub. Decent bar meals and terrace.

Rastelli's
Lake Road
Tel. 015394 44227

Price **A**

Family run, with especially good pizzas. Evenings only, closed Tuesdays.

★ *Jackson's Bistro*
St Martin's Square
Tel. 015394 46264

Price **A–B**

Jackson has long gone, but this has a cheerful atmosphere over two floors. Excellent value for money.

★ *Lighthouse Café and Restaurant*
Main Road
Tel. 015394 88260

Price **B**

A neat, metropolitan feel to this café-restaurant, which is well placed to catch the posh southerners as they swoop into Windermere. Dining room or bar for cocktails and snacks.

Broughton-in-Furness

The Square Café
Market Square
Tel. 01229 716388

A popular café with homemade food; good for cake or a light lunch.

Caldbeck

Watermill Café
Priest's Mill
Tel. 016974 78369

Healthy lunches and teas in a very tastefully converted watermill. Also craft shops, with people crafting away. Open occasional evenings for special dinners. Closed January and first few weeks of February.

Cockermouth

Norham Coffee House
Main Street
Tel. 01900 824330

A pleasant courtyard setting and atmosphere.

Coniston

Beech Tree House
Yewdale Road
Tel. 015394 41717

A former vicarage. Vegetarian food.

Bluebird Café
Coniston Boating Centre
Tel. 015394 41366

This neat little café just by the lake is kept in trim by the National Park Authority; it's next to their boating centre.

Jumping Jenny
Brantwood
Tel. 015394 41396

Good teas and lunches at John Ruskin's place. Open to non-visitors. There's a welcoming wood burning stove in winter.

Dent

Stone Close
Main Street
Tel. 015396 25231

Excellent lunches, teas and evening meals (these last by booking only), all in a 17th-century cottage, complete with flagged floors and cast iron range. Also does B&B.

Grange-in-Borrowdale

Grange Bridge Cottage
Tel. 017687 77201

A beautifully located tea room with terrific homemade cakes.

Grange-over-Sands

★ *Hazelmere Café and Bakery*
Yewbarrow Terrace
Tel. 015395 32972

Very popular since it was named best tea place in Britain. It offers a vast range of teas and good cakes and light lunches.

Grasmere

Miller Howe Café
Red Lion Square
Tel. 015394 35234

Daytime only, but the sort of refined take on tea and cakes that you would expect of the Miller Howe empire.

Villa Columbina
Town End
Tel. 015394 35268

Price **B**

Next to Dove Cottage, this is good for teas, cakes and light lunches in the day, and Italian dinners in the evening. Closed in January.

Hawkshead

Queen's Head Hotel
Main Street
Tel. 015394 36271

Price **B**

Good, straightforward food – this is probably your best bet for dinner in Hawkshead.

Kendal

★ *1657 Chocolate House*
Branthwaite Brow
Tel. 015397 40702

Chocoholics' heaven. There are dozens of versions of hot chocolate and chocolate cakes and a chocolate shop. Some non-chocolate-based food is available too.

Brewery Arts Centre
Highgate
Tel. 015397 25133

Price **B**

Café is open all day in the exhibition area – something to look at while you're guzzling. Evening meals are served in the Grain Store restaurant. The pizzas are especially good. Art on the walls there too.

Low Sizergh Barn
Sizergh, near Kendal
Tel. 015395 60426

Great tea room above the farm shop. Get a seat by the window to watch the cows being milked.

Keswick

★ *Abraham's Tea Room*
Borrowdale Road
Tel. 017687 72178

A conversion at the top of George Fisher's outdoor shop. Get those climbing boots on as it's 38 steps to get a cup of tea, but worth it. The building is fascinating – it was once the home of the famous Lakeland photographers – and the views are marvellous. Good light meals are available every day during shop opening hours.

Lakeland Pedlar
Henderson's Yard
Tel. 017687 74492

An excellent café with inventive vegetarian food, much of it Mediterranean. Daytime only, sometimes later in summer.

★ *Maysons*
Lake Road
Tel. 017687 74104

This self-service place is good for light daytime meals. Open some evenings in the summer too.

Old Sawmill Tea Rooms
Dodd Wood, Underskiddaw
Tel. 017687 74317

Part of the Mirehouse estate, but there's no charge to get in. Makes the best fruit cake in Cumbria. Open daytimes from Easter to October only.

★ *Swinside Lodge*
Newlands, just outside Keswick
Tel. 017682 72948

Price C

Set-priced, four-course dinners are served in a Georgian hotel.

Melmerby

★★ *The Village Bakery*
Tel. 017688 98437

A tiny village 10 miles (16 km) northeast of Penrith, so it's not exactly on the usual tourist round but is a wonderful stopping-off point if you're making the trek to Newcastle. There's an excellent café in a converted 18th-century barn. Home produce using locally ground flours and organic ingredients, much of it available to take away. Baking in wood-fired ovens. Open daily, but check for reduced times in winter. Definitely worth a detour and now getting the national recognition it deserves. Founder Andrew Whitley has written a good book on bread, *Bread Matters*.

Newby Bridge

Fell Foot Café
Fell Foot Park
Tel. 015395 31274

The National Trust's access point to the south end of Windermere. The café is in an old boathouse, which has undergone a revamp and provides good teas and light lunches. Gets busy during holidays. You can hire rowing boats. Open Easter to November.

Ravenstonedale

★ *The Fat Lamb*
Crossbank
Tel. 015396 23242

An old coaching inn set high on remote moorland. Pub and restaurant. You can't miss it.

Rosthwaite

Riverside Bar
At the Scafell Hotel
Tel. 017687 77208

Good pub grub. The hotel does posher meals.

Seatoller

★ *Yew Tree Restaurant*
Tel. 017687 77634

Price **B**

Café by day, restaurant with South African specialities (it's a long story) by night. A great surprise in a remote area. Owned by the Honister Slate Mine people. Closed November to January.

Skelwith Bridge

Chesters Café
By the River Brathay
Tel. 015394 32553

Recently refurbished into a very upmarket caff, with cakes and light lunches. By the Touchstone Interiors shop and the river.

St John's-in-the-Vale

The Tea Garden
Low Bridge End Farm
Tel. 017687 79242

Homemade everything, including lemonade and cakes, in a fabulous spot. Open Easter to November.

Staveley

Wilf's Café
Mill Yard
Tel. 015398 22329

In a family-friendly conversion of an old bobbin loft. There's a link to the adjacent Hawkshead brewery beer hall, and you can bring their beers through to have with your meal. Daytime only, but occasional evening events.

Windermere

Lakeland Ltd
Behind the railway station
Tel. 015394 88200

Nice lunches and teas in a very well-refurbished building housing the home furnishings emporium. It gets busy, so they operate a timed ticket system.

Renoir's Coffee Shop
Main Road
Tel. 015394 44863

One of Windermere's best cafés, with excellent home baking and friendly service. Tables outside.

Wicked Windermere
High Street
Tel. 015394 44954

Price **B**

A new Cumbrian restaurant where African restaurant Kwela's used to be. Does a, well, wicked Kendal mint cake crème brûlée. Open every evening.

Workington

★ *Old Town House*
Portland Street
Tel. 01900 871332

Price **B**

Not many tourists go to Workington, least of all to eat, but the Old Town House has a good atmosphere and good food and is reasonably priced. Situated at the corner of a surprisingly elegant little square. Makes you think you can't be in Workington.

More good pubs

The best of the rest of the pubs not mentioned above – 20 places that haven't yet succumbed to the gastropub revolution and where you can still get a decent pint as well as something to eat.

Bitter End
Kirkgate, Cockermouth
Tel. 01900 828993

A cosy local with good bar food and its own micro-brewery.

Black Bull
Coniston
Tel. 015394 41335

Coniston's best pub and home of the Bluebird beer.

Britannia
Elterwater
Tel. 015394 37210

Very popular with walkers. Stone-flagged bar and lovely outdoor area. Homemade food.

Dog and Gun
Lake Road, Keswick
Tel. 017687 73463

Keswick's best pub. Good beers and photos by the Abraham brothers on the wall.

King's Arms
Hawkshead
Tel. 015394 36372

On Hawkshead's main square. Good beers.

Kirkstile Inn
Loweswater
Tel. 01900 85219

This famous pub is loved by walkers. Own-brew beers.

Kirkstone Pass Inn
Tel. 015394 33888

Lakeland's highest pub and one of the cosiest. It gets cut off after a lot of snow, which isn't a bad thing if you're inside.

The Mortal Man
Troutbeck
Tel. 015394 33193

A cosy pub with rooms and noteworthy sign.

Newfield Inn
Seathwaite
Tel. 01229 716208

A pretty Duddon Valley pub. Wordsworth used to drop in.

The Old Crown
Hesket Newmarket
Tel. 016974 78288

The first community cooperative pub in Britain. There are fine beers from its own Hesket Newmarket Brewery.

Old Dungeon Ghyll
Great Langdale
Tel. 015394 37372

A classic walkers' pub and hotel; this is the place to swap stories of the fells after a long day's walking.

Pheasant Inn
Bassenthwaite
Tel. 017687 76234

A good walkers' pub with excellent beers.

Queen's Head
Tirril
Tel. 017688 63219

Good food and beers from its own Tirril Brewery.

The Sun Inn
Bassenthwaite
Tel. 017687 76439

A 17th-century pub with good bar meals.

Tower Bank Arms
Near Sawrey
Tel. 015394 36334

A National Trust pub, as featured in Beatrix Potter.

Wainwrights
Chapel Stile
Tel. 015394 38088

A great location and good local beers. Part of the Langdale estate.

Wasdale Head Inn
Wasdale
Tel. 019467 26229

The original Lakeland walkers' and climbers' bar, and still the best.

Watermill Inn
Ings
Tel. 015398 21309

Real ale fans' mecca, with 16 beers on tap at any time.

White Lion
Patterdale
Tel. 017684 82214

A good post-walk pub.

Woolpack Inn
Eskdale
Tel. 019467 23230

A no-nonsense walkers' pub with good beer and hearty food.

Beer and breweries

So much for the foodie places – now for the liquid stuff. The real stuff, of course, which real ale drinkers drool over while making skitty comments about that fizzy beer that the big breweries pump out everywhere. Alongside its revolution in food, the Lake District has seen an amazing transformation in its beer. A decade ago there were a couple of small breweries, but now there are more than 20, many of them picking up awards and exporting their brews all round the country. Helped by a few tax breaks and some very thirsty walkers, the independent and micro breweries are thriving.

It's ironic then that Cumbria's biggest brewery has sold up. **Jennings** was originally set up in the village of Lorton, but since 1874 it's sat majestically on the banks of the Cocker in Cockermouth, near the Castle. The brewery and its chain of 128 pubs were bought by brewing giant Wolverhampton & Dudley in 2005, but so far the owners seem content to let it be. And it remains very popular with enthusiasts and as much a part of the Lakes as Herdwick sheep. They produce an excellent range of beers, and you'll see their pubs all over the Lakes, but especially in the north. Bills itself as 'The Genuine Taste of the Lake District'.

Jennings runs regular tours to see the traditional brewing methods. Afterwards you can sample the produce, then stagger into the shop to buy Jennings leisure wear. What more could a beer enthusiast want? Tour times vary (tel. 0845 129 7190 or visit *www.jenningsbrewery.co.uk*).

Jennings is being increasingly challenged by the host of small breweries, and you'll find dozens of their different brews across the Lakes. Ten of the companies worth looking out for are noted below.

Barngates Brewery
Ambleside
Tel. 015394 36575 or visit *www.barngatesbrewery.co.uk*

Attached to the Drunken Duck, which offers all the beers on tap and in bottles. The brews are named after pub pets.

Bitter End Brewery
Cockermouth
Tel. 01900 828993 or visit *www.bitterend.co.uk*

At the back of the pub of the same name.

Coniston Brewery
Tel. 015394 41133 or visit *www.conistonbrewery.co.uk*

Ships its award-winning Bluebird bitter to supermarkets across the country.

Cumbrian Legendary Ales
Hawkshead
Tel. 015394 36436 or visit
www.cumbrianlegendaryales.com

Names its beers after Cumbrian heroes.

Dent Brewery
Tel. 015396 25326 or visit *www.dentbrewery.co.uk*

Brews from local spring water. It's a remote brewery but increasingly popular nationwide.

Great Gable Brewing Company
Wasdale Head
Tel. 019467 26229 or visit *www.greatgablebrewing.com*

Brews at the Wasdale Head Inn.

Hawkshead Brewery
Staveley
Tel. 015394 36111 or visit *www.hawksheadbrewery.co.uk*

A fast-growing firm with an excellent beer hall at Mill Yard, Staveley. Before you ask, they started life at Hawkshead but outgrew it.

Hesket Newmarket Brewery
Tel. 016974 78066 or visit *www.hesketbrewery.co.uk*

A cooperative brewery attached to the Old Crown Inn. Does tours.

Loweswater Brewery
Tel. 01900 85219 or visit *www.kirkstile.com*

Brewery of the Kirkstile Inn.

Tirril Brewery
Brougham Hall
Tel. 017688 63219 or visit *www.tirrilbrewery.co.uk*

A big exporter.

The Campaign for Real Ale is unsurprisingly active in Cumbria, and publishes a very good *Cumbria Real Ale Guide*, available in local bookshops. For more on their work, visit *www.camrawestmorland.org* or *www.westcumbriacamra.org.uk*. CAMRA also helps to organise beer festivals – there are annual events in Ulverston (late August or early September), Kendal (mid-October) and Whitehaven (mid-November). Several real ale pubs run their own festivals too – one of the best is in Boot every June.

Cider

Cider deserves a mention too. Cumbria has some very old apple varieties, and producers include Cock Robin. Based near Abbeytown, between Wigton and Silloth, they welcome visitors (tel. 07989 592566 or visit *www.cockrobin.org*).

The Lake District's specialist producers

Cumbria has loads of them, and more are springing up all the time. Some export their delicacies to foreign parts, like Fortnum & Mason's. Savoury Lakeland foods tend to centre around meat and are often found in smoked form – a good way of preserving food in days before refrigeration. Sweet products traditionally use lots of spices, which used to be brought in to ports on the west Cumbria coast and were highly regarded as a sign of wealth. A spice cupboard in your house was real status. Here are some personally tested recommendations.

Bakery products

There are lots of good bakeries, but the queen of them all is the Village Bakery of Melmerby near Penrith. In addition to delicious standard fare, they experiment with yummy new ideas. All organic (tel. 017688 98437 or visit *www.villagebakery.com*).

Charr

The Lake District's champion fish, a landlocked relic from the Ice Ages. A cross between salmon and trout and great on a barbeque. Found in a few good restaurants, though you'll more likely see trout.

Cumberland sausage

Traditional Lakeland fare, this is found across the Lakes and, unfortunately, ripped off by supermarkets. The proper Cumberland banger has a high meat content, no preservatives and plenty of spice. Some of the best are from Richard Woodall of Waberthwaite, near Millom (tel. 01229 717237 or visit *www.richardwoodall.co.uk*).

Grasmere gingerbread

The real stuff, baked since 1854 to a still-secret recipe and bought only from Sarah Nelson's Gingerbread Shop. Quite biscuity, but don't tell them so because they sell it firmly as cake. The smell in the shop is heavenly (tel. 015394 35428 or visit *www.grasmeregingerbread.co.uk*).

Handmade cheeses

A number of businesses have sunk under the weight of European legislation, but Thornby Moor Dairy of Thursby near Carlisle is still around and produces a good range (tel. 016973 45555). There's a great shop at Kirkby Lonsdale, gathering together some of the best local cheeses, called Churchmouse Cheeses (tel. 015242 73005 or visit *www.churchmousecheeses.com*; they do mail order).

Herdwick lamb

The Lake District's native breed is now enjoying something of a revival among discerning restaurants and pubs. The best supplier is Farmer Sharp, who runs a co-op of Herdwick suppliers and takes lamb and mutton down to Borough Market to impress London each week (tel. 01229 588299 or visit *www.farmersharp.co.uk*).

Ice cream

An obvious spin-off for dairies. The best producer is the Windermere Ice Cream and Chocolate Company, which makes 32 flavours with organic milk from Low Sizergh Barn (tel. 015398 22866 or visit *www.windermereicecream.co.uk*).

Kendal mint cake

Kendal's most famous export, beloved of walkers and of dentists in need of business. It's thought to have been created by accident when a Kendal confectioner spilt a pan. Manufacturers include Romney's (tel. 015397 20155 or visit *www.kendal.mintcake.co.uk*).

Rum butter

Cumbria's glorious combination of butter from the farms and rum from the west coast ports is good on scones, toast and Christmas pudding. It's traditionally eaten at Lake District christenings – the butter signifying the richness of life, sugar its sweetness, rum its spirit and nutmeg its spice. Dead easy to make.

Shrimps and cockles

The underrated produce of Morecambe Bay, cockles can be found on a few menus in Cumbria, but most are exported to

Europe. The top producer is Furness Fish in Flookburgh (tel. 015395 59544 or visit *www.morecambebayshrimps.com*).

Smoked meats, cheeses, fish, etc.

Look out for those that use traditional smoking methods and not nasty chemicals. For a good range try The Old Smoke-house at Brougham Hall, near Penrith (tel. 017688 67772 or visit *www.the-old-smokehouse.co.uk*).

Sticky toffee pudding

Now found on the menu of every other Lakeland caff or restaurant. It's a sweet sponge, usually served with hot fudge sauce. Several places lay claim to the original recipe, including Sharrow Bay, but its headquarters is definitely (and improbably) now the Cartmel Village Shop. They export it across the country and have people making it in the US too (tel. 015395 36280 or visit *www.stickytoffeepudding.co.uk*).

Westmorland damsons

For some reason they thrive in the Lyth Valley in the southern Lakes. Once a major industry for farms in the area, damsons are still widely used for jam, gin, sausages, chutneys and lots more. The Westmorland Damson Association organises an annual Damson Day celebration around the time that damson trees come into glorious blossom in mid- to late April (visit *www.lythdamsons.org.uk*).

Finally, **charcoal**. No, not for eating, but for cooking your delicacies. Fans of Arthur Ransome's books will know all about this stuff, traditionally produced in the Lakes from coppiced trees. A recent impetus from the National Park has prompted a little revival of the industry. Try Lakeland Charcoal of Finsthwaite, near Newby Bridge (tel. 07733 290801 or visit *www.lakeland-charcoal.co.uk*).

Any foodies wanting to get to know the best of the producers could do no better than take a tour with local food writer Annette Gibbons. A typical trip takes in local farmers and artisan producers and includes a nice lunch somewhere, costing £120 for a full day (tel. 01900 881356 or visit *www.cumbriaonaplate.co.uk*).

More information on Cumbria's food and drink can be had from a series of trails produced by the Cumbria Fells and Dales' Leader+ programme. They cover producers of honey, damsons, apples, sausages and beer among others. Tel. 017688 69533 or download the leaflets from *www.fellsanddales.org.uk*. Cumbria Tourism produces a useful booklet about the food and drink of the Lake District called, inevitably, *The Taste District* and available from TICs. Look out too for 'Made in Cumbria', the stamp of which shows that something is truly home-grown (tel. 015397 32736 or visit *www.madeincumbria.co.uk*).

Farmers' markets and food festivals

A good place to pick up the best of Lakeland produce is at one of the dozen or more farmers' markets around the county. They're also a fine way of supporting local farms, many of which diversified into selling produce after the foot and mouth crisis of 2001.

The best farmers' market is at Orton in the Eden Valley (second Saturday of each month; visit *www.ortonfarmers. co.uk*). There are also markets at: Brampton (last Saturday); Brough (third Saturday); Carlisle (first Friday); Cockermouth (first Saturday); Egremont (third Friday); Greenhead (second Sunday); Harrison and Hetherington (second Saturday); High Bentham (first Saturday); Kendal (last Friday); Penrith (third Tuesday); Pooley Bridge (last Sunday, held at Rheged from October to March); and Ulverston (third Saturday).

There are also a couple of big foodie festivals worth popping along to if you're nearby at the time. You can pick up lots of free tasters, and they usually have cookery demonstrations. The Cumbria Life Food and Drink Festival is held at Rheged in early May, with the Food Lovers' Festival at Crooklands near Kendal following in mid-June.

A Lake District dinner

Here's a three-course meal with its roots firmly in Cumbria. To start, potted shrimps. Then a tatie pot, the classic supper of Lakeland shepherds and farmers. And finally, sticky toffee pudding, of course. You're not likely to go hungry with this little lot, even if you've spent the day tramping the fells.

Morecambe Bay potted shrimps

8 oz (250 g) cooked Morecambe Bay shrimps
5 oz (150 g) butter
a pinch each of salt, cayenne pepper and nutmeg

Melt the butter, chuck in the shrimps and stir. Add the salt, pepper and nutmeg. Simmer for a few minutes, then tip the mixture into little pots. Spoon more melted butter on top to seal the pots. Leave to cool. Serve with hot brown toast.

Tatie pot

16 oz (450 g) potatoes
2 onions
1½ lb (700 g) neck of Herdwick lamb (or mutton if you prefer)
6 carrots
1 black pudding
14 fl oz (400 ml) stock or water
salt and pepper
butter or dripping

Peel and slice the potatoes and onions, trim the meat, chop the carrots and slice the black pudding. Arrange a layer of potatoes on the bottom of a big casserole dish, and place half of the lamb, onions, carrots and black pudding on top. Season well. Add another layer of everything, then finish with a layer of potatoes on top. Pour over the stock or water and dot with butter or dripping. Cook for 2 hours in a low oven (160°C, 325°F, gas mark 3), turning up the heat towards the end to brown the potatoes. You can leave it longer if you like. Serve with pickled cabbage.

Sticky toffee pudding

2 oz (50 g) butter
6 oz (175 g) white sugar
1 egg, beaten
8 oz (225 g) plain flour
6 oz (175 g) stoned dates, finely chopped
9 fl oz (275 ml) boiling water
1 teaspoon each baking powder, bicarbonate of soda and vanilla extract

For the topping
4 oz (120 g) brown sugar
3 oz (80 g) butter
4 tablespoons double cream

Mix together the butter and white sugar and whisk in the egg. Sift the flour and baking powder and mix that in. Dust the chopped dates with flour and cover with the boiling water, adding the bicarbonate of soda and vanilla extract. Add that mixture to the butter mixture and blend together. Transfer to a buttered cake tin and bake in a moderate oven (180°C, 350°F, gas mark 4) for about 40 minutes. While it's cooking, make the topping by heating together the brown sugar, butter and cream for a few minutes. Pour the mixture over the cooked pudding and put it under a hot grill until it bubbles. Serve with cream or ice cream. Or both.

CHAPTER SIX

Towns and Villages

Descriptions of the main towns and larger villages in the Lake District, plus their history and amenities

Lake District Towns

First, a guide to the big three tourist towns of the Lake District: Ambleside, Bowness and Windermere, and Keswick.

★★ Ambleside

Population 2,600 (at 2001 Census)

Beautifully located in the Rothay Valley, 1 mile (1.6 km) north of the head of Lake Windermere, Ambleside is more centrally situated than Bowness and is one of the major centres for the climbing and walking fraternity. It is good, too, for the general visitor and has more escape routes to the surrounding fells and lakes than anywhere else in the Lake District. It gets very, very busy in summer but, unlike some places, it doesn't die in winter and can still be quite lively and interesting when the winter fell-walking enthusiasts start arriving.

History

The name itself comes from the old Norse for riverside pastures, and the town has a long history because of its position at the crossing of many old packhorse routes. The Romans had a fort at Waterhead, 1 mile (1.6 km) south of the town. Probably built around AD 79, Galava fort protected the road that ran from Brougham over Hardknott to Ravenglass. Few stones remain, but the layout is still visible from the surrounding fells – especially Todd Crag on Loughrigg. Recent excavations have revealed more.

The town's most famous building is the Bridge House, which stands in Rydal Road, straddling Stock Beck. Local legend says that it was built by a Scotsman to avoid Land Tax, but it was actually the apple-storing house belonging to Ambleside Hall, when this part of the town was all orchard.

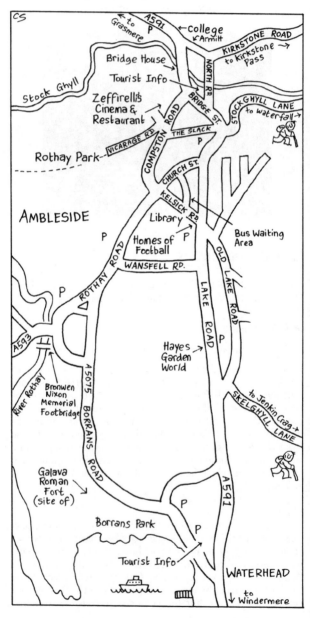

It is now a National Trust Information Centre but has also been a weaver's shop, family home, cobbler's and a tea shop. The oldest part of the town dates from the 15th century and is on the Kirkstone side of the river. This was once a centre for corn and bobbin mills, and restored waterwheels can be seen just below the bridge on North Road and next to the Bridge House.

Originally the railway was to have come right through to Ambleside (there were plans to carry it on up to Keswick and put a tunnel through Dunmail Raise), but it was shelved, and 19th-century tourists had to come up from Windermere by steam launch and charabanc. You can sometimes take a trip on a horse and cart from the steamer pier at Waterhead into the centre of Ambleside.

St Martin's, the teacher training college in the centre of town, was once named after its founder Charlotte Mason, one of Ambleside's most famous residents, but is now an arm of the University of Cumbria's empire. Other notable Amblesiders included the diarist and close friend of Wordsworth, Harriet Martineau, Dr Arnold of Rugby and W.E. Forster.

Amenities
Bus station opposite the library; Tourist Information Centre on Market Cross; Zeffirelli's cinema; lots of shops and cafés; a B&B at every other house; bike hire at Biketreks off Rydal Road or Ghyllside Cycles on The Slack. Waterhead has Windermere Lake Cruises, more cafés and shops. A little electric shuttle bus connects Waterhead with the town centre every half hour or so.

Highlights: Ten things to do
- Admire Beatrix Potter's drawings and other literary Lakeland memorabilia at the **Armitt Collection** on Rydal Road.
- Follow the Victorians by taking a stroll up to **Stock Ghyll** and admire the waterfall.
- Gawp at the **Bridge House** over the river and wonder how a family of eight ever squeezed in.
- Head north out of town to Wordsworth's home at **Rydal Mount**.
- Take any footie fans along to the **Homes of Football** on Lake Road – a fine gallery of Stuart Clarke's football photos, all of them for sale.
- Sample the best of Lakeland food at **Lucy's**, Lucy Nicholson's mini-empire of deli, restaurant and wine bar.
- Pick up some Lake District **art** at one of several galleries around the town.
- Time a visit to coincide with August's **Ambleside Sports**, a celebration of Lakeland sport, farming and tradition.
- Walk the 11 mile (17.7 km) **Fairfield Horseshoe**, one of the best ridge walks in the Lake District.
- Stock up on all your **walking gear** at one of the many outdoor clothing shops. Ambleside is sometimes referred to as the Anorak Capital of the World.

Also handy for ...
Windermere and adjoining towns via the ferries at Waterhead. Tarn Hows; Elterwater; Townend at Troutbeck; Loughrigg Fell; the Langdales; Skelwith Force. Good access to virtually anywhere in the south Lakes. The Kirkstone Pass connects Ambleside to Ullswater and the north Lakes.

★★ Bowness and Windermere

Population 8,200

This is the largest town in the National Park, and it can certainly seem like it on a bank holiday weekend when it becomes the number one tourist attraction of the Lake District – especially for day-trippers, because it is the only central Lake District town to have a railway station. The busy lake shore gives it the feeling of a seaside resort rather than an inland town, and it has many of the usual seaside amenities. But it manages, if only just at times, to avoid the worst of seaside squalor and things like amusement arcades, and it tries hard to remain dignified, despite the hordes.

History
Technically it is two towns, but they are virtually joined together and always considered as one. Bowness is an ancient village, right on the lakeside, centred around the 15th-century St Martin's Church. (Martin was a Roman officer who divided his cloak in half to help a beggar. Jolly kind of him.) The name Bowness comes from Bulness, meaning a promontory that looks like a bull's head. And it does, if you study the map, jutting out into the lake beside Bowness Bay.

Windermere was originally a little village called Birthwaite, about a mile away inland. It became known as Windermere only after the arrival of the railway in 1848. Wordsworth, fearing that the horrid Lancashire hordes would soon be rushing round the lake to gape at him at Rydal and so ruin his tranquillity, tried to stop the railway being built. He predicted that the little village would be inundated by 'The Advance of the Ten Thousand'. He was right. A veritable explosion took place and Bowness and Windermere changed almost overnight. It wasn't just the masses but the New Wealthy from Lancashire who built splendid mansions, many of them Italianate or Gothic fantasies, grand holiday homes to show off their own grandness.

There still is quite a lot of money around Windermere, and quite a few palatial homes and private yacht harbours, but many of the bigger Victorian mansions are no longer private homes. Two examples are Brockhole and Belsfield, now the National Park's Visitor Centre and a hotel respectively. Belsfield was build by H.W. Schneider, who used to commute each day to his industrial empire in Barrow, going on his own launch down Windermere to Lakeside, then by a special carriage on the Furness Railway to Barrow. Ah, those were the days.

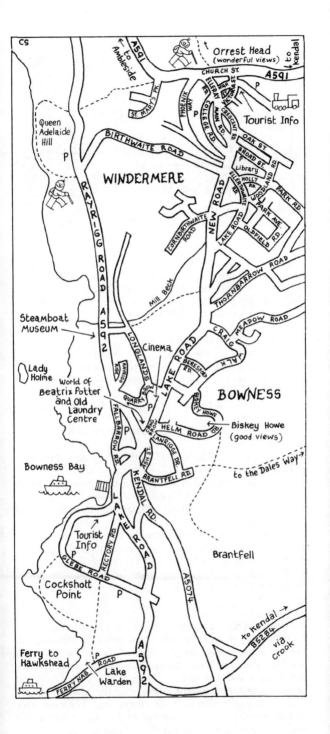

Amenities
Railway and bus stations; Windermere Lake Cruises; Tourist Information Centres on Victoria Street and Bowness Bay; masses of hotels and bed and breakfasts; shops; cinema; Old Laundry theatre and exhibition centre; bike rental at Country Lanes near the railway station.

Highlights: Ten things to do
- Take a **cruise** around the lake from Bowness Bay.
- Walk up **Orrest Head** for a brilliant view of the lake and, on a very clear day, of Morecambe Bay and Blackpool Tower.
- Walk south out of town and up **Brantfell** for more magnificent views.
- Enjoy an elegant **Lakeland afternoon tea** at luxury hotel Miller Howe.
- Introduce the kids to the **World of Beatrix Potter** at Bowness.
- Break away from the crowds and pop into **St Martin's Church** to enjoy the stained glass windows.
- Drive out of town to **Blackwell**, the magnificent Arts and Crafts house.
- Take a **swim**. You can get into the lake at various points, and there are regular organised swims. It's cold. Very cold.
- Have dinner at **Jericho's**, the best restaurant in town.
- Wait until the crowds have gone home and stroll along **Bowness Bay** at night for a lovely view of the lake.

Also handy for …
Lakeside, with an aquarium and the lovely grounds of Fell Foot Park, is a 6 mile (9.7 km) cruise down the lake. Beatrix Potter countryside is just across the lake on the car ferry. The National Park Visitor Centre at Brockhole is a short drive north, and a little way south is Blackwell, a restored arts and crafts house with wonderful views over the lake. The lovely quiet village of Troutbeck is a few miles away. For total peace and quiet only 5 miles (8 km) away by car, Kentmere is a pretty valley with fine walking along the Kentmere horseshoe.

★★ Keswick

Population 4,300

If Bowness, Windermere and Ambleside share the walkers and tourists of the south and central Lakes, then Keswick is the undisputed capital of the north. It has a fantastic setting, sandwiched between Derwentwater and Blencathra and Skiddaw, and it's sometimes regally referred to as the 'Queen of Lakeland'. In fact, it is most impressive when seen from a distance as bits of it nowadays scarcely live up to its promise. It has more bed and breakfasts and guesthouses per head of population than anywhere else in the country, and is the favourite centre for Lakeland climbers and serious fell-walkers. Always busy in the summer and only really attractive to walk round in the winter. The lakeshore has been much improved lately by the first class Theatre by the Lake.

History
The oldest building is Crosthwaite church at the northwest corner of town. The foundations date from 1181, but most of the fabric of the building dates from the 14th century and later. Inside is a memorial to Robert Southey, with an inscription written by his friend William Wordsworth. Canon Rawnsley, co-founder of the National Trust, is buried in the churchyard. Brandelhow, on Derwentwater, was the first property acquired by the Trust in 1902.

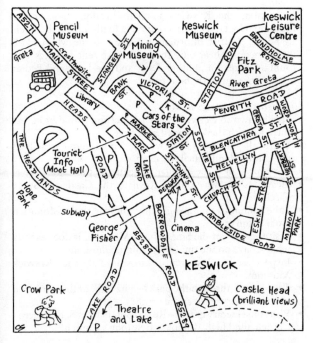

105

Originally a small market town, Keswick became prosperous with the arrival of the mining industry in the 16th century. Mining engineers were imported from Germany to look for copper, lead, silver and iron. They were treated with suspicion by the locals and forced to make their homes on Derwent Island, but they must have overcome the hostility because German surnames can still be found among the local population. The town also became famous for the black lead mined in Borrowdale, which prompted the creation of the Cumberland Pencil Company. A clue to another one-time important industry is in Keswick's name: it is derived from *kes* and *wic* meaning cheese and dairy farm. Southey and Samuel Taylor Coleridge lived in Keswick at Greta Hall. Overlooking the town is Windebrowe, where William and Dorothy Wordsworth lived for a short time before moving to Dove Cottage.

In 1865 the Cockermouth–Penrith railway line opened and put Keswick on the tourist map. Most of the town's central buildings are Victorian. The Moot Hall in the market square was built in 1813. Look out for an unusual one-handed clock. One visitor described it as a cross between an art gallery and a public lavatory, but it actually contains a Tourist Information Centre. The railway line no longer exists, unfortunately, and has been replaced by the horrid and unloved A66. This is one of the Lake District National Park Authority's notable failures: the Authority fought hard to stop it but were overruled by central government.

Amenities
Bus station; the Keswick Launch; headquarters of the Mountain Goat bus tour company; loads of small hotels and B&Bs; Tourist Information Centre in the Moot Hall; shops; cinema; Theatre by the Lake; bike rental at Keswick Mountain Bikes on Southey Lane and the Lakeland Pedlar off Bell Close car park; boat hire.

Highlights: Ten things to do
- Stroll down to Derwentwater for a **cruise** round or across the lake with the Keswick Launch
- Learn all you could ever wish to know about pencils at the **Cumberland Pencil Museum.**
- See what's on at the excellent **Theatre by the Lake.**
- Head a short way out of town to the **Castlerigg Stone Circle.**
- Take a minibus tour around the valleys with the **Mountain Goat** company.
- Visit the **Cars of the Stars Motor Museum.** It does exactly what it says on the tin. Or the mining museum.
- Inspect some Victorian curiosities at the **Keswick Museum.**
- Take a walk through the **parks** – Fitz Park at the north end of town, Hope Park at the south.
- Visit some **literary graves** – Robert Southey's at St Kentigern's Church and Hugh Walpole's at St John's Church.

- Walk along the **railway path** towards Keswick, reclaimed from the old branch line.

Also handy for ...
Three lakes – Derwentwater, Bassenthwaite and Thirlmere – are all within a couple of miles. If you're lucky you can see ospreys around Bassenthwaite. There's good access to the western lakes of Loweswater, Crummock, Buttermere and Ennerdale. Many of the Lake District's most famous fells, including Skiddaw and Blencathra, are close by, and Cat Bells, a fine climb for families, is the other side of Derwentwater. Borrowdale, with the Bowder Stone on the way, is a drive to the south.

Other Lake District hotspots

Next come the Lake District's second tier of towns and larger villages – six centres where you might well end up staying or spending some time. They are: Hawkshead, Grasmere, Coniston, Patterdale and Glenridding, Broughton-in-Furness and Caldbeck.

★★★ Hawkshead

Population 590

Set in lowland countryside near the head of Esthwaite Water, Hawkshead is generally reckoned to be the quaintest and prettiest village in the Lake District. Consequently it gets very crowded in midsummer. Cars are banned from the village itself, which is a good idea, but it does give the village something of the character of an open-air museum. It has an attractive muddle of squares and cobbled streets, overhung by timber-framed 17th-century buildings. It isn't too difficult to imagine what it must have been like when Wordsworth went to school here.

History
The name of the village is Old Norse and means 'Hauk's summer pasture'. An important wool town in the Middle Ages, it once contained seven inns. St Michael and All Angels' Church, up on the hill overlooking the village, is one of the most interesting Lakeland churches. There has been a chapel or church on this site since the 12th century, but the present building dates from about the 15th. Inside are decorations and painted texts dating from around 1680.

Ann Tyson's Cottage on Vicarage Lane in the centre of the village is identified by a plaque, but when William Wordsworth lodged with her, Ann Tyson lived at Colthouse, just outside the village. In 1548 William Sawrey, the vicar of Urswick, stayed at what is now the Old Courthouse. Local records say that he was besieged for two days by a 'tumult of insurrection', men armed to the teeth with swords, clubs and daggers. They demanded that he should come out 'for they would have one of his arms or legs before going away'. Eventually they were dispersed by neighbours, though why, or what it was all about, no one knows.

Highlights: five things to do
- Imagine Wordsworth behind his school desk at the **Hawkshead Grammar School**.
- See Beatrix Potter's watercolours and sketchbooks at the **Beatrix Potter Gallery**.
- Stroll round the interesting interior of **St Michael and All Angels' Church**.
- Walk a mile or two out of town to **Tarn Hows**.
- Sample the Lake District's beers on a mini **pub crawl** round the village's four excellent inns.

Also handy for …
The Rusland Valley; Grisedale Forest; Esthwaite Water; Coniston; Tarn Hows; Sawrey and Beatrix Potter country; the Claife Heights on the shore of Windermere. Hawkshead is best reached from the east by the Windermere ferry.

★★ Grasmere

Population 840

Grasmere is everyone's idea of a picturesque Lakeland village and is now forever associated with William and Dorothy Wordsworth. It looks very pretty, especially if seen from Loughrigg Terrace, looking down over the lake with the village against the background of Helm Crag and Dunmail Raise, but the tall surrounding fells can give it a damp, claustrophobic air, especially in winter. The village is almost wholly orientated towards tourists with cafés, gift shops and B&Bs. In winter it used to die completely, but the Wordsworth industry and the presence of sweater and jumper shops now encourage the village to stay open out of season. In summer it is overrun: the sports field becomes an unsightly mass of caravans, and the road into the village becomes blocked with coaches disgorging hordes of Japanese tourists in search of Dove Cottage.

For all this, Grasmere thinks rather a lot of itself, disdaining what it sees as the commercialism of Dove Cottage while at the same time feeding off the visitors it brings to the area. In 1979 a member of the Grasmere branch of the Women's Institute compiled a short history of the village, which contained the following sentence on the subject of 'off-comers': 'Grasmere is the poorer for the losses it has sustained during the last 25 years, losses of people who are not matched by the newer people who have come into the village, many of whom may be good and nice people but are not of the same calibre as their predecessors.' So, please don't spit or swear, especially near a resident.

History

An ancient road ran through the valley, and the village itself is really a string of hamlets along the old packhorse route to Whitehaven. The road used to come over White Moss and past Dove Cottage, which was originally an inn. The Wordsworths moved there in 1799, and the present main road was built in the 1830s. Coming from Ambleside, you encounter a rather nasty bend, just before coming into view of the lake, which is known locally as Penny Rock because blasting the rocks to put the road through added a penny to the rates. There is a corpse track over White Moss from Rydal, and coffins were once carried along here to Grasmere church. Up the hill, past Dove Cottage, there is a large, flat stone known as the coffin stone, where the bearers used to rest.

Most of the village buildings are 19th or early 20th century, though the surrounding farms are far older. The church, dedicated to St Oswald, dates from the 13th century and is the scene of one of Lakeland's rushbearing ceremonies on the Saturday closest to the saint's day (5 August). The Wordsworth family graves are in the churchyard, and there are still family connections in the valley.

The annual Grasmere Sports and Show is one of the oldest and most popular traditional events in the Lake District, showcasing wrestling, fell-running, hound trailing and the like. It probably dates back to Viking times and involves people from all over the north. At one time even Dove Cottage would close down on Sports Day, so that the staff could go along. Now they have to keep at it, catering for the hordes. It's held on the third or fourth Sunday of August.

Highlights: five things to do

- Take a **Wordsworth tour** of Dove Cottage, the attached museum and the family grave in St Oswald's churchyard.
- Hire a **boat** and row out across Grasmere lake.
- Pick up some famous **Grasmere gingerbread** at Sarah Nelson's shop. You'll smell it before you see it.
- See the work of Lakeland's most famous family of artists at the **Heaton Cooper Studio**.
- Walk out of town and up **Loughrigg Terrace** for wonderful views of the lake and valley.

Also handy for ...

Grasmere is a good base for most of the central fells, including some of the most famous Lakeland peaks like Helvellyn, Fairfield and the Langdale Pikes. Pretty (and quieter) villages, including Elterwater, Skelwith Bridge and Chapel Stile, are close. Grasmere is the traditional dividing line between north and south Lakeland, and Dunmail Raise connects the two, though if you're going south a nicer route is over Red Bank to Elterwater and Ambleside. This route is also handy for Coniston, Hawkshead and the Langdale Valley.

★ Coniston

Population 1,060

Probably the most disappointing of the major Lakeland villages, Coniston has a magnificent setting at the foot of the fells, but the grey, stone-built village has little character of its own and is almost wholly given over to the tourist industry. Its best feature is the way the Old Man of Coniston rises dramatically behind the houses when seen from the village centre. The road from the south can be rather dreary, apart from Blawith Common. Still, it's a good centre for walkers – though many climbers now seem to prefer the Langdales and Borrowdale – and Coniston Water offers plenty of activity. A good starting point for your visit is the Coniston Information Centre, run by the community since the closure of the official TIC and staffed by volunteers seven days a week all year round. Their website (*www.conistontic.org*) is helpful if you're planning a visit.

History

The name Coniston means 'king's town'. Coniston grew up in the 18th century as a mining village, though copper was mined locally as far back as Norman times. In the 16th century Keswick's German miners were brought in, and the ore extracted was sent to Keswick for smelting. The area around Church Beck is still referred to as Coppermines Valley, and the evidence of the activity is obvious in the landscape.

Coniston was once served by a railway line, which came up from Furness, and its closure rendered the village rather inaccessible compared to the central Lakeland villages. Its most famous resident was John Ruskin, and the 16th-century St Andrew's Church in the centre of the village contains his tomb. A regular summer visitor was Arthur Ransome, who got his inspiration for *Swallows and Amazons* here. And on the village green, just opposite the car park, a large, green-slate seat acts as a memorial to Donald Campbell, who died attempting the world water speed record on the lake in 1967. There's lots more information about his life at the Ruskin Museum (see Chapter 10).

Coniston's oldest building is Coniston Hall, a 16th-century place once associated with the area's largest landowners, the Flemings. It is now owned by the National Trust, although it's not open to the public.

Highlights: five things to do
- Swot up on Coniston's history and traditions at the **Ruskin Museum**.
- Take a cruise over the water on the **Gondola**, the National Trust's elegantly restored steam yacht.
- Take a **rowboat, canoe** or **dinghy** out on the lake from Coniston Boating Centre.
- Puff your way up the **Old Man of Coniston**, which towers over the village – the fell, that is, not the old boy in the village.
- Visit the grave of **Donald Campbell** at the new cemetery a few hundred yards from the church and the memorial to him on the village green.

Also handy for ...
Grisedale Forest; the Furness fells; Tarn Hows; the Duddon Valley; Hawkshead; Beatrix Potter's Hill Top at Sawrey; John Ruskin's house at Brantwood.

★ Patterdale and Glenridding

Population 460

These two rather shapeless villages at the southern end of Ullswater are separated by less than a mile. Patterdale is the prettier and is more of a real village. Glenridding is best used for access to the lake, the second-longest after Windermere and the range of activity thereon. But the setting of both is spectacular, surrounded on almost all sides by mountains with the only open view over towards the lake. They are superb centres for walking, with dozens of fells including one of the Lake District's most popular, Helvellyn, within striking distance.

History
The name Patterdale is a corruption of 'Patrick's Dale'. The patron saint of Ireland is supposed to have preached and baptised here once, and along the road towards the boat landing at Glenridding there is St Patrick's Well, which was once thought to have healing properties. Glenridding was a mining village until the mines closed in 1862. Lead was discovered in the area in the 17th century, and mining was at its height in the early 19th century, with Greenside being one of the best lead mines in the country.

Highlights: five things to do
- Cruise round Ullswater on one of the **lake steamers**, some of which have been in service since the 1850s.

- Drive out of Glenridding on the A592 to find the **daffodils** that inspired Wordsworth's most famous poem at Gowbarrow Park.
- Walk along the **lake shore** from Glenridding in the early evening, when the hordes of day-trippers have gone home.
- Get a head for heights on **Striding Edge** on the way to the top of Helvellyn.
- Stroll between Glenridding and Patterdale via **Lanty's Tarn**, a pretty patch of water with views over Ullswater.

Also handy for …
Ullswater; Aira Force; Gowbarrow Park; Brotherswater and Haweswater; Pooley Bridge and Dalemain at the north end of Ullswater. Patterdale is a great base for fells, including Fairfield, Place Fell and Helvellyn.

★★ Broughton-in-Furness

An old market town, built largely in the 18th century, Broughton has a quiet character, and the market square has hardly changed in the last two centuries. You can still see the old stone fish slabs. The market itself is on Tuesdays. Because it has been largely missed by the tourist hordes, Broughton is unspoilt and a friendly place to shop. The obelisk in the square was erected to commemorate the jubilee of George III. Nearby is Broughton Tower, built in 1330 as an old pele tower and now part of a residential estate with the grounds not open to the public. The Broughton family's associations with this area go back to before the Norman Conquest. The name Broughton means 'the hamlet by the stream', and the 'in-Furness' bit was added later to distinguish it from the innumerable other Broughtons dotted about the northwest. This Broughton is a good base from which to explore the Duddon Valley, Furness fells and Swinside Stone Circle.

★ Caldbeck

As Grasmere is to Wordsworth, so Caldbeck, in its own little way, is to John Peel, the famous huntsman and hero of the song. Set near open fells to the 'back o' Skidda', on the northern boundary of the National Park, it has a traditional village green, duck pond, a 12th-century church and an amazing river gorge called the Howk. Look out for the signs. Behind the church is St Mungo's Well. The churchyard has the bodies of two famous Lakeland characters: John Peel and Mary Robinson, the Beauty of Buttermere. Caldbeck is still a real, working village, not yet overrun by tourists, despite the development of gift shops and a café around Priest's Mill. The nearby fells are also quiet and uncrowded, even on a bank holiday weekend. It's the home of Chris Bonnington, the mountaineer. It's also handy for Mungrisdale, Bassenthwaite and the Solway Coast.

Lake District villages

There are pretty villages across the Lake District, but here are ten we think are particularly worth a detour.

★★★ Cartmel

A lovely little village, just west of Grange-over-Sands and just outside the National Park, with a beautiful square, an old village pump still standing and a nice river running through it. It's very picturesque and popular at weekends as it has several good pubs and a Michelin-starred restaurant, L'Enclume. It's most famous for the Priory, which dates back to 1188, though only the priory church and gatehouse remain (they're now in the care of the National Trust). The square is often spoilt by parked cars – the best place to park is through the village, by the racecourse, which hosts several big meetings each summer. The village is becoming a bit picture-book, but it's still less of an open-air museum than Hawkshead. It is famous the world over for sticky toffee pudding, available from the village shop.

★★★ Maulds Meaburn

Not in the Lake District proper, because it's across the M6 towards Appleby, but many discriminating Cumbrians consider this the county's prettiest village. Fascinating stone houses, each one different, on either bank of the River Lyvennet, with sheep grazing around. Black Dub, the spot where Charles II and his army took a breather on the way back from Scotland in 1651, is marked by a memorial south of the village.

★★★ Troutbeck

One of the Lakes' most famous villages. Strung along a hillside just north of Windermere, it is really a series of hamlets grouped about a series of wells. The cottages and barns date from the 17th century to the 19th, the finest of all being Townend, built in 1262 though largely 17th century, and now opened to the public by the National Trust from March to October. There are two old, restored inns, the sign to the Mortal Man being quite famous for its rhyme:

> O Mortal Man that lives by bread,
> What is it makes thy nose so red?
> Thou silly fool that look'st so pale,
> 'Tis drinking Sally Birkett's ale.

Note that there is another Lakeland Troutbeck, just off the A66 near Threlkeld. Even Pevsner got the two muddled.

WATENDLATH

★★★ Watendlath

A moorland hamlet of farms, set artistically beside a large tarn. It is situated to the east of Rosthwaite and was the remote, isolated setting for Hugh Walpole's 1931 novel *Judith Paris*. Now it is a magnet for tourists, and so to be avoided on summer bank holiday weekends. It can be reached by leaving the main Borrowdale road and crossing Ashness Bridge. Owned by the National Trust. Good teas.

★★ Askham

This ancient and pretty village is 5 miles (8 km) south of Penrith. Many houses date from between 1650 and 1750. Askham Hall is 14th century in parts and was developed on the site of a pele tower. It is now the home of the Earl of Lonsdale. Lowther Castle is only a façade – a Gothic mansion built in the 19th century rather than a genuine castle – and is now mostly ruins, not open to the public, though there are plans afoot to restore and rejuvenate it. Also on the estate is a park, the Lakeland Bird of Prey Centre and, in August, a major horse trials event. The village is handy for Haweswater, Penrith, Ullswater and the Eden Valley. There are two good pubs.

★★ Grange-in-Borrowdale

Not to be confused with Grange-over-Sands, though if you did you'd be some distance from where you wanted to be. This was once a grange of Furness Abbey. Only a small hamlet, but beautifully situated alongside the River Derwent. The tea room by the bridge is a good finishing point after a walk in the Borrowdale fells. It's one of Lakeland's prettiest villages.

★★ Hesket Newmarket

A proper northern hamlet, this is well off the tourist beat. Once an important market, now it is just a pleasant village built around a long green. Charles Dickens and Wilkie Collins stayed here in 1857 while they were on a Lake District tour, and the inn where they stopped is now a private home called Dickens House. Hesket Hall is a dull but odd building with a peculiar roof and 12 angular projections forming the walls. The corners of these projections are supposed to make an effective sundial. The Old Crown is a good pub (the first in the country to be run as a cooperative by villagers), with its own brewery attached.

★ Elterwater

Like many Lakeland villages, Elterwater is overrun in summer and most of the cottages are second homes. But the village green and water are lovely, and the bustling Britannia pub makes it a good place for recuperation after a Langdale walk. There's an artist's studio displaying watercolours of the area and a decent village store.

★ Ireby

On the northern edge of the Lakes, Ireby gained a market charter in the 13th century, but in time Wigton and Cockermouth proved too much competition for it. Look out for the original St James's Church, a simple Norman affair, stuck in a field a mile outside the village on the Torpenhow road (a new one was built in 1845). Ireby is good as a base for the Solway coast, Bassenthwaite and Skiddaw. The Lion is a nice pub with good beer.

★ Rosthwaite

A little hamlet of whitewashed buildings in the Borrowdale Valley, useful as a base for setting off for Watendlath, Seatoller, Langstrath and Sty Head. The footpath up to Watendlath used to be quite attractive but is now very heavily used. Prince Charles takes B&B at Yew Tree Farm in Rosthwaite when he comes to the Lakes. A couple of hotels serve decent food and beer, and there's a village shop.

Cumbrian Towns

Most of the above towns and villages are in the National Park, but there are many more on the fringes that you are likely to visit or at least pass through and that can be just as Lake Districty. In addition, a few more further afield are well worth seeing. Here are the main ones.

★★ Carlisle

Population 71,800

A bustling market and industrial town, Carlisle is Cumbria's capital city and the home of the County Council, Radio

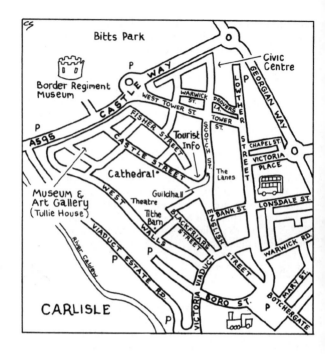

Cumbria, Border Television, Cumbria's only Football League team and a host of industries. It's not a huge place by southern standards, but it makes up for it with an exciting and confusing one-way system. The city has a long history, much of it reflected in the architecture. It also has a castle and Cumbria's only cathedral.

History

Carlisle became an administrative centre during the Roman invasion. Much of its subsequent history revolved around its proximity to the border, which was not always north of the city – there were times when Carlisle itself was part of Scotland, and the Scottish influence is still clear. The Romans called it Luguvalium and placed a fort at Stanwix, on Hadrian's Wall, which ran along the northern outskirts of the city.

There has been a castle at Carlisle since 1092, occupying a good strategic position that was easily defended. Throughout the Middle Ages it was continually plundered, attacked and generally demolished by marauding Scots. The castle became more and more important, and walls were built around the city. Mary Queen of Scots was imprisoned here in 1568 after fleeing from her own country.

Highlights and amenities

The castle still stands proud and is looked after by English Heritage. It also houses the Border Regiment Museum and the Carlisle Roman Dig, an exhibition showing off the finds of recent excavations. Carlisle has an excellent museum and gallery at Tullie House, a fascinating town trail and a neat cathedral, built in 1122 and hammered by the centuries of warfare. It has a good main line railway link with Newcastle, Scotland and the south, and its own small airfield. There's a leisure, arts and entertainment centre at the Sands and a flashy yet tasteful shopping precinct at the Lanes. The excellent Victorian covered market between Scotch Street and Fisher Street is open every day except Sunday. The best bits are around the Old Town Hall, Fisher Street and Castle Street, and the centre is now mainly pedestrianised. Hurrah.

★★ Cockermouth

Population 7,800

For some reason the National Park boundary line does a rather vicious loop around Cockermouth, excluding it from the park. Which is a pity, because it well deserves to be inside. Cockermouth is a fine little town, far easier for everyday shopping than Keswick and distinctly on the way up. Main Street, Market Place and Kirkgate are very attractive, and the area around All Saints Church, beside the River Cocker, is pretty. The church is good, although the wall-to-wall carpet looks a bit odd. Cockermouth has a nice community air about it, the worst aspects of the tourist industry being notably restrained. Perhaps there are advantages to being outside the National Park after all.

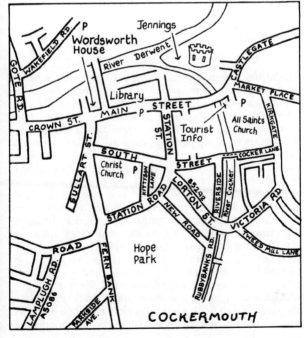

117

History

Cockermouth's most famous building today is undoubtedly Wordsworth House, a fine Georgian building that dominates the main street. William was born there in 1770. The other notable building is the castle, built originally in the 13th century, though much of what remains dates from a century later. Much of it is in ruins, though part is still lived in by Lady Egremont. It is rarely open to the public, except occasionally during the town's festivals. Cockermouth was subject to the usual cross-border warfare, and the castle was besieged by Royalists during the Civil War.

Highlights and amenities

Of all the towns lying just outside the Lake District, Cockermouth is probably the quietest and most interesting to escape to when the crowds of the central Lakes begin to annoy. Wordsworth House remains the town's main tourist attraction, but there's also a great printing museum and a good art gallery on Castlegate. The same street has the Quince & Medlar, an excellent vegetarian restaurant, and don't miss Market Place and Kirkgate. Cultural life is centred around the Kirkgate Centre, which puts on plays, films and music.

A good place to go on a rainy morning is the Lakeland Sheep and Wool Centre, just out of town; it's a good introduction to Cumbrian farming with sheepdog exhibitions. A good place for a rainy afternoon is Cumbria's longest serving brewery, Jennings. There are tours and samples of the beers; follow your nose to find it on Brewery Lane.

★★ Kendal

Population 27,500

Kendal has suffered a bit in the last few years. Whereas we rated it highly in the earlier editions of this book, nowadays Penrith seems the friendlier, livelier and more attractive place to visit and shop in. Kendal has been spoilt by the traffic and diabolical one-way system; take a navigator to make notes of likely parking places as you are swept past them, then aim for them the second time round. It's known locally as the 'Auld Grey Town', which is a fair description on a winter's day.

It is a shame, because Kendal is a busy market town and is quite lively culturally, largely thanks to the Brewery Arts Centre. The best parts are Kirkland (right at the end of the main shopping street) and the small lanes known as 'yards' off the main street. If you're coming in from the south park near the church then walk along the riverside and go up into the town centre via Kent Street and Market Place. In the town centre is the Westmorland Shopping Centre, which makes much use of local stone, while the Artisan shop attached to Booths is a good place to sample Lakeland food and drink. Shopkeepers moan that a pedestrianisation

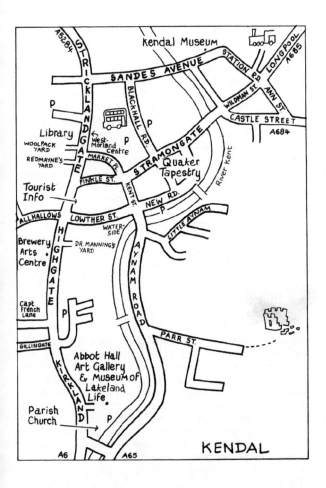

KENDAL

scheme and out-of-town superstores are ruining Kendal's character, but the town deserves a bit of a revival.

History
It used to be the largest town in the old county of Westmorland and is now the headquarters of the Lake District National Park Authority, despite being outside the National Park. There was once a Roman fort, called Alauna, just south of the town. It suffered from the marauding Scots (like everywhere else) but settled down a little during the 14th century and became famous for Kendal Green, a heavy cloth mentioned by Shakespeare in *Henry IV* ('Three misbegotten knaves in Kendal-green').

The castle, which stands on the hill to the east of the River Kent, was built by William Rufus and once belonged to Thomas Parr, whose daughter, Catherine, was the sixth and last wife of Henry VIII. Today it is a ruin but still commands a fine view over the town. More recent famous residents

119

include legendary fell-walker and author Alfred Wainwright, who was borough treasurer at Kendal for 20 years.

Highlights and amenities
Kendal has one of the best art galleries and museums in Cumbria, Abbot Hall, and one of the best theatre and film venues, the Brewery Arts Centre. The Museum of Lakeland Life, next to Abbot Hall, and the Kendal Museum are both excellent (see Chapter 10). There's a good leisure centre, and the town is reasonable for shopping of all kinds, including some unusual little shops tucked away from the main shopping centre. There's a market on Wednesdays and Saturdays. Kendal's not spoilt for restaurants, but there are plenty of good tea places. A railway station links to the main line station at Oxenholme, tucked away to the east of the town. It bills itself as the southern gateway to the Lakes, and road access to the rest of the area is pretty good once you're out of the town itself. Don't forget to pick up your mint cake, now one of the town's biggest exports.

★★ Whitehaven

Population 25,500

While Cockermouth and Penrith have crept into Lakeland and been accepted as one of us, the towns along the west coast have long been considered out of sight, if not off the map. Few tourists will linger long in Barrow unless they're visiting the Dock Museum or trying to find Furness Abbey or Piel Island, and even fewer will find much to detain them in Workington, apart from Portland Square. But hurry hurry to Whitehaven, before everyone else discovers it. At the moment, it's practically a tourist-free zone, and there you will mingle with proper ethnic Cumbrians.

History
For a little while back in the 18th century, Whitehaven was the nation's third port after London and Bristol, rich on coal exports, tobacco imports and the slave trade. The Georgian town had been laid out on a grid pattern by the Lowther family (still big in Cumbria) and was the first planned town in Britain. George Washington's granny lived in Whitehaven. John Paul Jones, founder of the American Navy, raided the town in 1778, the last occasion on which Britain was invaded from the sea.

Highlights and amenities
After some dismal decades of decline in the shipping and coal industries, Whitehaven is coming to life again. You can see it in the spruced-up Georgian streets and squares. It's not all the result of hand-outs and guilt money from nearby Sellafield – but civic pride and a new if gentler affluence. The Georgian bit is towards the harbour – Lowther Street, King Street, Roper Street. Once you've worked out the one-way streets

and managed to park, you can explore all the delights on foot. Pause a while to read the monster mosaic poem in the Market Place, then walk on to Michael Moon's amazing, tardis-like second-hand bookshop to compliment him – he wrote it. The entire walled harbour is now a conservation area. Walk out on Sir John Rennie's West Pier and inspect the lighthouse, built in 1832. Indoor delights include the Beacon and the Rum Story, covering local history and trade with the Caribbean, respectively. There's a lively market on Thursdays and Saturdays. And don't forget St Bees, 5 miles (8 km) down the coast.

★ Penrith

Population 14,800

A friendly, sandstone-built market town on the eastern fringes of the Lake District. Its character is rather muted,

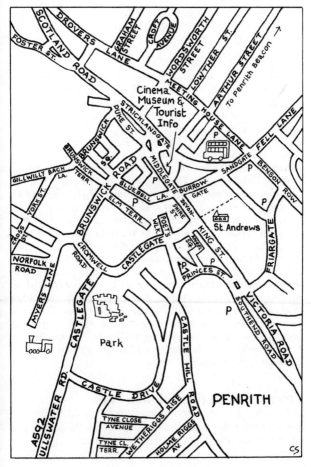

spoilt by traffic during the week. It's a little overlooked and forgotten compared with Carlisle, but is still a nice place for shopping, especially during the week and not a bad gateway to Lakeland proper. One of the best attractions is the view from Penrith Beacon, which stands on a hill overlooking the town, across the plain to the Lakeland fells.

History
The town dates back to Roman times and was beloved by the marauding Scots once the Romans had gone. It was the capital of the independent kingdom of Cumbria until 1070. An unusual castle, originally merely a defensive tower, was built around 1400 and enlarged in subsequent years, falling into disuse during the 16th century and providing a stock of building material for the local houses. The oldest and most interesting buildings are to be found around the church, and most of these date from the 1700s. William and Dorothy Wordsworth went to school in Penrith for a time, and William later wrote of the Beacon. This structure was once a link in a communication chain that ran the length of the country and was a useful early-warning system when the Scots were on the rampage again.

Highlights and amenities
Penrith makes a reasonable base for a Lakeland or Eden Valley holiday and is improving all the time. It has a station on the west coast main line, though trains from Carlisle to Oxenholme don't always stop there. The castle – now in sandstone ruins – is opened to the public by English Heritage and lies in the public Castle Park. The area around St Andrew's Church is very attractive. There is a cinema, the Alhambra, and a good theatre venue, the Penrith Playhouse. A nice bookshop, The Bluebell, is in Angel Square and has become a centre for the local community. There are also two olde worlde shops at either end of Market Square, which have somehow survived for over 200 years. J&J Graham, the posh grocers, is Penrith's answer to Fortnum & Mason and a good place to pick up Lakeland specialities, while Arnison & Sons, the drapers, established in 1740 and once the home of Wordsworth's grandparents, is in a magnificent time warp. Until fairly recently a sticker on the front door announced 'We stock nylons', and a visit is still a trip back in time. Tuesdays and Saturdays are market days. The latest excitement in the area is Rheged, a big visitor centre just outside Penrith off the M6. Start your visit at the Tourist Information Centre, housed in a 17th-century former school building on Middlegate.

Towns outside the National Park

Some of the other towns of note that lie on the wrong side of the National Park border are noted below.

★★ Grange-over-Sands

Usually billed as Cumbria's Riviera, this is a genteel Victorian town, once a sizeable holiday resort. If the waterfront was better, it might have become another Blackpool. As it is, it has become a popular retirement town, sometimes known locally as 'God's waiting room', though elderly newcomers sometimes regret their choice when they see the hills. The town is largely unspoilt and seems to be made entirely of grey limestone. Behind the town, on Hampsfell, is a spectacular limestone escarpment, now protected but once quarried extensively for building materials. On the escarpment is an odd structure known as Hampsfell Hospice, built for the 'shelter and entertainment' of walkers. On a clear day the views from the roof are fantastic, from Blackpool Tower to Skiddaw. The sands out across Morecambe Bay are very dangerous – the tide rarely reaches the town, but when it does it fairly races in – but a vastly experienced official guide takes parties across. There is a good promenade and a spectacular approach to the town across the sands by train.

★ Maryport

This was a village called Ellenfoot, until Humphrey Senhouse developed the port and called it after his wife, Mary. Sweet, huh? It was the birthplace of Thomas Ismay, founder of the White Star Line, which built the *Titanic*, and Joseph Lister, the surgeon. Today it's a smaller but somehow sadder version of Whitehaven, despite lots of new development in the harbour. In the town itself don't miss the quaint little maritime museum. Find the cobbled Fleming Square, walk on to the Senhouse Roman Museum on the north side of town, then down the cliff and back along the promenade. You'll probably meet no one.

★ Ulverston

A typical, friendly, northern market town, with a market cross, a nice old cobbled street and a nearby canal that gave the town its share of trade from the coast. Overlooking the town is the Hoad Monument to Sir John Barrow, a 90 foot (27 m) high imitation of the Eddystone Lighthouse. Look up and you'll see it. A public path up Hoad Hill leads to the monument and good views of the town and surrounding countryside. Ulverston is largely unspoilt but shows signs of decay, which is a great pity. It holds the world's largest collection of Laurel and Hardy memorabilia in a museum dedicated to them (Stan Laurel is the town's most famous son), and the Conishead Priory a little way out of town is well worth a visit. It's trying to gee itself up by becoming a festival town, with events most months of the year; visit *www.ulverston.net* for details.

CHAPTER SEVEN

Lakes

What to do on and around the 16 major lakes and the best of the tarns

There's some disagreement about this, but most experts say there are 16 lakes in the Lake District. The other bits of water are tarns. A few tarns, despite their lower status, are, in fact, bigger than one of the so-called lakes, but most tarns are very small, and some of them do not even have the dignity of being named. It's the 16 lakes that are the glamorous attractions – the crowd pullers.

Only one of the 16 is actually called a Lake, since all the rest already have the word 'mere' or 'water' in their name. Which is the lucky one? Read on …

Longest to shortest – the size of the lakes

	Length in miles (km)	Width in miles (km)	Height above sea level in feet (metres)	Maximum depth in feet (metres)
Windermere	10½ (16.9)	1 (1.6)	130 (40)	219 (67)
Ullswater	7½ (12)	¾ (1.2)	476 (145)	205 (62)
Coniston	5¼ (8.4)	½ (0.8)	143 (44)	184 (56)
Bassenthwaite	4 (6.4)	¾ (1.2)	223 (68)	70 (21)
Haweswater	4 (6.4)	½ (0.8)	790 (240)	198 (60)
Thirlmere	3½ (5.6)	½ (0.8)	583 (178)	158 (48)
Derwentwater	3 (4.8)	1¼ (2)	244 (74)	72 (22)
Wastwater	3 (4.8)	½ (0.8)	200 (61)	258 (79)
Crummock	2½ (1,6)	½ (0.8)	321 (98)	144 (44)
Ennerdale	2½ (1.6)	¾ (1.2)	368 (112)	148 (45)
Esthwaite	1½ (2.4)	½ (0.8)	217 (66)	80 (24)
Buttermere	1¼ (2)	½ (0.8)	329 (100)	94 (29)
Loweswater	1¼ (2)	½ (0.8)	429 (131)	60 (18)
Grasmere	1 (1.6)	½ (0.8)	208 (63)	75 (23)
Rydal Water	¾ (1.2)	¼ (0.4)	181 (55)	55 (17)
Elterwater	½ (0.8)	¼ (0.4)	187 (57)	50 (15)

First, four of the big lakes, distinguished from the rest because they offer cruises across them and lots of other water-based activity.

★★★ Derwentwater

It's a close-run thing between Derwentwater and Ullswater for the title of best lake. We think Ullswater just makes it, thanks to its magnificent scenery and variety, but Derwentwater has been called the 'Queen of the Lakes' and it is nicely compact and very pretty. Friars Crag, less than a mile from the centre of Keswick, has one of the finest – and most popular – views in the country, looking across the lake and down into Borrowdale.

The name means the 'lake of the river which abounds in oak trees'. The shores are still heavily wooded and are largely in the care of the National Trust. It is only 3 miles (4.8 km) long but, at 1¼ miles (2 km), the widest of the lakes. (Most of them have a superlative of some sort, if you search hard enough.) The average depth is only 18 feet (5.5 m), which means that this is one of the first lakes to freeze over in cold winters. It's famous for skating.

Derwentwater has eight islands. Lord's Island used to be the site of the house of the Earl of Derwentwater, hence the name, and St Herbert's is named after the disciple of St Cuthbert who made it his home and prompted a procession of monks and friars on pilgrimage. Another 'island', in the southwest corner, is marked on some maps as Floating Island, and it appears only every three years or so – a mass of weeds and rotting vegetation, which pops to the surface in dry weather and when buoyed up by marsh gases. It's more of an event than an island. Derwent Island was home in the 16th century to some of Keswick's miners, and the lake was once used for transporting charcoal, graphite and ore. The house on the island is privately let by the National Trust, but it opens it up for visits on a handful of days in summer (tel. 017687 73780 for details). The lake has interesting and often rare wildlife and is one of only two lakes supporting the vendace fish, a relic of the Ice Age.

Getting on the water
The Keswick Launch runs services around the lake from Keswick Piers just outside the town, stopping off at six places along the way. The launches are unlike those on Ullswater or Windermere, being a lot smaller and with no pretensions to being called steamers. Between mid-March and mid-November launches leave every 30 minutes, either clockwise or anticlockwise, and the service is cut to half a dozen journeys on weekends and school holidays only for the rest of the year. A clockwise round trip, which takes about 50 minutes, takes you to the piers at Ashness Gate, Lodore Falls, High Brandlehow, Low Brandlehow, Hawes End and Nichol End. It's a good way of seeing the lake and shoreline, but the

launches themselves can be noisy and uncomfortable (tel. 017687 72263 or visit *www.keswick-launch.co.uk*).

There are useful private launch sites for canoes, sailboards, dinghies and the like at the Keswick Launch base (above); Derwentwater Marina at Portinscale; Nichol End Marina; the Lake District National Park Authority car park at Kettlewell near Lodore; and the National Trust land opposite Barrow House Lodge near the B5289. There's a 10mph (16kph) speed limit, enforced by wardens. You can hire boats at Keswick Launch, Lodore, the Derwentwater Marina and Nichol End. Anglers need a permit, available from Keswick's Tourist Information Centre or the post office.

Other attractions
There are pleasant walks to be had from all of the piers along the Keswick Launch route, and you can complete a 10 mile (16 km) circuit of the lake with only a short stretch on the busy road. The path is narrow on the western side and can quickly become congested in summer, though it usually has the best views. A good vantage point for the lake is Cat Bells, an easy climb from Hawes End or High Brandlehow piers. There's more fine walking in the Newlands Valley and Borrowdale, both close by.

★★★ Ullswater

Windermere may be bigger and busier, and Derwentwater may be more compact, but Ullswater has variety and grandeur, and it's bordered by some of the best walks in the Lake District. If we had to pick just one lake for amenities and beauty, it would be Ullswater. Wordsworth agreed – he reckoned it had the best mix of beauty and grandeur.

At the Pooley Bridge end it is gentle, flat, almost boring, but as you work your way along its length the landscape around becomes more picturesque and then, finally, you get the grandeur and magnificence of the southern end at

Glenridding. A good view is also to be had from Kirkstone Pass, looking down with Brothers Water in the foreground.

Ullswater is a serpentine lake, snaking its way through the landscape for 7½ miles (12 km). It is best explored from the southern end, where the lake is dominated by St Sunday Crag, Place Fell, Fairfield and Helvellyn. Walk along the path on the eastern shore from Howtown to Patterdale and you'll appreciate Ullswater at its best. The opposite side has the main road and is usually crowded in summer.

During the 1960s Ullswater was the subject of a battle between the National Park Authority and Manchester Corporation, which wanted to extract water to feed the reservoir at Haweswater. As a compromise, the pumping station was hidden completely underground at the northern end, and most visitors will not even know it exists. The name comes from the first Lord of Ullswater, a Norse settler called Ulf. Ullswater is a public highway and was once used for transporting miners and ore from Glenridding. At the foot of the lake is a hill called Dunmallet, which was once the site of an Iron Age fortification.

Getting on the water
The delightfully named Ullswater Navigation and Transit Company runs four Ullswater Steamers around the lake, from Glenridding to Pooley Bridge via Howtown. It takes about an hour to go the whole length. The boats resemble the cruisers on Windermere, and, as it is for them, steamer is a courtesy title only since they all run on diesel. One boat, *Lady of the Lake*, was first launched in 1877, and *Raven* 12 years later. Services run all year round, with eight or so departures a day from Glenridding in the summer, reducing to three in the winter. There's a bar on board and the odd special themed cruise (tel. 017684 82229 or visit *www.ullswater-steamers.co.uk*).

Anyone can launch a private boat on Ullswater, sail or motorised, and there's none of the registration bureaucracy of Windermere, though a 10mph (16kph) speed limit applies on all parts. It's a particularly good lake for sailing. Launches include a public site at Howtown, National Trust land north of the steamer pier at Glenridding (no powered craft) and Ullswater Yacht Club, as well as Glenridding and Pooley Bridge, where you can also hire various craft. The Glenridding Sailing Centre offers tuition. Fishing is free with a rod licence.

Other attractions
Gowbarrow Park, now owned by the National Trust, has the daffodils that inspired William Wordsworth's poem and hugs the northwestern side of the lake. The popular falls at Aira Force are close by. The villages of Dacre to the north and Askham to the east are worth a visit. Helvellyn, probably the Lake District's most popular mountain, is best accessed from Glenridding at the southern end, and you can combine a walk along the shore with a climb up Place Fell. Sharrow Bay, Lakeland's most luxurious hotel and with a Michelin-starred restaurant, is on the eastern shore if you've got money to burn.

Windermere Lake from Old England Hotel

★★★ Windermere

Not just Cumbria's largest lake, but England's too, at 10½ miles (16.9 km) long and 1 mile (1.6 km) wide. It is named after a Norse hero, Winand or Vinandr, and has always been a busy highway, probably used by the Romans for ferrying troops and then later used for transporting iron ore, charcoal and passengers. For the last 80 years or so the boats have all been purely pleasure bound, but there are still hundreds and hundreds of them. In summer they glisten from afar like tadpoles, with hardly enough water to go round, or so it often appears.

After a long public inquiry, a 10mph (16kph) speed limit was introduced on Windermere in 2005. The Lake District National Park Authority argued that the fast power boats that had become popular on the lake were out of keeping with the aims of a National Park, and it was supported by environmental groups and the Friends of the Lake District. Opposing them, naturally enough, were power boat users and water skiers, who campaigned very hard to preserve the status quo, arguing that Windermere was big enough to be shared by everyone with a bit of common sense. Despite their threats to do so, few people have flouted the speed limit, and the lake has undoubtedly become a much quieter place since it was brought in. The flip side is that some nearby hoteliers and shopkeepers have seen their incomes slide, as the power boaters and water skiers go elsewhere for their thrills.

Windermere is still alive with people enjoying other aquatic diversions, and it is a beautiful lake, with wooded shores, dramatic mountain views looking east and north, and little islands dotted around. The Bowness end swarms with visitors, but you can quickly escape from the crowds by crossing on the ferry to the western side and walking along the shore. There is no road, nor any towns or villages along the western shore, and you can walk a lakeside path most of the way, gazing across at the mansions and masses on the other side.

Getting on the water

At one time there were several public cruisers working the lake, but after a few takeovers the uninspiringly named Windermere Lake Cruises (WLC) is now in sole charge. This has at least made timetable linking and booking much more straightforward, and many of the historic boats are still in action.

WLC provides a regular service up and down the lake, from Waterhead at the north end to Lakeside at the southern tip, but the busiest departure point is Bowness. A full-length one-way trip takes an hour and a bit and is a great way of getting the feel of the lake and surrounding area. Boats run all year, but with a slightly reduced service in winter. In summer you can also take circular cruises round some of the islands, and some boats stop at Brockhole. There are endless permutations of fares, including a 24-hour Freedom of the Lake ticket that allows you on and off as you please. Local residents can get a discount card. You can also buy tickets to connect you with the railway at Lakeside or tickets that allow you on buses at either end of your journey. For more information and timetables tel. 015395 31188 or visit *www.windermere-lakecruises.co.uk.*

The Windermere Ferry meanwhile provides a service between Bowness on the eastern shore and Ferry House near Sawrey on the west. There has been some sort of ferry on this route for about 500 years, and Wordsworth went across on his way to school in Hawkshead. These days the ferry pulls itself across the lake by means of some ingenious chains below the surface. It only takes seven minutes and saves motorists a 10 mile (16 km) detour round the tip of the lake, but queues can quickly build up and eat into the time you've saved. From April to October a connecting bus whisks you on from Ferry House to Beatrix Potter's Hill Top, Hawkshead and Grisedale Forest. The ferry costs £3.00 for a car and passengers, or 50p for pedestrians, and runs from early morning to late evening all year round (tel. 01228 607653).

Private usage of the lake has changed since the 10mph (16kph) speed limit was introduced, and it's subject to by-laws brought in by the Lake District National Park Authority. Some busier parts of the lake, at the tips and in the

middle, have a 6mph (10kph) limit. In addition, all power-driven boats must be registered and are subject to an annual charge for using the lake. For individuals wanting to launch a boat, access can seem very daunting and difficult, not least because the eastern side seems to be full of large private houses. But it is possible to launch from a number of sites, including the public slipway at Ferry Nab and the private Windermere and Waterhead Marinas. The Lake District National Park Authority's Windermere Registration Scheme can register your boat (tel. 015397 24555); the Lake Patrol team can advise on the confusing regulations (tel. 015394 42753).

Lighter craft, like dinghies, canoes, windsurfers and so on, can also launch from the National Trust's Fell Foot Country Park at the south end of Windermere or from the much quieter western shore between Ferry House and Wray Castle, also owned by the National Trust. You can hire rowing boats at Bowness, Waterhead, Low Wood and Fell Foot Park, and several companies provide sailing tuition. One of the best for small boats is the council-run Lakes Leisure Windermere on the eastern shore (tel. 015394 47330 or visit *www.lakesleisure.org.uk/windermere*).

Some islands are free to access, but you're not allowed to camp on any of them. Swimming is quite popular, but don't underestimate how cold it is, even on a blazing August day. There are occasional organised swims, and the record for the length of the lake is four hours. If you prefer to sit on the shore, you can fish the lake with a rod licence (with landowner's permission on private stretches of the shore).

Other attractions
Belle Isle is the largest of the 20 islands on Windermere, and you can see it from Bowness. It was originally the home of the Curwen family and is now privately owned. You can't land there, but you can glimpse the house through the trees if you're passing by boat. The National Trust owns Wray Castle, just north of the Ferry landing stage on the western shore, with grounds open to the public. The National Park Visitor Centre at Brockhole is worth a visit, as is the Steamboat Museum (see Chapter 10; it's closed for refurbishment at the time of writing).

★★ Coniston Water

If you travel along the busy road near the western shore, Coniston can be a little disappointing. You can see the lake, but it is against a background of low fells and forest plantations. This is also the most touristy route, with ice cream vans in every lay-by. It is quieter and more satisfying along the narrow road on the eastern shore, and from here you can see Coniston Water at its best, with the Old Man and its neighbours rearing up magnificently in the background. (This often happens with the lakes. You get there, wonder what all the fuss is about, trundle about a bit – and then suddenly it hits you.)

The lake is 5¼ miles (8.4 km) long and ½ mile (800 m) wide. It has a couple of small islands, owned by the National Trust, including Peel Island, which features in Arthur Ransome's *Swallows and Amazons* as Wild Cat Island. On some very old maps Coniston appears as Thurston's Mere, which derived from an Old Norse name. It has been a public highway for centuries, and ore mined at the head of the lake used to be carried down to the foot and then transported to the quay at Greenodd. The lake is famous as the scene of Donald Campbell's attempts at the world water speed record, and it was where he died in 1967. There is a memorial to him in the village, an exhibition dedicated to him in the Ruskin Museum (see Chapter 10) and photographs of his attempts in his favourite pubs, the Sun and the Black Bull. There's an ongoing project to restore Campbell's *Bluebird* (more details at *www.bluebirdproject.com*). Since the 10mph (16kph) speed limit was introduced on Windermere, Coniston has hosted the long-running annual Power Boat Records Week each November, though ongoing grumbles about safety and noise might put future events in jeopardy.

Getting on the water

The best way to enjoy the water anywhere in the Lake District is ★★★ **The Coniston Gondola**, and it is the star attraction of this particular lake. The steam yacht was launched from Coniston Hall by the Furness Railway Folk in 1859, and ran a regular service up and down the lake for nearly 80 years. When it was eventually retired, its engine was sold to power a sawmill and its hull became a houseboat. It was washed ashore in 1963 and lay derelict until the National Trust started taking an interest in the mid-1970s. With some daring, they began to restore her, and the unique and beautiful craft they created has been back in service since 1980. It can carry over 80 passengers, is decked out with luxurious upholstery and fittings and is the only silent method of powered public transport anywhere in the Lake District. A trip on it is highly recommended; sit at the front, though, because there can be specks of soot at the back.

The *Gondola* runs daily between 11.00am and 4.00pm from April to October. A leisurely circuit of the lake takes about an hour, stopping off at Brantwood on the eastern shore, and costs £6.00 (children £3.00). The service is sometimes suspended if the weather is bad. For more details tel. 015394 41288 or visit *www.nationaltrust.org.uk/gondola*.

The Coniston Launch is a less grand way of touring Coniston, but it is a pleasant enough ride and covers the whole lake. It runs every day from mid-morning to late afternoon, hourly in the summer and reducing in winter, down to weekends only in December and January. There are a couple of different routes and occasional themed or evening cruises (tel. 015394 36216 or visit *www.conistonlaunch.co.uk*).

Launching a private boat is restricted to the Coniston Boating Centre at the northern end, run by the Lake District National Park Authority. You can also hire rowing boats, quiet electric launches, dinghies, kayaks and canoes from here (tel. 015394 41366). There's a nice café nearby if you don't want to get wet. There is a speed restriction of 10mph (16kph) over the whole lake, so take it easy in that rowing boat. Fishing is permitted if you have a rod licence.

Other attractions
The star of Coniston's shoreline is Brantwood, John Ruskin's home, on the eastern bank. There are walking trails along this part of the shore, and several nice little car parks tucked among the trees from which to join them. Nearby Tarn Hows and Esthwaite Water are worth a visit, as is Hawkshead, 2 miles (3.2 km) from the north end.

The next dozen

Now the 12 remaining lakes, each of which has its own appeal despite – or perhaps because of – their lack of public transport across them. They're listed in order of star rating, our favourites first.

★★★ Buttermere

The name is a dead giveaway and means 'the lake by the dairy pastures'. It is a perfect little lake. You can walk right round it, and the views are superb. The early tourists used to rave about it being the 'quintessence of natural beauty', and if you're based in the north Lakes and have time for only one low-level, easy family walk, do this one. Park in the village and follow the footpath across farmland to the shore. Go round anticlockwise and along the north shore you'll enter a short tunnel, cut through the rock; the story goes that the local landowner had it blasted through because he was annoyed at not being able to walk all round the lake. You'll also pass Sourmilk Gill, a magnificent waterfall in full spate. The whole walk round won't take you much more than two hours, but try to avoid it on bank holiday weekends when it turns into a scrum, as do the pubs in the village. If you're feeling lazier, you could always park at the southern end and look across the water to High Stile and Haystacks.

Getting on the water
No motorboats are allowed, but you can hire rowing boats. Permission to launch small boats, canoes and windsurfers can be got from Dalegarth Farm, 1½ miles (2.4 km) south-east of the village (tel. 017687 70233) or from Wood House (tel. 017687 70208).

★★★ Grasmere

Everyone likes Grasmere. And with all that fame and literary name, how could we begrudge it three stars? It is a delightful little lake, completely surrounded by fells and nice to look at

133

from every angle. It has one island, centrally placed, no piers or steamers, and on the west side the fields come right down to the water's edge. The only things that spoil it are the A591, which thunders along the east side, and the 'beach' at the foot of the lake under Loughrigg Terrace, which can get busy in summer. Lots of people stop along the A591 to take photographs. Don't. If you want to be different, park at White Moss, then walk over the old road towards Dove Cottage. About halfway you'll see a seat in some woods on your right, from which you get a good, if less panoramic, view of the lake with Silver How as its backdrop. When the lake is still and the sun is shining in the early morning, the island seems to be sitting on a mirror and the view is absolutely magical. Another classic view is from the top of Loughrigg Terrace, with Dunmail Raise in the background.

You can walk right around the lake – it's about 4 miles (6.4 km) – although you are on that horrid road a lot of the way. There is a pleasant little wood at the southern end. The island belongs to the National Trust and it was used by William and Dorothy Wordsworth for picnics, while the stone barn was used to shelter sheep, taken across in flat-bottomed boats. William got the inspiration for many of his poems on and around the lake. The name Grasmere simply means 'the lake with the grassy shore'.

Getting on the water
No powered craft are allowed on the lake. Rowing boats can be hired from the Faeryland Tea Garden between March and October (tel. 015394 35060), and arguably the best place from which to see Grasmere vale is from a boat in the middle of the lake. Or you could row over to the island with a picnic, though no camping is allowed.

★★★ Rydal Water

A reedy little lake, usually mentioned in the same breath as Grasmere. You can get a good view of both of them from the road if you whiz past in your car, but it's definitely worth a stop.

The river that flows out of Grasmere enters Rydal Water, then flows out at the foot down to Waterhead. If you are keen, you could canoe all the way from Grasmere to Lakeside at the southern tip of Windermere, although the walk back wouldn't be much fun. The river, the Rothay, gave the lake its former name, Rothaymere or Routhermere. It gets its current name from Rydal village, though it isn't actually in Rydal 'dale' at all. It's one of the smallest lakes, just ¾ mile long by ¼ mile wide (1.2 by 0.4 km), but it can be absolutely superb first thing in the morning or in winter when there is no one else about. Wordsworth loved it, and in summer it can get busy with people on his trail.

There's a lovely old bridge just to the south called Pelter Bridge, where you can turn off the A591 on to the Upper Loughrigg road. Park here and walk up the lane back to the lake. The view from the bench as you come into sight of the lake is a classic and especially lovely in winter. Carry on and walk right round the lake up White Moss, then follow the road back.

Getting on the water
No public launching of boats is allowed, although you may see the odd rogue canoeist. The 'beach' on the south shore is good for swimming, but it's cold. Obviously.

★★★ Wastwater

After Ullswater this is our second choice lake. If you have time for only two, Wastwater provides the perfect antidote to the busy, over-populated lakes.

Wasdale was the original name, meaning 'the valley with the lake', so the 'water' part is, strictly speaking, redundant. It doesn't matter – this is the deepest, most dramatic and most haunting of all the lakes. It is well over towards the coast, and the only way to it by car is over the tortuous Wrynose and Hardknott Passes or from the west coast. Approach through Greendale and you suddenly come within sight of a view that is in almost every book on the Lake District – the famous Wastwater screes. Nearly 2,000 feet (610 m) high, they plunge into the lake, presenting a sheer wall that looks vertical. It's not, and there's a path along the foot of the screes, but it's exceptionally tough going, and if you look up from it you'll feel dizzy. It's best seen on a still, sunny day when the screes are reflected in the lake and can look frightening. Look up and you'll see another familiar view – Great Gable flanked by Kirkfell and Lingmell. This is the emblem on the National Park badge.

Wastwater's inaccessibility makes it a quiet, unspoilt lake, a favourite starting point for walkers and mountaineers. The road is usually quiet, making for a good walk along the entire length of the west shore, and there is lay-by parking along it. At the head of the lake is the tiny village of Wasdale Head, with the Wasdale Head Inn, famous as the unofficial headquarters of the Lake District mountaineering fraternity. It was once run by Will Ritson, renowned as the biggest liar in England for the tall tales he told guests (see Chapter 14).

Don't miss St Olaf's Church, a little further on, hidden in a field behind a clump of fir trees, and one of the smallest and most spectacularly located churches in the country. In the little graveyard are memorials to dead climbers, killed on Scafell, Gable and the Himalayas. If these don't put you off, some of the best walking in the Lake District can be had from here.

Getting on the water
You can canoe or row on the lake, but you'll need a permit and numbers are limited. The National Trust warden can advise (tel. 019467 26220). The lake is popular with divers because of its depth and clear water.

★★ Crummock Water

The name is Celtic, hence its Scottish sound, and means 'crooked lake'. It is separated from Buttermere by a narrow, ½ mile (800 m), strip of land, and in the ancient past they were probably joined as one lake. It is bigger than Buttermere and very attractive, but nothing like as busy, and the contrast between them is striking. The approach from Loweswater along the eastern shore is a very pretty road, with the lake in the foreground against Mellbreak and Ling Crags. There is a footpath along the west shore, going from Buttermere village to Loweswater, and this gives some excellent views up the valley. Scale Force waterfall is a short diversion away from the path. The lake is now owned by the National Trust.

Getting on the water
There is no public launch site, but small dinghies, canoes and boards can be launched from access land at several points. Numbers are limited, and permission must be sought and paid for from Wood House, which also handles fishing permits (tel. 017687 70208).

★★ Ennerdale Water

Like Wastwater, Ennerdale Water is on the western flanks of the Lake District and is one of the wildest and remotest lakes. It has a good name for solitude and quiet, with the result that you might meet lots of other people who have also gone there to be alone. The Forestry Commission has recently rather drawn people's attention to it by promoting the valley's forest trails. The valley is dominated by the Commission's plantations, but at least they have kept out the cars and allow free access. You can walk all around the lake, although things get a little scree-y on the southern shoreline. Park at Bowness Knott, where the road ends at the northern tip of the lake, and walk along the shore to the southern foot of the lake – a good place for picnics – and then back by the other side.

Ennerdale Water is actually a reservoir, but the dam is hardly noticeable. Amenities are few, apart from the car park and picnic points, and there are no hotels, pubs or villages along it. Ennerdale Bridge, 1½ miles (2.4 km) west, has a couple of pubs and a shop. Access from the central lakes is difficult and means either coming down via Cockermouth or heading towards the coast from Buttermere, leaving the fells and turning back in again, but this inaccessibility has its advantages, and it is the only completely road-free lake in the whole of the Lake District. Every other shore – even Wastwater – has a road along at least part of its shore. So it makes a perfect, peaceful circular walk with easy going most of the way, even with children. Allow about four hours. If you're feeling more energetic, the Ennerdale horseshoe – taking in High Stile, Haystacks, Great Gable, Kirk Fell and Pillar, among many more – is a classic and strenuous Lakeland hike.

Getting on the water

Ennerdale Water is owned by United Utilities and only limited private canoeing or kayaking is allowed. Access is by free annual permit, but you'll have to plan a bit in advance (tel. 017687 72334 or write to The Old Sawmills, Thirlmere, Keswick CA12 4TQ). Fishing permits are available from the same place.

★★ Loweswater

Probably the most forgotten of the 16 lakes, which is a great shame as it's very pretty. It is the only lake whose waters flow in towards the centre of the Lake District. There, that's one for the record books.

The car park on the road at the foot of the lake has room for only about 20 cars. At little more than 1 mile (1.6 km) long and less than ½ mile (800 m) wide, it is one of the smallest lakes and, at only about 60 feet (18 m) deep, one of the shallowest, which means it is one of the first to freeze over in winter. Loweswater means the 'leafy lake', referring to the woods that flank one side. It's a nice, gentle lake, though looking east over it there are some rather grand views. The small car park at the southern end Maggie's Bridge, leads you to a footpath right around the lake or, if you prefer something more gentle, go into the woods along the west side, which are owned by the National Trust and provided with plenty of seats. It is popular with locals as a Sunday afternoon sort of a place.

When you're visiting Loweswater, make sure you take in the Lorton Valley, which has some of the most attractive, lush scenery in the northern Lakes, and don't forget that Crummock Water and Buttermere are just around the corner. The three lakes go together, making a perfect string of pearls. With clever car parking, you could walk them all in a day, sticking each time to the roadless shores and taking in refreshments at the pubs in Buttermere and the Kirkstile Inn in the village of Loweswater. Combined, the hat-trick of circuits are 15 miles (24 km) or so of walking. What bliss.

Getting on the water

The National Trust hires rowing boats from Watergate Farm at Waterend if you want to admire the tranquillity from the water (tel. 01946 861465). Otherwise no craft are allowed. The farm issues fishing permits too.

★★ Thirlmere

Another reservoir. Thirlmere was once two much smaller lakes, called Leatheswater and Brackmere, with a footbridge across their narrow middle. In 1879, to much consternation from the likes of John Ruskin, the area was bought by Manchester Corporation Water Works to supply the industrial northwest. A dam was built at the north end and the water level raised by 54 feet (16.5 m). It is now called Thirlmere, which means the lake with the hollow – the hollow presumably being where the two earlier lakes joined. It is now 3½ miles (5.6 km) long and ½ mile (800 m) wide.

Thirlmere is, in fact, quite a pretty lake, very clear and pure, and despite being coniferous, the woods along the west shore have a wild look about them. The lake is best appreciated from the lovely little road that threads its way through the trees along the west shore line. From the A591 it can look rather barren, especially in midsummer when the water level drops, leaving a ragged, white scar around the rim of the lake. One of the best and most peculiar viewpoints is at Hause Point, about halfway along the west road. You have to climb some metal steps and find yourself on top of a rock along with a seat. The view to Dunmail Raise is good, although Helvellyn is uninspiring from this angle.

The lake's owner, United Utilities, has opened up a lot more of it to the public lately. There is access at most of the lay-bys along the west road and from the Station Coppice car park halfway along the east side. There are forest trails on each side, and on the west side is a footpath, constructed by the British Trust for Conservation Volunteers, which leads to Raven Crag, an excellent viewpoint.

Getting on the water
United Utilities' policy of full public access extends to the lake. No powered craft are allowed, but dinghies, canoes and sailboards are all permitted without the need to get permission or pay a fee. Rod licence holders can fish the lake.

★ Bassenthwaite Lake

This is it – the only true 'lake' in the Lake District; the others are all mere 'meres' or 'waters'. But just to confuse matters, Wordsworth called it Broadwater. It is one of the largest lakes but also one of the shallowest – 4 miles (6.4 km) long but just 70 feet (21 m) deep at most. It is the most northerly of the lakes and has no real settlement on its shores. Apart from the hideous A66, which blasts its way up the west side, the shores are relatively unspoilt, and because the lake is now owned by the Lake District National Park Authority it should be kept that way.

Towering over the lake at the Thornthwaite corner is a craggy white rock that looks down over the A66. This is known as The Bishop, because legend has it that a bishop once tried to ride up the screes at this point – either to demonstrate his faith in God or as the result of a drunken bet, depending on which story you believe. Either way, his horse wasn't up for the challenge, falling and plunging them both to their deaths. The local Swan Hotel whitewashes the rock every year.

Bassenthwaite can look very mysterious – which is how Tennyson saw it when he stayed by its shores and was inspired by it in his poetry. One of the best views of the lake and the surrounding countryside is available from Dodd, on the east side, and there's a path running the length of the west shore. The only access to the east shore is at Mirehouse, a stately home open to the public and with a wooded walk in the grounds. The car park near the south end of the lake is good for Whinlatter Forest, and Powter How at the extreme south end is a pleasant woodland walk.

Many of Bassenthwaite's visitors are bird lovers, drawn by the 70 or so species that can be found around the lake. The big attraction is Bassenthwaite's ospreys, which arrived unexpectedly in 2001 and have returned every year since. Fair-weather Lakes tourists that they are, they usually arrive in April and head off for Africa in August or September. There's a viewing platform at the Forestry Commission's Dodd Wood centre, where you can watch the birds swoop over and around the lake. There's a live video feed of the ospreys' nest at nearby Whinlatter Forest Park Visitor Centre and webcams at *www.ospreywatch.co.uk*.

Getting on the water
There is no public right of navigation on the lake, and access is limited by the National Park Authority to conserve the area's wildlife. All power craft are banned, and there are several no-boating zones, but permits to launch dinghies, canoes, windsurfers and rowing boats can be obtained from the Keswick Tourist Information Centre (tel. 017687 72645). The launching point is at Peel Wyke on the western side, just off the A66. You need a permit to fish, too; they're also available from Keswick.

★ Esthwaite Water

Wordsworth knew this lake well as a boy, but nowadays it can be easily missed if you're rushing up to Hawkshead. It's not a particularly spectacular location, but conventionally pretty, surrounded by low fells and minor roads. In some ways it's similar to Rydal or Grasmere, but without the crowds and cars. A public footpath runs from near the village to the shore at the northwest, and down in the southwest, a couple of miles from Hawkshead, is a good car park and access point.

Getting on the water
Rowing boats are the only craft allowed on the lake, and the only public launch point for them is the car park on the southwest side. The water is packed with trout, making it particularly popular for fishing, and the Esthwaite Water Trout Fishery hires boats and runs courses. If you don't catch anything you could always buy trout from the shop and pretend it was all your own work (tel. 015394 36541 or visit *www.hawksheadtrout.com*).

★ Haweswater

One long reservoir: 4 miles (6.4 km) long and ½ mile (800 m) wide. It *used* to be only 2¼ miles (4 km) long, with the attractive dairy farming village of Mardale and the renowned

Dun Bull Inn at its head. Then, in 1940, the Manchester Water Corporation stepped in, spent £5 million on building a 120 foot (37 m) high dam, and turned Haweswater into a much bigger reservoir to serve the northwest. Mardale is now under the water, though in very dry weather its remains sometimes poke their way back to the surface. The story of Mardale's sinking is told in *Haweswater*, a very good novel by Sarah Hall.

Haweswater is one of the most isolated and difficult lakes to reach, accessible only from the northeast and southeast sides and lying in wild and unspoilt countryside. It's rather lonely, and if you're in the area for only a short time you might not think it's worth it, but it's loved by Lakeland experts. And bird lovers too, since England's only known golden eagles have been spotted here for many years.

There's a fine lakeside path that dips in and out around Haweswater, and you'll probably not see anyone else the whole way, except perhaps near the Haweswater Hotel, the modern replacement for the Dun Bull Inn, halfway along the western shore. You can park at Burnbanks at the northern end or Mardale Head at the southern end, but the best way to discover Haweswater is to park at the head of the Kentmere Valley and walk over the Nan Bield Pass.

Getting on the water
There's no access. Enjoy the scenery instead.

Elterwater

This is a peculiar little lake, the smallest of the 16, and in fact it often gets omitted altogether in favour of Brothers Water. Tucked away at the foot of the Langdales, you get glimpses of it as you travel along the B5343. It doesn't have much to offer in the way of walking but is best reached by parking in the car park at the eastern end, crossing the road and entering the wood. A footpath runs along the side of the lake and up to the little village. Its chief distinction is the good view this path gives you, looking over the lake to the Langdales. Pleasant enough for a quiet stroll, but not really typical Lake District. The name is rather nice though: *Elter* is Old Norse for 'swan', so this is 'swan lake', and migrating swans still call in.

Getting on the water
No access.

Tarns

So much for the lakes. Now for their less famous, less popular little brothers, the tarns. It's impossible to tell how many there are because the smallest have no names, and some come and go depending on how wet the weather is. Two of the tarns, Brothers Water and Devoke Water, are as large as the smaller so-called lakes and are sometimes added to their number. Another, Tarn Hows, is more visited than most of the Lakes.

Tarn enthusiasts should look out for a few books. *The Tarns of Lakeland* by Lakeland artist W. Heaton Cooper includes paintings or sketches of 103 tarns. *Exploring Lakeland Tarns* is by Don Blair, who lists 213 with a checklist to get you started on your own voyage. *Tarns of the Fells* is a collaboration between the Cumbria Wildlife Trust, the Friends of the Lake District and the Freshwater Biological Association. Or, if you really want to get to know the tarns, you could do as two Grasmere gentlemen did in the 1950s and take a swim in 463 tarns in the Lake District – the number they considered proper and permanent tarns. You might, as they did, have to break the ice to get into some of them or dodge landowners wondering what you're up to, but what an achievement it would be. While you plan your first swim, here's our pick of ten of the bigger, better known tarns, all of them worth considering for a visit.

★★★ Blea Tarn

Say that you have been to Blea Tarn and the response is likely to be: 'which one?' There are a few. The prettiest and most accessible lies between Little and Great Langdale and is found by following the B5343 along Great Langdale until it becomes a minor road and begins to climb. At the top there's a car park on the left and one of the best tarns in Lakeland on your right. Magnificent on a sunny day.

There's another Blea Tarn above Boot in Eskdale. It's accessible only by a bit of a trek on foot, but it's very pretty. A third is southeast of Watendlath, high up to the west of Thirlmere. Set in a bog and very boring, it's worth mentioning only because it is higher than the other two.

★★★ Easedale Tarn

As tarns go, this deserves three stars because it is one of the nicest and easiest to get to, and it has one of the best approach marches, right alongside Sourmilk Gill with its beautiful tumbling waterfalls and small ponds. Great for a hot summer day. The tarn lies northwest of Grasmere village; just opposite the green is a road leading to Easedale car park. The tarn itself has a rather sombre setting, though there are lots of good views back down the valley. The mass of stones on the left as you come within sight of the tarn are the remains of an old refreshment hut. A painting, showing what it was once like, is hanging in Dove Cottage. William and Dorothy Wordsworth knew and loved this little hidden tarn and valley.

★★★ Innominate Tarn

A tarn that was given a name to show it hasn't got one, if that makes sense. It has an unparalleled location on the top of

Haystacks and is one of the most tranquil spots in the Lake District. Its claim to fame is that this is the spot where Alfred Wainwright had his ashes scattered.

★★ Grisedale Tarn

One of the largest and deepest tarns, Grisedale Tarn is set in splendid scenery. It is on the Grisedale route to Dollywaggon Pike and Helvellyn, so it's for dedicated fell-walkers only. The pass was once a packhorse route through to Penrith. Nearby is a rock bearing an inscription to commemorate the parting of William Wordsworth and his brother John, who died at sea five years later without William ever seeing him again. The inscription was put there at the insistence of the energetic Canon Rawnsley, though you might have to search a little to find it.

★★ Red Tarn

On Helvellyn, this is the highest and most magnificently sited of all the tarns in the Lake District. It lies in the depths of an immense bowl, formed by Helvellyn, Striding Edge and Swirrel Edge. At only 85 feet (26 m), it's not as deep as it appears. In the last century a dam was built to supply the mines at Glenridding.

★★ Tarn Hows

One of the most popular places in the entire Lake District. You see it on postcards all over the area, and it's thought to get a million or so visitors a year. It can feel like they're all there at once in the summer.

Tarn Hows lies between Hawkshead and Coniston and is advertised on some signposts simply as 'The Tarns'. It's a beautiful tarn, lush and very chocolate box, with one of the most delightful views in Lakeland. It's also home to some of the country's few remaining red squirrels. It's only ½ mile (800 m) long, surrounded by woods and with a footpath all the way round. To the west the immense bulk of Wetherlam looms.

It's usually referred to as a manmade tarn, but there used to be several much smaller tarns in its place, called Monk Coniston Tarns, until the local landowner built a dam and converted the marshy ground into one big tarn with two little islands. The present name really refers to the farm to the southwest. It has been in the hands of the National Trust since 1930 – it was donated by Beatrix Potter – and the Trust does much to control the level of erosion. But with the number of footbridges, paths, fences and picnic spots springing up it is becoming more artificial every year. Avoid it on bank holiday weekends and during the summer holidays, or go very early. It is at its best in winter, when it can be very beautiful and sometimes good for skating.

★ Devoke Water

As large as Rydal and sometimes promoted to the realms of the lakes, Devoke Water is rather out of the way in an austere moorland setting, due east of Ravenglass. It is approachable only by foot. From the central Lakes it involves a long drag over the Wrynose Pass, and it's hardly worth going all that way unless you're into Bronze Age settlements – there are 400 ancient cairns and 'hutments' in evidence around the tarn, dating from around the time when the area was first cleared of forest. Much loved by Norman Nicholson for its desolate feeling. The name – meaning 'dark one' – says it all really.

Alcock Tarn

This small, partly artificial tarn is on the fell to the east of Grasmere. There's a path to it on the road to White Moss, above Town End, and it's a good objective for an afternoon stroll. Not spectacular, but there are some good views from round about, taking in Coniston, Langdale and Helvellyn mountain ranges. It used to be called Buttercrags until a man named Alcock dammed it and stocked it with trout.

Brothers Water

Another tarn that is sometimes classed as the 16th lake at the expense of Elter Water, an idea that seems to come in and out of fashion. It lies just to the south of Ullswater, forming a well-known view from the Kirkstone Pass, and it may once have been part of the lake. A footpath skirts its shores, and you can park at Cow Bridge for a pleasant stroll between the woods and the water on the western side, though with Ullswater beckoning a couple of miles to the north you might not think it worth stopping for. It used to be called Broadwater, and it's said to have got its present name when two brothers drowned in it while skating in 1785.

Loughrigg Tarn

On the west side of Loughrigg Fell, this tarn is passed by the road from Grasmere over Red Bank. Wordsworth said it had 'a margin of smooth green meadows, of rocks, and rocky woods, a few reeds here, a few water lilies there', which just about sums it up. It's pleasant to come across but not worth going to a lot of trouble to seek out. You can camp at Tarn Foot Farm at the south end.

Mountains

The top ten mountains and fells in Lakeland with some recommended walking routes, plus our pick of the dales, passes, waterfalls and views

THE BORROWDALE VALLEY FROM GREAT END "ROGUE HERRIES" COUNTRY. 899.

If you accept 3,000 feet (914 m) as the minimum height for a mountain, the Lake District has four: Scafell Pike, Scafell, Helvellyn and Skiddaw. Or three if you do as many do and count Scafell and Scafell Pike as one, though they have separate summits. Here's the big Lakeland top ten:

1. Scafell Pike 3,210 feet (978 m)
2. Scafell 3,162 feet (964 m)
3. Helvellyn 3,118 feet (950 m)
4. Skiddaw 3,053 feet (931 m)
5. Great End 2,968 feet (910 m)
6. Bow Fell 2,959 feet (902 m)
7. Great Gable 2,949 feet (899 m)
8. Pillar 2,929 feet (892 m)
9. Nethermost Pike 2,923 feet (891 m)
10. Catstye Cam 2,920 feet (890 m)

This list excludes a few peaks that we count as part of other summits: Symonds Knott, Ill Crag and Broad Crag on Scafell Pike and Helvellyn Lower Man on Helvellyn.

As well as being the highest, Scafell Pike, Helvellyn and Skiddaw are also the most popular mountains, though figures to prove it are naturally non-existent. They haven't quite got to the point where a turnstile is needed on the top, though on busy days it would ease congestion a bit, as there is often a queue to stand on the final cairn.

Note All our routes in this chapter are purely rough guides and must be used with a good map and compass.

The Big Four Mountains

In height order.

★★★ Scafell Pike and ★★ Scafell

3,210 feet (978 m) and 3,162 feet (964 m)

Scafell Pike is England's highest point and the hardest to get to of all the popular Lake District's mountains. It's also the one that has seen some terrible accidents, but the one that you can boast most about – if you honestly get to the top. It's not really very difficult, but it does involve a long, slow climb. The weather is likely to be very different on top – usually worse – so be well prepared with stout footwear, some extra layers of warmth and good rainwear. Despite its challenges, it's not unusual to see some first-time visitors scaling it in flip-flops and T-shirts and, near the top, pondering the error of their ways.

It's part of a range of peaks known as the Scafell Pikes or the Scafell massif, and you have to work your way over or round them before you finally start climbing the big one – hence the relatively long time needed to get up compared to some others that happen to be nearer to civilisation or a car park. But that just makes Scafell Pike all the more special. Samuel Taylor Coleridge did it in 1802, carrying a pen and a bottle of ink with him. He wrote a letter on top, making his the first recorded ascent, and then ignored all the easy paths by hurrying down via Broad Stand, which is not to be recommended (see below).

The actual summit of Scafell Pike is not very exciting or pretty, being rather bleak, barren and stony, though on a clear day the views are sensational. On a warm summer day it'll also be swarming with walkers celebrating their achievement and having their photos taken. By contrast, the top of nearby Scafell is often empty, though the occasional person has scaled it by mistake, having got it mixed up with its bigger brother.

A ravine on the north side, called Piers Gill, is about the most dangerous part of Scafell Pike. In 1921 a walker fell down it, breaking both ankles, and lay at the bottom for nearly three weeks. He was finally found by chance by three walkers, having been kept alive by a pool of water near where he fell.

Routes
The shortest and quickest but steepest route is from Wasdale Head, going up Lingmell Gill, but if you're coming from central Lakeland it's a long drive to Wasdale.

Another way is from Seathwaite in Borrowdale. Walk straight up the valley for about 1 mile (1.6 km) until you hit Stockley Bridge, then cut right up Sty Head Gill for Sty Head Tarn. You'll probably see hordes of walkers by the tarn, socks and boots off, resting or guzzling picnics. Once over Sty Head Pass, you hit a long, open walk, which takes you along the western flank of Scafell Pike, a route sometimes known as the Guides' Walk or the Corridor. It finally takes you straight up to the summit, over rougher, rockier ground but still not too difficult. On the way back, if the day is clear and you feel confident, try coming down the other side via Sprinkling Tarn, then on again to Sty Head. The round trip should take about six hours, and on a hot day you can celebrate with a dip in the ice green, marvellous marble water at Stockley Bridge.

Scafell Pike and Scafell look close on the map, but combining the two is surprisingly tricky. Between them is the notorious Broad Stand, a 30 foot (10 m) drop that should be enough to put you off the direct route. Walking on to Scafell via Foxes Tarn instead involves a bit of detour and more ascent and descent, but it would take a good deal longer if you got stuck on Broad Stand.

★★★ Helvellyn

3,118 feet (950 m)

Often regarded as the finest of the 'big four' by Lakeland experts, for its brilliant views, exciting summit and exhilarating ascents. But in some ways it's the most dangerous, and it seems to have more accidents than any other Lakeland mountain. But Wordsworth climbed it safely when he was 70. Makes you sick. Unlike him, you're unlikely to be alone on a climb of Helvellyn, and the most popular routes up can get congested from very early on summer mornings. It's less busy but still popular in winter, when the snowy slopes attract serious walkers and a handful of skiers; there's a hut and tow lift on the slopes of nearby Raise.

The summit is exposed and can get bitterly cold, but there's a shelter where you can get your breath back and scoff your sandwiches, and the all-round views are fantastic. The number of memorials dotted around the upper slopes can be alarming. One of them near the summit shelter is in honour of two pilots who, for some reason, thought it would be a fun challenge to land a plane there in 1926. They got off safely, unlike Charles Gough, who was killed in a fall in 1805 and is remembered with a memorial stone. His dog was still standing watch by his body when it was discovered, an act of fidelity that inspired poets, including Wordsworth and Walter Scott. Accidents continue to happen, especially on Striding Edge, and it's not a mountain for those with any nerves about heights.

Routes
From the King's Head Inn at Thirlspot you can cross Helvellyn Gill to join the route up from Swirls car park, gaining Helvellyn via Lower Man. From the little church and car park at Wythburn follow the path through the forestry plantation, up the side of Combe Gill on to Swallow Scarth and Helvellyn on your left. Or from Grasmere, follow the old packhorse road up Great Tongue to Grisedale Tarn. Fairfield is on the right and Seat Sandal on the left. Climb up Dollywaggon Pike in front of you, then on over Nethermost Pike to Helvellyn. It's steep at first, but it makes a good expedition, with fine views all round.

Probably the most popular route up is from Glenridding, though only experienced walkers should tackle the upper reaches if the weather is bad. From the car park follow the lane on the other side of the beck and take the fork in the path marked Lanty's Tarn. Follow the zigzag path to the pretty tarn. Go down the hill, through a small plantation and up on to the ridge, taking the right hand path up the fellside. Grisedale Valley is on your left. Once you're on the ridge, cross over the stile and take the left-hand path on to the infamous Striding Edge. The edge is narrow and involves some scrambling, but this can be avoided by taking the well-trodden path a little lower down. Red Tarn is on the right. It gets its name from the way it appears dark red in colour when the sun rises, and there's always a crowd to watch the sun come up on Midsummer Day. Getting off the Edge and on to Helvellyn proper involves more scrambling, and the path up to the top is steep.

After you've enjoyed the views and your lunch, the usual way down is via Swirral Edge on the opposite side of Red Tarn to Striding Edge. There are great views as the path leads down to Mires Beck and on to Ullswater, and despite the crowds it can be a peaceful on a summer day. Once you're at the bottom, the path on the right of the beck leads you back to the car park at Glenridding. Swirral Edge is also a good way up if you're nervous about Striding Edge.

★★★ Skiddaw

3,053 feet (931m)

Some climbing types are rather scornful about Skiddaw, dismissing it as easy-peasy – nowt more than a stroll, with no hairy bits where real men can break their legs. All true. It is a modest, rounded and rather cuddly sort of mountain, but it makes an excellent walk all the same. How nice not to walk in fear or dread, as you can on Helvellyn, and how reassuring to think that even if the mist comes down or it grows dark, you should be perfectly safe. Just follow the crowds.

Skiddaw dominates the northern fells and is a landmark for miles around. People who live beyond it describe themselves as living 'back o'Skiddaw'. It was the first popular mountain climb in Lakeland, and that lovely open path from the Keswick side has been used by millions for over 150 years. You could probably take a pram up it. In the last war motor bikes and army vehicles went up it. No bother. In 1815 Wordsworth and Southey took their respective families up for a bonfire party to celebrate Waterloo, with the servants carrying up roast beef and plum pudding. It's that sort of friendly place. Handy for parking, too. 'Such massive strength and such beauty of outline rarely go together,' said Wainwright. 'Here, on Skiddaw, they do.'

Routes
There are several ways up. From the Bassenthwaite Lake side you can get up it from Millbeck or High Side. Or you can approach it from the rear – the eastern side, which is hidden from Keswick and hardly used, though it means a long but exciting walk from Dash Falls. If you do this route, look out for Skiddaw House, an amazing building stuck literally in the middle of nowhere, once used by shepherds and now a rustic but peerlessly located bunkhouse (visit *www.skiddawhouse. co.uk* for more information).

But by far the most famous, popular and dramatic route up is from Keswick. Follow the little road off the A591 towards Underscar and Applethwaite, then take Gale Road up to the end of it. The car park here will probably be full, so come back and find some space on the road. The drive is a bit of a cheat, because you've knocked off almost 1,000 feet (300 m) already – real climbers start from Keswick and climb Latrigg first – but it's a useful headstart if you have children in tow. The beautiful and enticing grassy slope right in front of you takes you up Jenkin Hill, and you rise very quickly with good views back over your shoulder to Keswick and Derwentwater. After that first steep climb it's a long but easier walk to the summit. The top can be freezing, so take warm clothes. It can all be done in three hours, even with the children or a family dog.

The best of the rest

Another top ten – more of the bigger summits, all worth attempting sometime.

★★ Blencathra

2,847 feet (868 m)

Or Saddleback, as it's also known, though not by Lakeland aficionados. Dramatic and curvy in profile, Wainwright called it 'a mountaineers' mountain'. The adventurous can park at Scales and follow the footpath along Sharp Edge, perhaps the most exhilarating ridge walk in the Lake District but one to be avoided in the wet because some stretches involve hair-raising scrambles. Scales Tarn is down to the left as the path leads on to the summit. You can return by Hallsfell, which is quite steep. A shorter and easier route is from the Blencathra Centre, reached from Blease Road in Threlkeld. From the car park follow the footpath over Knowe Crags, returning the same way.

★★ Bow Fell

2,959 feet (902 m)

One of Wainwright's six best fells, along with Scafell Pike, Pillar, Great Gable, Blencathra and Crinkle Crags, Bow Fell hosts some of the best views anywhere in the Lake District. Park in the National Trust car park in Langdale and walk up Mickleden, which is nice and flat, passing under Pike o'Stickle. Take the left path at the fork and go up Rossett Gill. Go beyond Angle Tarn and turn left up Ore Gap, which takes you on to Bow Fell. On a clear day the views are fantastic, stretching as far as Ingleborough in the Pennines and even Snaefell on the Isle of Man. For the return, head south for the Three Tarns and take the left path down the Band back into Langdale.

★★ Crinkle Crags

2,816 feet (858 m)

Well named, and its distinctive succession of peaks make for a spectacular sight from the Langdale Valley floor. But what look like small creases in the summit from down below are actually quite steep and challenging ups and downs when you meet them close to. The quickest and easiest route up is from the Three Shire Stone at the top of Wrynose Pass, going over Cold Pike.

For a fuller day's outing park in Langdale and follow the track beyond the end of the road to Stool End Farm, turning left at the fork up Oxendale. Go up Brown Gill and over Grey Knott, then on to tackle the crinkles. The scrambling is mostly easy, though there is one difficult steep section, which may be climbed with care; otherwise take the footpath to the left of it. Continue along the top of the crags, to Shelter Crags and down to the Three Tarns. Here, take the path back down to Langdale, taking the right fork down Hell Gill, into Oxendale and the farm again. It's an interesting and varied route with great views all round, but in misty weather it can get quite confusing. Take particular care around Long Top, the next top after the awkward section, where it is easy to descend into the Eskdale Valley by mistake.

★★ Fairfield

2,863 feet (873 m)

A meeting point of several ridges and thus a stop on many hiking itineraries. From Grasmere take the path near the

Swan Hotel up Stone Arthur and on to Great Rigg and Fairfield. From Patterdale follow the long bridleway up Grisedale to Grisedale Tarn, and take the very steep and not very pleasant path to the summit; or take the more direct footpath over St Sunday Crag. Return by the ridge off Hart Crag over Hoggil Brow, though you have to walk the last mile along the road back into Patterdale.

Fairfield is the central nail on the Fairfield Horseshoe, a long but easy walk from Ambleside and one of the classic hikes of the Lake District. From the town go up the Kirkstone Road a little way, then left up Nook Lane right to the end, passing through a farm to Low Sweden Bridge. Follow the clear path on to Low Pike and then High Pike, Dove Crag and the summit of Fairfield, a boulder-strewn area but with great views down the valley. Return by Great Rigg and Heron Pike down to Rydal Mount. The footpath takes you through Rydal Hall and Park and back into Ambleside for a well-earned pint.

★★ Great Gable

2,949 feet (899 m)

One of the most distinctive peaks in the Lake District and featured on the emblem of the Lake District National Park. The surrounding crags are popular among rock climbers. For mere walkers there are paths up from Wasdale, Seathwaite and Honister, the last being the easiest over Brandreth, Grey Knotts and Green Gable. From Seathwaite walk up Sourmilk Gill on to Green Gable, descending to cross the aptly named Windy Gap and on up a steep ascent to Great Gable. There are good views into the Wasdale Valley and of the Scafells. Westmorland Cairn, a short diversion from the summit, is well worth a visit and gives probably the most spectacular view of the Lakeland crags, down into Great Hell Gate and to Tophet Bastion.

★★ Pillar

2,929 feet (892 m)

A dramatic and rugged mountain with a surprisingly flat, grassy and spacious summit. It takes its name from Pillar Rock, one of the great challenges of Lakeland rock climbing. From Wasdale, follow the bridleway up Mosedale and over Black Sail Pass. Then it's an easy walk up on to Pillar, noticing Robinson's Cairn on the right, which marks the climbers' traverse to Pillar Rock. (John Robinson was one of the pioneers of Lakeland rock climbing.) Pillar is part of the famous Mosedale Horseshoe walk, which also takes in Steeple and Yewbarrow, but unless you're doing that it's best to take the same route down, because others are very steep and only for the sure footed. Pillar is also possible from Ennerdale, following a long path from the Bowness Knott car park through the forestry plantations.

★ Harrison Stickle

2,403 feet (736 m)

The highest of the Langdale Pikes, the rocky and dramatic profile of which soon become familiar to Lake District visitors. The Pikes are a good deal shorter than most of the mountains proper, but they manage to command their sky-line in a way no others can match.

Harrison Stickle and its neighbours look tantalisingly close to the civilisation of Great Langdale on the map, but it's a short, sharp shock of a climb. Park at the National Trust car park and take the path from the far end up the hillside along a stream. You'll reach Stickle Tarn. Follow the path to the left of the tarn and up again, turning left on the ridge path to cross Harrison Stickle. You can come back the same way, but if you want to tick off the other Langdale Pikes you can carry on the path and come back via Loft Crag.

★ High Street

2,718 feet (829 m)

Perhaps Lakeland's busiest mountain through the ages, its flat top and ridges having lent themselves to a Roman road to march soldiers along and even a popular high-altitude racecourse. From Hartsop walk beyond the end of the little road up Hayeswater Gill to Hayeswater, on to the Knott and along the ridge to High Street. The cairn on Thornthwaite Crag, a mile or so on from the summit, is about 14 feet (4.2 m) high and one of the most remarkable in the Lake District. Walk beyond here and down into Threshthwaite Cove, quite steep and a bit tricky, along the beck back to Hartsop. Alternatively, you can climb from Kentmere via the Nan Bield Pass or from Troutbeck up the Garburn road, though both are long walks.

For the best route park at the southern end of Haweswater, walk up the Gatesgarth Pass then right on to Harter Fell and along the ridge, crossing over the Nan Bield Pass. The tarns down on the right are Small Water and Blea Tarn. Carry on over Mardale Ill Bell and on to the summit. Descend by walking north a short distance and down Long Stile and Heron Crag; then it's a short walk by the lakeshore back to the car park. Enjoy the great views over the fells and into the Longsleddale, Kentmere and Haweswater Valleys.

★ The Old Man of Coniston

2,635 feet (803 m)

This towers over the village and lures visiting walkers. The slopes are scarred by quarrying, but it's still a grand mountain with a couple of pretty tarns beneath the top. For an easy, very pleasant walk park in Coniston village and go across the old railway bridge up the steep metalled road that leads on to the Walna Scar Road bridleway. Bear right and follow the footpath to Goat's Water. Dow Crag is the impressive rock face on the left. Follow the path past the tarn and out of the hollow and right on to the summit of the Old Man. There are great views out towards the coast and back inland towards Windermere. Go down by the steep footpath to Low Water tarn and through the jumble of relics from the coppermines, down into Coppermines Valley, where there are a few houses and a youth hostel. Follow the track back into the village.

★ Steeple

2,687 feet (819 m)

One of the best named fells in the Lake District and a fairly dramatic climb whichever way you tackle it. Some people consider it part of Scoat Fell, but its distinctive, exposed top earns it a place on its own. And it sounds good to say you've climbed a steeple.

Steeple is just about as inaccessible as mountains get in the Lakes, and even the quickest route requires a lot of legwork. Park at Bowness Knott, where the road runs out on the northern side of Ennerdale, and cross the river where the lake ends. Carry on along the valley by the river for another 1½ miles (2.4 km), then cut right, through the forest along Low Beck. The path soon gets steeper and leads to the top, a small and rather dizzying spot. For a different way down continue on to cross Scoat Fell, then bear right back towards the forest and Ennerdale.

Fells

Even though they never grew into proper mountains, the fells of the Lake District can provide just as much pleasure and even danger as their big brothers. Here are our top ten tops around 1,000 to 2,000 feet (300–600 m) high.

★★ Castle Crag

980 feet (299 m)

A small crag with old slate quarries, north of Rosthwaite in Borrowdale. Its modest height and accessibility make it a popular one for families, but be warned that some of the paths through the mounds of slate near the top require a bit of scrambling.

Park in the car park at Rosthwaite and walk to the end of the road, passing through a farmyard. Follow the track right of the river, eventually crossing to the left. Follow the riverbank path and turn left through a gate up the track by the side of Broadslack Gill to the old slate workings. Turn left up the track over the spoil heaps, up a steep path on to Castle Crag. There are marvellous views all round at the top.

★★ Cat Bells

1,481 feet (451 m)

This is an excellent family climb with good paths and great views as a reward for a steep ascent. From the road leading south from Portinscale to Grange-in-Borrowdale, park at Gutherscale car park on the western side of Derwentwater. Follow the crowds and the erosion control signs up the steep fellside to the summit. There are very good views in all directions, especially into Newlands Valley. If you're feeling energetic you can continue from Cat Bells on the same path to cross Maiden Moor and High Spy; it's one of the best ridge walks in the Lake District. But if you or your kids have had enough, descend by taking a left turn at the crossroads of footpaths and dropping down to Hause Gate and Manesty. Walk south a short distance and turn off left, then take the path leading through the woods and beside Derwentwater, back to Hawes End and the car park. Alternatively, take the road north for a glimpse of Hugh Walpole's fine house at Brackenburn on the way back.

★★ Harter Fell

2,129 feet (649 m)

One of the less well-trodden fells with a fine sense of isolation. There are routes from Eskdale and Hardknott Pass, but a good half-day walk can be had from the Forestry Commission car park at Birks Bridge in the Dunnerdale Forest. Follow the track through the plantation to an old farm and turn right up the gill, which eventually leads on to the summit. The summit is craggy and provides a good playground for children. Good views to the Scafells and Dow Crag range.

★★ Haystacks

1,959 feet (597 m)

The name alone is enough to make this a favourite fell for many, and it's the one Wainwright chose to have his ashes scattered on. The easiest approach is from Honister. Park in the youth hostel car park, follow the track towards the quarries but turn left after a few yards up the steep fell path. Follow this to Blackbeck Tarn and on to Haystacks.

If you prefer, park at Gatesgarth at the south end of Buttermere, follow the Scarth Gap Pass, turn left at the top and on to Haystacks. This is a nice gentle walk, with good views over Buttermere and Crummock Water and across to Gable and Ennerdale Valley. There are several lovely tarns on and around the top. For a circular walk, descend via Warnscale Beck.

★★ Helm Crag

1,299 feet (396 m)

One of the best known fells in the Lake District, at least by sight. It's also known as the Lion and the Lamb from the shape of the summit crags if you look at them from the right direction. It's a popular walk from Grasmere, but the summit and views more than make up for any crowds.

Park where you can on the north side of Grasmere and head up Easedale Road beyond Easedale House. Carry on up the steep path on to Helm Crag and climb both pillars on the summit before continuing along the ridge over Moment Crag (pausing here – at least for a moment) to the old boundary fence. The fence itself is no longer there, but the posts and one stile remain. Cross over the stile (everyone does) and turn south to Codale Head, and down to Codale Tarn and Easedale Tarn. Finish off by going down Sourmilk Gill back to Easedale. A nice walk with varying scenery and views.

★★ Lingmoor

1,530 feet (466 m)

For a short but rewarding walk from the car in the Langdales start at the car park opposite Blea Tarn. Walk down the hill towards Langdale a short distance and follow the path on to Side Pike. Walk up the hill and on to Brown How, where there are good views of the Langdale Valley and the Coniston fells. Lingmoor is a bit of a surprise, because once you've gained height it can be seen that it opens out into a moorland-type plateau, complete with tarn.

★★ Loughrigg Fell

1,101 feet (336 m)

Also known simply as Loughrigg. Another family favourite, with easy slopes, varied terrain and a sense of achievement when you get to the top, even if it's barely 1,000 feet (300 m). Park in the car park on the A591 between Rydal Water and Grasmere. Cross over the River Rothay through the wood on to the terrace. It's an easy plod, with lots of seats, and the terrace swarms with visitors in summer. Follow the terrace to the gate and turn left up some steep steps. The real summit is the one with the trig point. Considering it's a fairly short walk, there are spectacular views from the top.

★ King's How

1,290 feet (392 m)

More of a hill than a mountain or fell, but a lovely climb with maximum views for minimum effort. Situated at the Jaws of Borrowdale, this gives you the perfect introduction to one of Lakeland's best valleys. Park at the Bowder Stone car park on the B5289, about 5 miles (8 km) from Keswick. Turn right along the road and after 440 yards (400 m) or so turn right up a path that winds up to the summit for views of Derwentwater, Bassenthwaite Lake and surrounding fells.

King's How was bought by the National Trust as a memorial to King Edward VII after his death in 1910, and there's a memorial slab to him just below the summit.

★ Walla Crag

1,234 feet (376 m)

A craggy outcrop that looks formidable from the valley floor but turns out to be an easy family walk and a gentle induction into Borrowdale. Park in Great Wood car park on the B5289 a couple of miles south of Keswick and follow the signs, turning left through the woods and heading towards Rakefoot Farm on to the fellside. Pass through a gate, keeping the boundary wall on your right-hand side. There are fine views over the Borrowdale Valley and the higher fells, like Grisedale Pike and Skiddaw. Descend the same way or – if you're sure-footed – by Cat Gill, which is very steep.

★ Yewbarrow

2,058 feet (630 m)

A fell shaped like the upturned hull of a boat. There are rough outcrops around the top that put off a lot of walkers, while others are distracted by nearby Great Gable or Scafell Pike instead, which gives those who do make it up plenty of space to enjoy the views over Wastwater and the Scafell range. It's only a couple of miles walk to the summit from Wasdale Head. Walk down the road along the northern shore of Wastwater to Overbeck Bridge – you can park your car there if you prefer, but the walk will loosen you up for the climb. The path from here leads up along the left side of a wall and takes you between the rocky outcrops of Dropping Crag and Bell Rib and through the Great Door on the way to the top.

Dales

And now ten dales to explore, by foot or by car, which are attractive and interesting in their own right but which also offer fairly easy walks and explorations for those sensible people who want to leave their cars and strike out on their own.

★★★ Borrowdale

One of the prettiest valleys in the Lakes, there are spectacular views but it can get crowded in the summer. It's a southern extension of the Vale of Derwentwater with a variety of scenery and contrasts. A good area from which to walk: low-lying and higher fells are easily accessible and so are many valley walks. The drive around the west side of Derwentwater provides good views of the lake. There are good low-level walks up the Langstrath Valley with a number of pretty dubs along the beck, and Greenup Ghyll. Borrowdale seems to come to an end just beyond Grange, where the slopes of Grange Fell and Castle Crag come together to give barely enough room for the river and road to pass through. These are the famous Jaws of Borrowdale. Don't be put off – the valley opens up beyond and continues a long way down to the village of Seatoller and then up to Seathwaite.

★★★ Langdale

The most popular valley in the Lake District. Technically, it consists of two dales, joining at Elterwater and separated by Lingmoor Fell, called Great Langdale and Little Langdale. Great Langdale is the more popular, and the little winding road that runs its length is sometimes crammed with cars in midsummer. It has dramatic scenery, especially during the drive up the valley, the Langdale Pikes suddenly rearing up in front of you. There are many walks on to the higher fells, with lower fells at the Elterwater end of the valley. Little Langdale is charming, though not quite as spectacular.

For low-level walks in Great Langdale, try Oxendale and Mickleden, both of which give a sense of being among the mountains. At the head of the valley the Old Dungeon Ghyll is a famous meeting place for climbers and walkers, and the nearby Stickle Barn provides a good café and bar. Make an early start if you want a decent parking spot; the National Trust car park can fill up quickly. Avoid the new houses at Chapel Stile. Ugh.

★★★ Wasdale

The most inaccessible valley in the area and therefore one of the quietest, even at the height of the season. Mobile phone and TV reception are still poor to non-existent, which you may or may not think an advantage. The Wasdale Head Inn is famous for its association with the development of rock climbing, and it continues to be a place where walkers and climbers swap stories of the day's adventures over a pint. Wastwater is the most foreboding of the lakes, and the whole valley has a brooding air about it. There's great climbing all around, and it's an excellent walking base for the Scafell range and Great Gable.

★★ Duddon Valley

Also known as Dunnerdale, this is the valley of the River Duddon. Wordsworth wrote 35 sonnets on this charming river. The whole valley is lovely, with plenty of car parking and pleasant walks on the surrounding fells, and it's ideal for picnicking and swimming. At the northern end is Birks Bridge, a little packhorse bridge in a renowned beauty spot.

★★ Eskdale

Although Eskdale is very popular with tourists, only the lower half – from Boot – is really well explored. A beautiful valley, its head lies at Esk Hause in wild and dramatic scenery, the foot among the plains and sand dunes at Newbiggin. The road traverses only about 4 miles (6.4 km) of the dale itself. To explore the foot of the valley at its best, leave the car at Ravenglass, take the railway to the Dalegarth terminus and walk back, detouring to follow the River Esk through lovely woods and pastures.

★★ Vale of Lorton

Not technically a dale, more a sequence of valleys, but it's the lushest, prettiest part of the northern Lakes. It's best to explore it from Cockermouth to get the full shape and extent. Coming from Keswick, you can get into it over the Whinlatter Pass, hitting the village of Lorton, where you turn left and follow the River Cocker upstream. Very gently and subtly, three marvellous lakes carefully unfold themselves for your inspection. First, there's Loweswater, then bigger Crummock Water and finally the most popular of the three, Buttermere. Go right to the end of the valley and you can get back towards Keswick, over Honister Pass this time. Excellent walks all the way, either round lakes or up the surrounding fells, with some nice hamlets and pubs to explore along the way.

★ Ennerdale

One of the few Lakeland valleys not properly accessible by road. Despite attracting more people lately, it retains a wild and isolated feel. The head of the dale is spectacular, with Steeple and Pillar rising above the dark conifer plantations. The road goes along the north shore of the lake as far as Bowness Point, and thereafter it's for walkers only. There are Forestry Commission trails among the woods. It helps if you like conifers.

★ Longsleddale

Not far north of Kendal but another relatively undiscovered and unspoilt part of the Lakes, just tucked inside the south-east corner of the National Park. The fells here are rolling rather than dramatic, more typical of the southern half of the Lakes than the north. The road along the River Sprint ends at Sadgill, but there's a pleasant walk carrying on north up to Haweswater or west into Kentmere and Ambleside. Longsleddale's claim to fame was that it was part of the inspiration for Greendale, the picture postcard valley served by Postman Pat; his creator, John Cunliffe, lived for a time in Kendal.

★ Martindale

Tucked between Ullswater and Haweswater, this is also tricky to get to by road and is all the better for it. You can park at Patterdale or Hartsop and walk east to it, or a road will take you some of the way down, to Dale Head. The magnificent High Street ridge running north to south gives views down into the valley.

★ Swindale

This can be reached from Bampton or Shap, though only by tracks or on foot, making it a real walker's valley. It's lovely and long, usually forgotten by the hordes. Rolling fells provide plenty of interest with low-level and higher walks, especially on to the ridges, and there are good views down into the neighbouring valleys.

Passes

Lakeland has several dramatic mountain passes for cars. Some are famous, and two are notorious. All of them are exciting and great for those lazy motorists who never leave the wheel but want to go home and boast that they have scaled the Lakeland heights. But do not underestimate these roads, especially in bad weather when ice or snow can make them treacherous and the mist cuts visibility to next to nothing.

★★ Hardknott Pass

1,291 feet (394 m) at its highest point

The Lake District's most exciting road. It's hair-raising in places, with one-in-three gradients, sharp bends and a delightful sheer drop on the west side. It's worth trying for the dramatic views, but only if your nerves, brakes and engine are in good order. It can also get very busy in summer, with numerous hold-ups as motorists shuffle about on the steep bits to get past each other. Cyclists are advised by a sign at the top to dismount and walk the descent, but you're allowed to cycle up it if you've got the stamina and the gears. At one time you could regularly watch 2CVs being pushed up by groups of students on rag week. Just below the summit, on the Eskdale side, there are parking places to access the Hardknott Fort, which stands guard over this once Roman road and should not be missed. The pass is a very handy link from the western side of the Lakes to the east, via Cockley Beck where it meets the ...

★★ Wrynose Pass

1,281 feet (391 m)

Probably the more famous of the Big Two, though staff at Tourist Information Centres frequently get asked the way to Rhino Pass or even Buffalo Pass. It's notoriously steep and narrow, and there are places where it is impossible for two cars to pass. The passing places that are provided are not parking places, and anyone using them as such deserves to have their handbrake released. At the summit is the Three Shires Stone, which used to mark the meeting point of Lancashire, Westmorland and Cumberland before it all got turned into Cumbria. The place where traditionalists shed a few tears.

★ Honister Pass

1,176 feet (359 m)

From Seatoller, in Borrowdale, to the southern tip of Buttermere. There are one-in-four gradients in places, and it gets narrow on the Buttermere side, though it's not too difficult for motorists. Increasing numbers of people use it for access to the Honister slate quarry and attached visitor centre.

★ Kirkstone Pass

1,489 feet (454 m)

The highest of the Lake District's passes, connecting Ambleside with Ullswater. This is the pass all the TV crews rush to when snow begins and they want to show everyone that the Lake District is snowed in. From Windermere the road is good, with a long, interesting descent to Patterdale. To get to the pass from Ambleside, you go up a very narrow, steep road, aptly called the Struggle (it begins almost opposite the Bridge House). In the 19th century travellers used to have to leave their coaches and walk alongside the horses up this part. It's not quite as bad as that today, but there are some sharp bends to trap the unwary. At the top is the Kirkstone Pass Inn, the third highest pub in England and a refuge for walkers and motorists alike. It has been cut off by snowfalls for weeks on end in the past.

Newlands Pass

1,100 feet (335 m)

The most direct route from Keswick over to Buttermere village. It starts off looking easy and yummy looking, through Beatrix Potter-type country, but gets steep and wild at the top.

Whinlatter Pass

1,043 feet (318 m)

Links Braithwaite, near Keswick, to High Lorton. A nice, easy route to Loweswater, Crummock Water and Buttermere, and a scenic alternative to the A66 if you want to get to Cockermouth and are in no hurry. It's the easiest of the passes, although there are occasional steep sections. Going up from the Keswick end, there are good views over Bassenthwaite with parking places. A lot of the view is obscured, however, as you enter the Forestry Commission's Thornthwaite Forest.

Waterfalls

Most Lakeland becks or streams have a force or waterfall of some kind. Many of them are small, hidden and unsung. They do their own gentle singing – tra la, gurgle, gurgle – and get a bit more vociferous after heavy rain. They are also ideal for a shower after a walk in the fells – a bit cold, sure, but the tingling, refreshed feeling afterwards is great. Here are ten of the finest and most famous.

★★★ Taylor Gill Force

Above Borrowdale, at Stockley Bridge. Park at Seathwaite and follow the path to what the experts generally consider to be Lakeland's finest waterfall. A spectacular setting with an ambling mountain stream transforming itself into a 140 foot (43 m) cascade. It can be seen from below the bridge, but for the best views follow the path to the right of the falls.

★★ Aira Force

Probably the most famous and visited of the Lake District's falls. On the west side of Ullswater, near Dockray, the falls are a short, pleasant walk from the public car park. The main force falls 70 feet (21 m) from below a stone footbridge. You also get a good viewpoint from the path, which ends just below the falls. If the sun is shining, look out for the rainbow.

★★ Dob Gill

This beautifully situated little cascade is in the trees on the western shore of Thirlmere. There's parking on the shore road 1 mile (1.6 km) north of Wythburn, but you're likely to be the only visitor to these falls. Upstream is Harrop Tarn.

★★ Esk Falls

There are lovely waterfalls all along the River Esk, and the best are found towards the top. Park on the Hardknott Pass near the castle and take the footpath up; it's a fine walk.

★★ Scale Force

The Lake District's longest waterfall, at 172 feet (52 m). A path leads from Buttermere village, and the falls are hidden in a narrow, tree-lined gorge. More for real waterfall collectors than the average visitor.

★ Lodore Falls

At the southern end of Derwentwater, Lodore Falls are easily reached from the road, but perhaps the best way to view them is by boat from the lake. This 40 foot (12 m) cataract is in a chasm surrounded by woods and crags. The land is owned by the nearby hotel of the same name, and there is an honesty box by the falls, which must be unique for a natural feature of this kind.

★ Measand Beck Forces

A small but pretty series of waterfalls where the Measand Beck empties into Haweswater on the northwest side. Park at the south end of the reservoir and enjoy them on a walk all the way round.

★ Sourmilk Gill, Seathwaite

The best of several places of the same name in the Lakes. There are numerous falls as the Gill descends from the fells. A short walk from Seathwaite in Borrowdale, it's great after heavy rain – and since this little village is reputed to be the wettest place in England that's quite often.

★ Stock Ghyll Force

On the fellside behind Ambleside, this delightful little water-fall is easily reached by walking from the town centre up the road that runs behind the Salutation Hotel. A nice, wooded walk to a 90 feet (27 m) cascade flowing under a stone foot-bridge. Not spectacular, but very pretty. This was a popular walk for Victorian waterfall enthusiasts.

Skelwith Force

Only a small waterfall, just a drop of 16 feet (4.8 m), but nicely situated on the River Brathay. Just above the mini-empire of slate galleries, shop and café at Skelwith Bridge.

Best views

Our top ten viewpoints have been chosen because they're either good, brilliant or simply classics. In our own, un-humble opinion.

★★★ Border End

At the top of Hardknott Pass, this is a short walk to the north up the fellside. There are spectacular views across to Scafell and Scafell Pike, over the River Esk.

★★★ Whinlatter Pass

From the brow of the hill, looking north across Bassenthwaite Lake.

★★ Castle Crag

One of the best viewpoints in the Borrowdale area, with marvellous views all round. A short climb and maximum reward for effort.

★★ Corney Fell

From the summit, looking northwest to the Isle of Man.

★★ Orrest Head, Windermere

Just above Windermere village. Brilliant 360 degree views. This is the first Lakeland vantage point climbed by Wainwright, and he obviously liked what he saw.

★★ Place Fell

Brilliant views over Ullswater and also to the south.

★ Ashness Bridge

Looking over Derwentwater. This is a view to be found in every postcard rack.

★ Gummer's How

At the southeast end of Lake Windermere. The summit gives a view up Windermere and into the Lakeland fells.

★ Loughrigg Terrace

Looking down into Grasmere Vale, with Helm Crag and Dunmail Raise in the background. A classic.

★ Wastwater

From anywhere on the northern side looking over to the screes.

CHAPTER NINE

Walks

*Where to put those feet – especially family feet –
with not too much danger, on the fells and
in the forests. And some advice on what to do
if you do put a foot wrong*

I like a walk to be round. I don't like dragging straight up, only to come straight down again the same way – that's for fell-runners. A sort of circle is best, slowly up a valley, through a gap, easily on to the top, then round the other side, preferably near a lake, back to base, without repeating one step. I don't like it too steep, especially coming down. It hurts the old knees. I like variety, smooth bits and rough bits. I don't want any roads, but I do like paths I can find easily, especially those grassy swards that look as if the Great Gardener in the sky had taken his celestial lawnmower to the side of the fell. I definitely want views, especially a lake, and I want to feel impressed by myself – look how far we've got, haven't we done well. I like a top that is a top, with a cairn we can crouch beside, scoffing the while. And back at the beginning, I like the thought of a pub or hotel nearby, for emergencies, such as more scoff.

My wife hates screes, so we are not allowed anywhere near them, certainly not. On family walks the children have their own requirement: it must be a new walk, one we haven't done before. Oh, the hours I have spent studying the Ordnance Survey maps and the Wainwright books, getting further and further afield, trying to work out new routes that will keep us all happy. Many of those books of family walks are full of the obvious stuff, often lifted from each other, which any idiot can work out for themselves, such as round Grasmere, or Friar's Crag. I don't want them as easy as that. I like a walk that can spread itself across the day, with two hours up, a picnic and lots of rests, then two hours to stroll back. The joy when we find a new one, which we like to think we have created, carving it out of the contours, shaping it in our minds. And after all these years, we still manage to find them. So here's a dozen of them – all simple and fun, and chosen for scenery and ease of walking, with a variety of pleasures.

They're all possible with a relatively fit family party – and a good map, of course. They make a pleasant change from the more arduous mountain and fell climbs of the previous chapter (and don't forget them, of course, when contemplating possible family outings). Right, best feet forwards.

★★★ Buttermere

A lovely, easy lakeside walk with good views. It's about 4 miles (6.4 km) and will take 2½ hours at a leisurely pace.

Park at Buttermere's main car park by the Fish Hotel. Take the rough farm road to the left of the hotel and across the plain over to the lake. Cross the footbridge and follow the left-hand path around the lake's southern shore. Just past the head of the lake, go left across the fields and join the road by Gatesgarth Farm. When the road joins the lake, watch out for a footpath on the left, which takes you back to the shoreline and on towards the village.

★★★ Ullswater

Our all-time favourite walking area is around the far shore of Ullswater – the bit where there's no road. It has all the sights and sensations you could want, and all in a fairly short space. You can either park up at Howtown and do a circular walk or get there on the lake steamer. Either way, you are in for sheer pleasure. Both routes are about 10 miles (16 km) of easy walking.

Route 1
Park on the grass by the little church of Martindale above Howtown and walk back down the little twisting road, away from Howtown and into Boredale. It starts off like easy Beatrix Potter country, all smooth and rounded, but as you proceed up the valley the fields and farmhouses run out and it gets wilder and emptier. The road runs out after 1½ miles (2.4 km), but continue climbing up to the head of the valley, through the Boredale Hause or pass. The path is clear and the walking easy, though it gets a steeper towards the end. Once over the top, bear right and head down towards Patterdale. Admire the views, then pick up the path that leads north along the shores of Ullswater. It skirts along the flanks of Place Fell, then twists and turns with the shape of the lake, giving a different but equally wonderful view at every angle. There are plenty of benches and other places to stop, rest and admire the lake. After 3 miles (4.8 km) along the shore you'll reach Sandwick. If you're tired, turn right up the little road back to the car, but if you've got energy left you can carry on around the shore, doing a circle of Hallin Fell. You'll reach

the pier at Howtown, from where it's a short walk back up to the car. The perfect walk.

Route 2
Park at Glenridding and catch the steamer to Howtown (tel. 017684 82229 or visit *www.ullswater-steamers.co.uk* if you want to check times). On leaving the pier, turn right through several gates and go on to the fellside path above Waternook. The path soon drops down to the shore of the lake, entering woodland for a while under Hallin Fell. Cross the beck at Sandwick and follow the road for a short while, before turning right on to the footpath, leading back to the shoreline. The next mile is through attractive open and wooded slopes. Below Silver Crag the path divides; keep right, by the lake, and follow it back to Patterdale. The road takes you back to Glenridding.

★★ Arthur's Pike, Ullswater

A quiet, unusual way of seeing a familiar view. This perfect round walk of about 4 miles (6.4 km) will take three hours or so with lots of stops on top to admire the brilliant views of Ullswater. Nice, easy beginning, just to warm yourself up, then the satisfaction of a brisk climb. Always uncrowded. Not many know this walk.

Park at Howtown, if you can, which means getting to the pier before the crowds or, if you're cheeky enough, parking at the hotel and telling yourself you're going to be a guest once you've done the walk. Or you could get the steamer over after parking at Glenridding. Go through the hotel grounds to Mellguards, then left through a gate and on to a long, very easy grassy path, which hugs the side of the hill (Swarth Fell), almost parallel with the road to the left below. Just after the little reservoir thingy, cut up steeply through some ferns and climb up to White Knott, which is the first cairn. All very easy. It looked hard from below, but come on, you'll be on the top in no time. Carry on to Arthur's Pike itself, following the cairns, then continue to Bonscale, a lovely ridge walk, but take care not to come down into Swarthbeck Gill. When you're above Fusedale, then cut right, zigzagging down the grassy slopes, heading back to Howtown Hotel.

★★ Barrow

No, not that beautiful town, but, like Arthur's Pike, a relatively unknown fell, yet right within top tourist country. On a bank holiday weekend, when the world and his wizened granddad is doing Cat Bells, try Barrow instead. It's a very satisfying round walk, with impressive views and no hard climbing, of four and a bit miles (about 6.4 km).

Park in Braithwaite village, just off the A66 west of Keswick. Leave as if heading for Newlands, turning right off the road at Braithwaite Lodge Farm. It looks private, but head straight up to it and then on and up the hill in front of you, trying to ignore the sound of the A66 below in the distance as it will soon disappear. Having reached the top of Barrow, where the views of Derwentwater are magnificent, you can either head back – if the weather is bad or the party is lazy – by going right, down on the path to High Coledale. But better still, carry on, veering to the left of Stile End and round Outerside (no need to climb either). You'll emerge above Coledale. Cut right down the grassy slopes to the valley bottom, heading for the old mines around Force Crag, then straight along the very good Coledale Beck track all the way back to Braithwaite. Time perhaps for a drink in one of the two pubs, or drive straight to Keswick and lash out at Maysons on something more substantial.

★★ Derwentwater

An easy, 3 mile (4.8 km) walk along the west shore, with good views of the surrounding fells and the islands on the lake.

Park in Keswick and take the launch over to Hawes End (the anticlockwise launch will take ten minutes (tel. 017687 72263 or visit *www.keswick-launch.co.uk* for times). Follow the lakeshore footpath left, leaving the shore for a short while but then reaching the edge of the lake and the Low Brandelhow landing stage. Another ½ mile (800 m) through the woods takes you to the next landing stage, High Brandelhow. Here bear right up some steps, pass through a kissing gate and then keep left between the cottage and boathouse. At the next fork in the path go right across some rather boggy ground and join another path going left back to the shore. Follow the footpath until it joins the road, then go left along it for a short while, back to the Lodore landing stage. You can catch the launch back to Keswick from here.

★★ Gowbarrow

Yes, another Ullswater stroll, but this time on the main road side, where it is very attractive but hard to work out a decent family amble without hitting either millions of other families or the main road. This one does the job. It's an easy, satisfying three hour family stroll with great views, the famous waterfall to take in and Wordsworth's daffodils to look out for in season.

Park at the National Trust's Aira Force car park. Depending on the crowds, go up and explore the waterfall at once or save it for later. The walk proper begins by heading right over a stile, aiming for the towers of a house called Lyulph's Tower. As you climb the flank of Gowbarrow Fell there are excellent views of Ullswater. Wordsworth's daffodils are between the road and the water. Eventually start going up above a stream, following a wall, to the top of the fell. It's usually empty on top, because the softies will have stuck to Aira Force. Back along the top and then descend by a steep but easy grassy path, which children usually try to slide down, the fools, to Aira Force.

★★ Easedale

This one goes uphill a bit, in fact it is quite steep in places, but it makes a good family walk if you take your time. It should take about two and a half hours.

From Grasmere village go along Easedale Road for ½ mile (800 m) until you reach a footpath signed Easedale Tarn. (If the road peters out you've gone too far.) Go along the obvious track and at the small gate take the path directly up the hill in front of you. This follows Sourmilk Gill, which has some nice waterfalls and pools, and leads up to the tarn. You can walk all the way round it, though it can get a bit boggy at the head.

Follow the beck back down the hill, this time on the opposite bank. Watch out for a footpath on your left, marked by small cairns. This leads down to Far Easedale Gill. Cross by the footbridge and follow the stream down. Eventually you'll reach a gate and a track that becomes Easedale Road, taking you back into Grasmere.

★★ Loweswater

One of Lakeland's forgotten lakes – this is a good place to escape the midsummer hordes. This is a dead easy 4 mile (6.4 km) walk that should take about two and a half hours. There are good views of Mellbreak and, from the fell road, the Isle of Man.

Start at the Kirkstile Inn and follow the road past the church, towards Loweswater lake. Turn left at the road junction and then straight on, signposted Ennerdale and Mockerkin. Follow the narrow, twisting road (beware boy racers) for just under a mile until you reach the fell road. Turn right up here and follow this uphill, towards Mosser. There are good views from the top. At a prominent footpath sign after about ¾ mile (1.2 km), turn left and go downhill to a farm gate. Follow the track back to the road you left earlier. Turn right and then, just past the second entrance to the Grange Country House Hotel, left. Follow the bridleway to Hudson Place Farm.

Keep to the main track. By the farm, turn on to the gravel track and then through the left hand of two gates. This track takes you down to the lake. A nice grassy path follows the shore, through Holme Wood, and brings you to Watergate Farm. Follow the track left, across several fields, and it brings you back to the road. Turn right at the road junction for the inn.

★★ Mirehouse

A lovely, easy walk, only 3 miles (4.8 km) and done in a couple of hours. Try to go when the house is open (Wednesdays and Sundays from Easter to October, plus Fridays in August).

Park at Dodd Wood car park and leave via the path that crosses the stream behind the Old Sawmill tea rooms. Join the forest road and turn left for a few yards before turning right and walking uphill along a narrow track. This levels out and then descends through the trees to bring you out on the A591 beside the Ravenstone Hotel. Turn right in front of the hotel and cross the road, soon reaching a footpath on the left side. You're now on the route of the Allerdale Ramble, and the path leads down some steps and across a series of fields until you reach a minor road. Go straight across it and follow the path again, through the fields to St Bega's, a spectacularly located church on the shores of Bassenthwaite. Then follow the stream towards Mirehouse, with Dodd rising impressively behind it. The path continues through Mirehouse's grounds back to the A591 and the car park.

★★ Rydal Water

A good three-hour walk, which can be combined with a visit to Rydal Mount or extended by a couple of hours by nipping up to the top of Loughrigg Fell instead of hugging the lakeshore. It's very popular walking country in the high season, so go early or late in the day if you want to beat the crowds.

Park at White Moss car park between Grasmere and Rydal on the A591. Cross over the Rothay via the footbridge and go south along the western shore of Rydal Water. Where the path splits, the lower path goes alongside the lake and the upper takes you a little way up the fellside and past Rydal caves (two disused mines, carved out of solid rock and perfectly safe, though you can easily get inside only the larger of them). The path rejoins the A591 at Pelter Bridge. Turn left, cross carefully and take the path that leads up to Rydal Mount. By the Rydal Hall buildings, pick up the footpath (an old packhorse route) that leads back to White Moss.

★ La'al Ratty

A beautiful riverside walk, covering about 3½ miles (5.6 km) in total. It's good for children and grown-up steam buffs, who will love the train ride. Allow about two hours. Check train times at the station or in advance or you might get stuck (tel. 01229 717171 or visit *www.ravenglass-railway.co.uk*).

Park at Dalegarth station in Eskdale and walk back along the road towards Hardknott. Turn right at the crossroads, beside Brook House, and follow the lane to St Catherine's Church and the River Esk. Turn left along the riverbank and follow this very pretty route for about ¾ mile (1.2 km) until you come to a hump-backed stone bridge (Doctor Bridge). Cross over and head back on the other side of the river towards Dalegarth. The track climbs away from the river, through a farm and then meanders across several fields. Continue through a wood and across a campsite, via a rather impressive footbridge across Stanley Gill. Cross the track, into the next field and through more woods until you enter an attractive park. Follow the tarmac track by the river to the minor road at Forge Bridge. Cross the bridge and continue to the road junction, beside the King George IV pub. Turn left and walk to the railway station at Eskdale Green, from where you can enjoy the short train ride back to Dalegarth.

★ Muncaster Castle

A super walk that's well away from the crowds. It's about 3½ miles (5.6 km), so allow about two hours, plus time to visit the Castle (it's open daily from February to mid-November).

Park at Ravenglass railway station and leave via the footpath at the back, behind the terminus of the La'al Ratty railway line. This track takes you past the amazing Roman ruin of Walls Castle, once a bath house and now the tallest standing Roman building in the north of England. Continue along the track to Walls mansion, which isn't a Roman anything, and then turn left to Newtown House. Look out for the footpath on the left that takes you through a conifer plantation and up to a field. The path peters out, but use that as an excuse to run to the top of the hill in front of you for superb views across the valley to the fells of Lakeland, and across to the Isle of Man if it's a clear day. Head towards Dovecote Wood at the other end of the field, and pass through a gate in the wall into the grounds of Muncaster Castle. Go downhill through an amazing bamboo plantation until you arrive at the Castle. The right of way goes straight up the drive to the A595, but if the grounds are open you can detour right for more wonderful views. Once back at the A595, turn left for ? mile (1.2 km) until you reach Home Farm on the left. Follow the footpath through the farmyard and across fields to bring you back to the track leading to Walls Castle. Retrace your steps back to the station.

Forest walks

Forests and woodland cover about 12 per cent of the Lake District National Park, over half of the area belonging to the Forestry Commission. These aren't, strictly speaking, natural features of the landscape, and the Commission has earned itself some bitter enemies with its policy of covering the fells with dark, regimented conifers. To balance this, they have opened up more of their plantations to the public, providing waymarked walks and setting up centres to explain what they are doing. The Forestry Commission has two main forests where this has taken place – Grizedale and Whinlatter – plus some nice developments for the public in other areas. They're great for walking at any time of year.

★★ Grizedale Forest Park and Visitor Centre

The best known forest in the Lakes, and one the Forestry Commission feels very proud of. One of the first to be opened up to the public, and at the time of writing it was undergoing a £5 million facelift to update some of the tired facilities and revamp the visitor centre. It's due to open in 2008.

It lies between Esthwaite and Coniston. The main access points have car parks and toilets, and there is a visitor centre just north of the village of Satterthwaite. It gets a quarter of a million visitors a year, putting something of a strain on the narrow roads around it.

There are a handful of forest trails, including several good short ones for families and one exploring some of the spots featured in Arthur Ransome's *Swallows and Amazons*. The Silurian Way, a 9½ mile (15 km) waymarked trail, is a good way of exploring the area. Look out for the 90 or so forest sculptures, which are a brilliant diversion in the woods. They're often well camouflaged and have to be sought out; the visitor centre can provide a map of them as well as details of the artists, some of whom, like Andy Goldsworthy, have gone on to become very well known. There are mountain bike trails through the forest and a bike centre where you can hire bikes. It's a good way of keeping them off the fells.

The Visitor Centre has displays relating to the forest industry, a shop with crafts, leaflets and trail maps, and a café. No doubt much more after its revamp. It's particularly good late in the year, when they sell Christmas trees and organise lots of festive fun for children. It's open daily all year round from 10.00am to 5.00pm; 4.00pm in winter (tel. 01229 860010).

★★ Whinlatter Forest Park and Visitor Centre

The forest lies over to the west of Bassenthwaite Lake, and the Whinlatter Pass goes through it. It's advertised as England's only mountain forest, and it's lovely in autumn.

The visitor centre at the top of the pass is a starting point for a number of good walks, which give some great views over Derwentwater and Keswick. There are good children's trails – you can get certificates to prove they finished them – plus a couple of cycling and orienteering trails. Walks lack the excitement of Grizedale's sculpture trails, but the terrain is generally more interesting. The visitor centre has hands-on displays with lots of things to push, pull, watch and wonder at. Inside there's an audio-visual presentation in Cumbrian dialect (very brave), and outside there's a giant badger sett to walk through. There are also an adventure playground, a book and gift shop and a café. From May to September they have a live video link to the osprey nest at Bassenthwaite (see Dodd Wood, below), and there are regular events both outdoors and in. Open daily all year round from 10.00am to 5.00pm; 4.00pm in winter (tel. 017687 78469).

★ Dodd Wood

On the eastern shore of Bassenthwaite Lake, Dodd Wood is leased from the Mirehouse estate. There's an excellent walk that leads you to the top of Dodd, giving a good view over Bassenthwaite and the fells, and three more trails around the woods. Details are available from the Old Sawmill Tea Rooms, which is open daily from Easter to October for very good homemade food.

Dodd Wood also has Osprey Watch, a viewing platform to spot the ospreys that make their home round the lake between mid-April and August each year. Staff are on hand to tell you more about them (tel. 017687 78469 or 017687 74317 for the tea rooms; visit *www.ospreywatch.co.uk* for osprey information).

★ Ennerdale

One of the most dramatic Lakeland forests. Cars must be left at Bowness Knott car park. The main trail, Smithy Beck, goes along the edge of Ennerdale Water and is clearly waymarked. Openings in the trees reveal fine views, and keep your eyes peeled for red squirrels, deer and herons. The golden and green colours are stunning in autumn. The 14 miles (22.5 km) of forest roads are popular with cyclists (tel. 017687 76816).

★ Thirlmere

This is under the auspices of United Utilities, which has made a big effort to be more user-friendly in the last few years. There are nature trails at Swirls on the eastern shore and Launchy Gill and Harrop on the western side. Park at Armboth for Launchy Gill and Dobgill Bridge for Harrop. There's open access to the fellside above the forests (tel. 017687 72334).

The National Trust owns many other major woodlands, and good walks can be had in and around several of them.
- **Coniston** Park-a-Moor and Nibthwaite Woods on the east shore.
- **Derwentwater** Great Wood on the east shore, Manesty and Brandelhow on the west shore, and Friar's Crag, which has good wheelchair access.
- **Grasmere** South of the village beside River Rothay.
- **Tarn Hows** Trail dipping in and out of woodland by the water.
- **Windermere** Claife Heights, on the west shore between Hawkshead and the lake.

Other walks

You may be surprised to learn that Cumbria has any trees left standing, the amount of paper used these days to produce walk leaflets, guides and the like, but although some walks are quite contrived, linking some strangely unrelated places and ideas, others are much more useful and worth pursuing.

Some of the best walks are put together by the Lake District National Park Authority, which has a series of leaflets of walks in different areas, including plenty that link up well to public transport. There's also *Miles without Stiles*, a very good collection of walks suitable for people with buggies or wheelchairs or who don't want to be up and down and clambering over fences all the time. You can pick up the leaflets at Brockhole or other information centres, or download in advance at *www.lake-district.gov.uk*.

The LDNPA also runs an excellent programme of **guided walks**, led by knowledgeable rangers or locals and varying from short strolls to all-day hikes. They go all over the Lakes and have special wheelchair-friendly programmes, and they're particularly good because you don't need to worry about getting lost and arguing about which is the right direction. Most of them are free, but you'll need to book for popular ones. Look for details in the National Park's *Out and About* brochure, or from the events department (tel. 015397 92895).

If you want to hire a private guide to take you on a walk, there are plenty available. Blue Badge Guides are available via Cumbrian Discoveries (tel. 017684 84811 or visit *www.cumbriandiscoveries.co.uk*). Cumbria Tourist Guides will put together a walking tour based around anything from agriculture to Wordsworth; visit *www.cumbriatourist-guides.co.uk* for a directory of their members.

The best mountain guides reach standards set down by the British Association of Mountain Guides; for a list of local members, visit *www.bmg.org.uk*. Mark Scott, a LDNPA ranger and mountain rescue man, runs a programme of guided walks all year round and offers a personally tailored service too (tel. 01229 466096 or visit *www.classicfell-walks.co.uk*).

The Cumbrian coast is especially good for **wildlife walks**, thanks to all the mudflats and saltmarshes. Large numbers of wintering waders and wildfowl can be seen, in some cases more than in any other spot in the world. You might also see rare animals, like natterjack toads. The Cumbria Wildlife Trust runs frequent guided walks to some of the more interesting spots, and their people provide expert guidance to the animals along the way. A donation to funds is welcomed in return. Tel. 015398 16300 or visit *www.cumbriawild-lifetrust.org.uk* for schedules. The National Trust also has a leaflet for a nature walking trail at Arnside Knott on the coast, where you can spot rare birds and butterflies.

After Cornwall, Cumbria is probably the most interesting county in England for **geology** walks. In fact, American geologists come all the way here for things they can't get at home, like fluorites. Even an amateur with no knowledge can soon spot bits of the stuff, scattered over the fells. The northern fells just south of Caldbeck are good for finding specimens – especially Roughton Gill, Carrock Fell and Driggeth. Beware the old mine workings; they can be dangerous. Very good for pyromorphites, malachtite, pyrite and campylite, if you're lucky. The west coast, round Beckermet and Frizington, is also rich in haematite and barites.

The National Park offers six leaflets exploring 36 of Cumbria's best archaeological sites, some themed by area and some grouping together prehistoric and industrial locations. They are available from TICs. Another good guide to the area's geology, complete with guides and maps, is Robert Prosser's *Geology Explained in the Lake District* (Fineleaf Editions).

It's becoming quite popular to link old places along **historical trails**. They're often outside the Lake District, but that can sometimes add to their attractiveness, not to mention their peace and quiet. They include the following.

The Border Reivers Trail
A walk around many of the places in Cumbria most closely associated with the border wars and includes lots of pele towers.

The Cistercian Way
This covers the 33 miles (53 km) from Grange-over-Sands to Piel Island, with lots of monasteries en route.

The Hadrian's Wall Path
A coast-to-coast National Trail passing through a bit of the county and following the great wall and Roman forts.

Lady Anne's Way
A 100 mile (160 km) trek from Anne Clifford's birthplace in Yorkshire to Brougham Castle, with several of her Cumbrian properties in between (see also Chapter 14).

The Miller's Way
A 51 mile (82 km) walk from Kendal to Carlisle, set up to mark the 150th birthday of Carrs breadmakers and based on the journey of company founder Jonathan Carr. A route guide to go with it can be got from *www.carrs-flourmills.co.uk*.

Leaflets for most of these and other trails are available from TICs. Great Guided Tours offers history-based tours of the Lakes, especially along and around Hadrian's Wall (tel. 01228 670578 or visit *www.greatguidedtours.co.uk*).

Industrial trails are fairly common. Don't mock. Carlisle had its industrial revolution before Lancashire, and those west coast towns led the nation at one time in coal and shipping and town planning. There's lots of interesting Victorian industrial stuff to be seen, and good ones include the Whitehaven Trail, the Carlisle Industrial Trail and the Haematite Trail from Barrow, an 18 mile (29 km) route taking in the iron mining heritage of the Furness peninsula.

Jim Reid, a man who likes walking and drinking, put his passions together in **The Inn Way**, a 90 mile (145 km) circular walk starting and finishing in Ambleside. The route takes in no fewer than 44 pubs over seven days, though some people probably take a good deal longer to stagger round. One reviewer called it 'Wainwright with booze'. The book is available from most bookshops or at *www.innway.co.uk*.

More long walks

If you've exhausted all those short family walks and still have some energy left, you could try one of the following.

The Cumbria Way
A 72 mile (116 km) walk from Ulverston to Carlisle, taking in the shores of Morecambe Bay and passing through the heart of the Lake District. You could do it in a week, taking in bed and breakfast places or youth hostels along the way. It was set up by the Ramblers Association and is easily followed. If you're after a companion guide, try John Trevelyan's *Cumbria Way* (Dalesman) or Anthony Burton's *The Cumbria Way* (Aurum Press).

The Cumbria Coastal Way
This 180 mile (290 km) walk from Silverdale in the south to Gretna on the Scottish border was set up by the county council. It takes in lots of fine estuary sands. A guide is Ian and Krysia Brodie's *The Cumbria Coastal Way* (Cicerone Press).

The Allerdale Ramble
From Seathwaite to the Solway Firth. There are different ways of connecting them up, but the distance is usually about 55 miles (88 km). Use Jim Watson's *The Cumbria Way and the Allerdale Ramble* (Cicerone Press).

The Wainwright Memorial Walk
Starting and finishing in Windermere and taking in every major summit, valley and lake over 100 miles (160 km) or so (you don't have to climb every fell though). Devised by the great man and quite frequently followed in his honour.

The Westmorland Way and *the Cumberland Way*
From Morecambe Bay to Appleby and Appleby to Ravenglass respectively.

Other popular epic routes passing through Cumbria include the *Pennine Way* and Wainwright's *Coast to Coast* walk.

Walking tips and accidents

What should you do if something awful happens when you're out walking? You wouldn't be the first to have an accident. As more and more people pile on to the fells, the accident rate has increased enormously. The Lake District Search and Mountain Rescue Association keeps a grisly but fascinating diary of call-outs attended by its various teams, and in 2006 its members attended 396 incidents involving 493 people. There were 28 deaths and 202 injuries.

Call-outs are often cased by people getting lost or coming down a fell in the wrong place. A large number of accidents occur as the result of a slip on wet grass, so footwear with a good grip is essential. Of the annual deaths, about half are due to natural causes, like heart attacks, and most of the rest occur on the heights in snow or ice, often when climbers are well-equipped but are either foolhardy or caught out by unexpected conditions. It's worth carrying an ice axe and crampons if you plan to go on the high fells in snow – and even more important to know how to use them.

In the event of any accident, at any height, you should summon help by six long whistle blasts or torch flashes, repeated after a minute. This is the recognised distress signal on mountains. Telephone for help if you can, having made the injured person comfortable and administered first aid. Mobile phones have made this much easier, though it's not always possible to get a signal on the fells, in which case you should send someone to find the nearest phone box or farm. Dial the Police on 999, who will call out the nearest Mountain Rescue Team. You will be asked for details of the accident, injury and location. Work out your grid reference on the map if you can; it will make sending help much easier.

The Lake District has 12 individual mountain rescue teams in all, with permanent bases at Keswick, Coniston, Cockermouth, Ambleside, Kendal, Furness, Penrith, Patterdale, Wasdale, Millom and Kirkby Stephen. When a leader is contacted he puts out an emergency call to all his members

from his base headquarters. As soon as the first four arrive, usually including a doctor, they set off with first aid and radio equipment. Teams are staffed by volunteers and funded entirely by donations, and the 500 people who give up their time free of charge do a brilliant job. There is more information about their work and details about how you can support them at *www.ldsamra.org.uk*.

Maps and grid references

Just in case you have forgotten – tut tut – this is how you work them out. Grid references are always given in a group of six figures, such as 342 152, which in this case is the summit of Helvellyn. They refer to a precise, tiny and imaginary square on an Ordnance Survey map.

To find a grid reference, look for the square number at the top or bottom margins of your map. Now imagine the length of each square is divided into ten. So if your site is two-tenths of the way into square 34, as in this instance, your first three digits are 342. Now do the same vertically, looking for the square number in the side margins and further dividing that square into ten. In this instance your site is two-tenths of the way into square 15, giving you the three digits 152. So your full grid reference is 342 152.

If you need some tuition to get to know your maps, the Lake District National Park Authority has just the thing. They run frequent friendly Map and Compass training sessions and are experienced in helping complete novices, so don't be shy. There are also special events for young navigators. Check the LDNPA's *Out and About* magazine or tel. 015397 92895 for dates. The LDNPA also offers tips for keeping out of trouble in the fells and runs a Step Out, Stay Safe event, which runs through basic safety procedures.

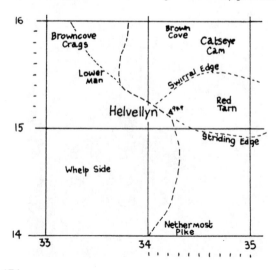

CHAPTER TEN

Museums and Galleries

*Town by town, village by village – the best
of the bunch for rainy days*

The Lake District has a surprisingly large number of museums and galleries for such a small area, and not all of them are simply about Lakeland fells and sheep. I bet you didn't expect to find the largest collection of Laurel and Hardy memorabilia here, or Napoleon's teacup, or the world's longest pencil. A lot of museums are now transforming themselves into highly imaginative interpretative centres, with audio-visual displays and light, airy buildings. But in some ways the ones that are being left behind can be the nicest – old fashioned and badly laid out, but ideal for pottering for an hour or two.

Here's our pick of Lakeland's best museums, with some fine galleries thrown in too. We've tried our very best to give correct opening hours and prices, but they do change from time to time and it's best to ring in advance if you're planning a special visit. And if you're particularly keen to see somewhere at it's best, go when it's sunny; these museums are obvious places to visit on rainy days and can get very full. Opening months are inclusive, so when we say May to October, for instance, it means from the start of May to the end of October. Last admissions are usually half an hour before closing time. Although most museums and galleries have special rates for children, the precise age at which a child ceases to be a child and becomes an adult varies from place to place, within a range of 5 to 15, so always check.

We have arranged the listings alphabetically by town or village. See also our listings of literary homes (Chapter 11) and stately homes (Chapter 12).

Ambleside

★★ The Armitt Collection

Rydal Road
Tel. 015394 31212 or visit *www.armitt.com*

Open all year round, daily, 10.00am to 5.00pm

Admission £2.50, children £1.00

It all began with three Brontë-type sisters, Marie Louisa, Annie Maria and Sophia Armitt, who devoted themselves to writing and the arts. They founded a library in 1912 that was subsequently supported by the great and the good of the times, such as Canon Rawnsley, Beatrix Potter, Arthur Ransome and G.M. Trevelyan, and as other locals donated their books and papers it began to build quite a collection.

The Armitt owns the largest collection of fungi water-colours done by Beatrix Potter (that was an early passion, before she wrote *The Tale of Peter Rabbit*), as well as early Lakeland photographs, rare books of literary and Cumbrian interest, literary manuscripts and archaeological relics. It has paintings by the German artist Kurt Schwitters, who lived for some time in Ambleside, and material about John Ruskin and Harriet Martineau. The museum shows off the best of the collection, and a separate library with thousands of volumes is open on Tuesdays and Fridays or by arrangement. Look out for the early Lake District guidebooks (then marvel afresh at this one).

★ The Homes of Football

Lake Road
Tel. 015394 34440 or visit *www.homesoffootball.co.uk*

Open all year round, Wednesday to Sunday, 10.00am to 5.00pm

Admission free, though there may be a small charge for special exhibitions

This gets a star if you like football, but not if you don't. Rather different from the Armitt, but it counts as art and a gallery, even if it is all about footie. Stuart Clarke's photo-graphs of thousands of grounds, players and fans around the world have toured the country, but this is their permanent home. There's something from just about every club you can think of, from Premier League champions down to Amble-side FC. His excellent photos are available to buy, framed, unframed or as postcards.

Barrow-in-Furness

★★ The Dock Museum

North Road
Tel. 01229 894444 or visit *www.dockmuseum.org.uk*

Open April to October, Tuesday to Friday, 10.00am to
5.00pm, and Saturday and Sunday, 11.00am to 5.00pm;
November to March, Wednesday to Friday, 10.30am to
4.00pm, and Saturday and Sunday, 11.00am to 4.30pm

Admission free

This smart and spacious museum is built over a Victorian
dry dock. It covers the working and social life or Barrow,
once the world's leading iron and steel centre and still pretty
big in shipping. The museum does the town's fascinating
history justice with three storeys of exhibits, many of them
high on interaction. Ship models give an idea of the vast scale
of the town's industry, and there's interesting material on the
railway network that once served it.

The museum is very nicely designed, and the once rather
empty space is filling up. There's a constantly playing reel
of six short films on different aspects of the town, and frequent special exhibitions, themed events and workshops.
Top marks to Barrow for making it all free. Café, shop,
adventure playground and walkways linked to the Cumbria
Coastal Way.

Carlisle

★★★ Tullie House Museum and Art Gallery

Castle Street
Tel. 01228 534781 or visit *www.tulliehouse.co.uk*

Open all year round, daily, Monday to Saturday, 10.00am
to 5.00pm (4.00pm November to March), Sunday, 12.00pm
to 5.00pm (4.00pm November to March)

Admission £5.20, children £2.60

Carlisle's award-winning cultural wonderland was greatly enlarged in the early 1990s and again in 2002 with a Millennium Gallery. It's clear how much care and imagination have gone into the exhibits, from the Romans to the railways. It manages to be fun yet tasteful and informative, well laid out for young and old, and well worth a couple of hours of anyone's time.

There's good material on Carlisle's history in the crossfire of centuries of Border strife, with nods to the influence of the Scots, Celts, Romans, Vikings and Normans and interesting stuff on the Reivers and the Roman Wall. Great sound effects. Lots on Lakeland wildlife, and don't miss the battle arrows in the glass, overlooking the Castle. The gallery's displays change all the time, but it's particularly good on pre-Raphaelite paintings and 20th-century British art. It's amazing to find works by Burne-Jones, Millet, Pisarro, Whistler, Augustus John, Paul Nash, Stanley Spencer and L.S. Lowry in a small provincial city like Carlisle. Tullie House got many of them on the cheap when the very shrewd Sir William Rothenstein became its London art adviser, and it's benefited from some generous bequests. Works by Antony Gormley and Sebastiao Salgado bring it bang up to date.

The museum and gallery are easy to find, just past the Cathedral before you get to the Castle. Restaurant, souvenir shop and always lots on – special exhibitions, lectures, films, concerts and much more. Before leaving, examine the original Tullie House, Carlisle's only remaining Jacobean building. The ornate lead drainpipes are works of art in themselves.

★ Border Regiment Museum

Carlisle Castle
Tel. 01228 532774 or visit
www.kingsownbordermuseum.btik.uk

Open April to September, daily, 9.30am to 5.00pm; October to March, daily, 10.00am to 4.00pm

Admission £4.20, children £2.10 (includes admission to Castle)

The museum is part of the Castle, which is well worth a visit in itself (see Chapter 13). The Border Regiment has served in battles all over the world for the last 300 years – from the Duke of Marlborough's days, the Napoleonic wars to the two World Wars. Displays cover all the conflicts, with medals, uniforms, photographs, trophies and letters. The regiment's roots are well explained, making this of particular interest to those with local connections, but it'll be of interest to any military fan. The full name, by the way, should be The Border Regiment and the King's Own Royal Border Regiment Museum (making it The Longest Museum Title in Cumbria).

★ Cathedral Treasury

Carlisle Cathedral
Tel. 01228 548151 or visit *www.carlislecathedral.org.uk*

Open all year round, daily, 7.30am to 6.15pm (5.00pm on Sundays)

Admission free

The museum, in a superb underground gallery, houses all the treasures from the cathedral and Carlisle's parishes – ancient copes, historic plates, silver, books and so on. There are also displays telling the story of Christian Cumbria.

★ Guildhall Museum

Next to the Old Town Hall
Tel. 01228 534781 or visit *www.carlisle.gov.uk*

Open April to October, daily, 12.00pm to 4.30pm

Admission free

Built in 1405, this, the last remaining medieval timber-framed building in Carlisle, is now beautifully restored. There are eight rooms, displaying the work of various guilds that once used the building – shoemakers, tanners, butchers, weavers, merchants. Now partly looked after by Tullie House, five minutes' walk away.

★ High Head Sculpture Valley

High Head Farm, Ivegill, south of Carlisle
Tel. 016974 73552 or visit
www.highheadsculpturevalley.co.uk

Open all year round, daily except Wednesdays, 10.30am to 5.00pm

Admission £2.50, children £1.50

A bit of a trek to get to, but a fairly unique attraction. There's a good gallery with regularly changing exhibitions, but the main draw are the big outdoor sculptures, carved by Jonathan Stamper and other artists, and arranged around the estate. They're not to everyone's tastes, but seeing them out in the open is quite striking, not least for the cows (it's a working dairy farm too). Trails link the sculptures, and Stamper has ambitious plans to build it into a major art centre. Good farm shop, tea room, children's play area and – somewhat bizarrely – a health and beauty spa complete the complex.

Solway Aviation Museum

Carlisle Airport
Tel. 01228 573823 or visit
www.solway-aviation-museum.co.uk

Open April to October, Saturdays, Sundays and bank holiday Mondays, 10.30am to 5.00pm

Admission £3.50, children £1.75

This small collection of local aircraft memorabilia is displayed in a modest building at Cumbria's only airport, but it's enthusiastically cared for by a team of volunteers. Photographs and equipment chart 70 years or so of aviation history, and there's a display on Blue Streak, Britain's first ballistic missile that was test-fired nearby. Outside are several planes from the 1950s and 1960s, including a Glostor Meteor, Canberra Bomber and Vulcan Bomber. You can climb into some of them.

Cockermouth

★ Castlegate House Gallery

Opposite Cockermouth Castle
Tel. 01900 822149 or visit *www.castlegatehouse.co.uk*

Open March to December, Friday to Monday, 10.30am to 5.00pm (2.30pm to 4.30pm on Sunday), or by arrangement

Admission free

A commercial gallery specialising in northern English and Scottish artists. You don't have to buy, of course – just admire the art and savour the ambience. There are ten or so exhibitions a year, and stars of previous shows have included Picasso, Lowry and Winifred Nicholson. Even if the current exhibition doesn't interest you, the house itself is well worth a peep, because it's one of Cockermouth's larger Georgian gems, just opposite the Castle. There's a walled garden with sculptures. There are several more galleries in Cockermouth, including Percy House and Neo Gallery on Market Place, the former with a big emphasis on Cumbrian artists.

★ The Printing House

Main Street
Tel. 01900 824984 or visit *www.printinghouse.co.uk*

Open all year round, daily except Sundays and bank holiday Mondays, 10.00am to 4.00pm; hours can vary according to staff availability, so ring in advance if you're planning a special visit

Admission by guided tour £2.75, children £2.00

Like several museums in the Lake District, this is a real labour of love. David Winkworth has been collecting printing presses, machines and typefaces for decades, as a sort of spin-off from his antiquarian bookshop business. You have to go through the shop to get to it, but it turns out to be surprisingly spacious. Shows the history of printing from

1800 onwards, with lots of good memorabilia and hands-on excitement. Relics include Imperial and Columbian Eagle presses, dating from the 1830s.

Coniston

★★★ The Ruskin Museum

Yewdale Road
Tel. 015394 41164 or visit *www.ruskinmuseum.com*

Open March to mid-November, daily, 10.00am to 5.30pm; mid-November to February, Wednesday to Sunday, 10.30am to 3.30pm

Admission £4.25, children £2.00

A constantly improving and expanding museum offering a great introduction to some of the people, industries and heritage of the Lake District. There are interesting displays relating to Ruskin, including paintings, sketches and his mineral collection. But the museum has broadened its repertoire to take in other aspects of local life, like copper mining, slate quarrying, lace-making and farming. There's interesting and accessible stuff on local geology and the art of dry stone wall building (there's an example outside). And it's built an exhibition of photos and memorabilia relating to Donald Campbell, who was killed on Coniston Water in January 1967 as he tried to break the world water speed record. There's an ongoing project to rebuild Campbell's *Bluebird* craft and display it here; you can monitor progress at *www.bluebirdproject.com*. An eclectic but brilliant museum.

The Ruskin Museum is right in the centre of the village, so parking is pretty hopeless. Use the main car park and walk back.

Finsthwaite

★★ Stott Park Bobbin Mill

1½ miles (2.4 km) north of Newby Bridge
Tel. 015395 31087 or visit *www.english-heritage.org.uk*

Open April to October, Monday to Friday, 10.00am to 5.00pm

Admission £4.20, children £2.10

A major site of what used to be one of the Lake District's most important industries. Unlike many such places, this is not a restoration but the real thing. The mill was built in 1835 and produced hundreds of thousands of bobbins a week when the Lancashire cotton industry was at its peak. When it declined, it turned out things like hammers, handles and pulleys instead, and it was still in action right up until 1971.

It was later bought by English Heritage to be preserved as a museum.

The massive mill building houses much of the original machinery, including the old water turbines and steam engines, which are cranked into life several times a week. The friendly staff – some of whom worked here – give guided demonstrations and tours, and there are displays and a gift shop. A fantastic place, unique and well worth leaving the tourist track to find. Combine a visit with a pleasant walk through the woods up to Finsthwaite High Dam, where you can circuit the water before heading back.

Flookburgh

★ Lakeland Miniature Village

Winder Lane
Tel. 015395 58500 or visit
www.lakelandminiaturevillage.com

Open all year round, daily, 10.30am to dusk

Admission £3.00, children £1.50

Another of those potty creations, the result of one man's passion. A village of over 120 buildings, houses, bridges and wishing wells, mostly in local Coniston slate, all in miniature at a couple of feet high, and all made entirely by hand by Edward Robinson. It claims to be Cumbria's only miniature village, if only because no one else would want to do it.

Robinson made his first building for charity 15 years ago, and it was admired so much that he started making more. And more. Now it's taken over his garden and life, and he's not finished yet. Many of his buildings are based on well-known Lakeland buildings, such as Hill Top, the home of Beatrix Potter. The National Trust is not amused by his version. Can you patent the shape of a building? He also makes them to order. It's easy to scoff, but the workmanship is excellent, faithful to the style of local architecture and building over the years. The Oriental Tea House fits in less well though.

Grasmere

★★★ Wordsworth Museum

Next door to Dove Cottage, just off the A591
Tel. 015394 35544 or visit *www.wordsworth.org.uk*

Open all year round, daily except early January to early February, 9.30am to 5.30pm

Admission £6.50, children £4.10 (including admission to Dove Cottage)

One of the best and most professional museums in the Lake District, keeper of the only Designated Collection in Cumbria (which means it's jolly important internationally). It has the best collection of original Wordsworth manuscripts in the known universe. Look out, too, for a copy of Dorothy's notebook, where she kept her famous journal. Not all the manuscripts are in William's own hand – he used to get Dorothy or his wife, Mary, to write out his poems before going through them to make corrections. It is fascinating to compare his handwriting later in life with a handwritten poem composed when he was at Hawkshead Grammar School – it got much worse.

The display is brilliantly presented and it's all in chronological order, telling the poet's life story, so don't worry if your knowledge of Wordsworth is confined to a single poem about daffodils. You can also see his possessions, including a coat and waistcoat mounted on a dummy torso so that you can get an idea of his size. It's not all Wordsworth: you can see paintings of some of his contemporaries, and there are items devoted to local history too.

There are regular special exhibitions, many of them very good indeed, and the adjacent Jerwood Centre lets scholars pore over the original manuscripts. There are courses and events, though the future of these is currently under review; contact the Wordsworth Trust for the latest details. There's the 3°W Gallery of new artwork. And then there's Dove Cottage, of course. Visit the museum first: it'll help you appreciate the cottage more. There's limited parking for the museum if you're very early, but otherwise it's best to park in the village and walk back. The museum can get very busy on wet days; if you want to avoid the crowds, get there early or at lunchtime.

★ Heaton Cooper Studio

Opposite the village green
Tel. 015394 35280 or visit *www.heatoncooper.co.uk*

Open all year round, daily, 9.00am to 5.30pm (from 12.00pm on Sundays, and to 5.00pm in winter)

Admission free

The gallery and studio here were built up by father and son Alfred and William Heaton Cooper from 1905. They're two of the Lake District's most famous artists, and you'll almost certainly have seen their paintings on postcards and prints. The gallery shows off some of their best work, including dramatic mountain landscapes, and there's material by other members of the family. It sells prints and artists' materials.

Hawkshead

★★ Beatrix Potter Gallery

Main Street
Tel. 015394 36355 or visit *www.nationaltrust.org.uk*

Open March to October, Saturday to Wednesday (plus Thursdays from June to August), 10.30am to 4.30pm

Admission by timed ticket £3.80, children £1.90

This 17th-century building was once the legal offices of William Heelis, Beatrix Potter's husband, and it's been nicely converted by the National Trust into an excellent little gallery to show off her original watercolours. The display changes every year, but there's always a good selection of work from her classic children's story books and some bits and pieces connected to her personal life, farming and National Trust links. It's nice to be able to compare the printed illustrations with the early sketches and drawings. There's obviously a demand for drawings of Peter Rabbit *et al.*, but it's a shame that's mostly to the exclusion of her other watercolours like her flower paintings, which are exquisite. For more of these, visit the Armitt Collection in Ambleside. There's also a recreation of Heelis's office, complete with his desk ledgers and period files. The gallery can get very busy on wet days, especially since the film adaptation of Potter's life stoked even more interest in her, and you may have to wait your turn for a while. Inevitably, there's a shop (open mid-February to Christmas).

★ Hawkshead Grammar School

Main Street
Tel. 015394 36735 or visit
www.hawksheadgrammar.org.uk

Open April to October, Monday to Saturday, 10.00am to 1.00pm and 2.00pm to 5.00pm; Sunday 1.00pm to 5.00pm (closes 3.30pm every day in October)

Admission £2.00, children free

This was once a sizeable school, opened in the 16th century and still educating into the 20th. Its most famous alumni is William Wordsworth, who was one of 100 or so pupils here in the 1780s. The school is a lovely old building, though now painted up and looking somewhat different from how it did in Wordsworth's day. Inside you can see the desk where he carved his initials. (Or at least, that's what they tell you – they're very hard to make out.) The main room is a schoolroom set out as it was in Wordsworth's day, and upstairs there is a small library and a small exhibition on the history of the school. Lots of quills and pens, and there's also the headmaster's study (potential for an exhibition of canes through the ages?)

The helpful curator will answer any questions about the school and Wordsworth, and can tell you why boys at the school were allowed to smoke and drink. Go early when few visitors are about if you want to make the most of his local knowledge. It's a nice, relaxing little museum, surprisingly quiet even in summer. The school is dead easy to find as it's opposite the main car park.

Holker

★★ Lakeland Motor Museum

Holker Hall, on the B5278 between Haverthwaite and Cark
Tel. 015395 58509 or visit
www.lakelandmotormuseum.co.uk

Open in 2008, January to October, daily, 10.30am to 4.45pm (4.00pm in January and February), but see below

Admission £7.00, children £4.50; joint tickets available for other Holker attractions

Has grown – and grown and grown – out of one man's passion for old cars and parts. Over 30 years it's gathered over 120 cars and motorbikes and some 30,000 'automobilia' exhibits, like Princess Margaret's scooter, illuminated petrol pump signs and toy cars. There's a recreation of a 1920s garage and workshop, stuffed with old tools and equipment. Prize exhibits include a 1922 Bentley, and they also have an East German Trabant, driven over when the wall came down and probably expired where it now resides. One of the best things is the Campbell Bluebird Exhibition, complete with replica Bluebird (not to be confused with the real thing, which is currently being restored for the exhibition at the Ruskin Museum in Coniston).

It's all fascinating and fun stuff, with a powerful whiff of nostalgia as you walk through. It helps if you like cars and engines, obviously. The friendly manager will lift up the bonnets if you ask nicely. The museum is in the grounds of Holker Hall and admission is separate to the rest of the Holker attractions, though you can park in the main car park. But 2008 is likely to be the museum's last year at Holker Hall. Having outgrown the space there, it has got planning permission to develop a brown-field site at **Backbarrow**, where it hopes to open its doors around Easter 2009. Ring or check the website for progress.

Kendal

★★★ Abbot Hall Art Gallery

Abbot Hall, off Kirkland by the parish church
Tel. 015397 22464 or visit *www.abbothall.org.uk*

Open all year round except mid-December to mid-January, Monday to Saturday, 10.30am to 5.00pm (4.00pm from November to March)

Admission (to all exhibitions) £5.00, children £4.00

The Gallery is in an immaculate Georgian building, set in a small park along with some of the oldest buildings in Kendal. It's one of the loveliest settings in town, right by the river and looking up towards Kendal Castle. Built in 1759 at a cost of £8,000, it has been open as an art gallery since 1962 and is now restored to its original decorative splendour.

Just because Kendal is not a major city, don't expect a small, provincial gallery; this is generally reckoned to be the finest gallery in the northwest and one of the top 20 in the whole country. Downstairs houses a small but impressive collection of 18th- and 19th-century paintings, including several by George Romney, displayed along with period furniture, porcelain and glassware. It's set out in such a way that you feel as if you're wandering around someone's stately home – only without all those ropes. Upstairs the house becomes a more traditional art gallery setting to display the contemporary collection, with works by Kurt Schwitters, David Hockney and Stanley Spencer and one of the biggest public gallery collections of work by Lucian Freud. There are three or four special exhibitions each year, always imaginative, challenging and well worth looking out for. There are talks from one of the curators most Thursdays at 2.00pm about what's currently showing, and regular lectures and other events too. Excellent café, good bookshop and free car park (go through the main council car park off Kirkland). All in all, this is one of the best galleries anywhere (and yes, that includes you, London).

★★★ Museum of Lakeland Life

Abbot Hall, off Kirkland by the parish church
Tel. 015397 22464 or visit *www.lakelandmuseum.org.uk*

Open all year round except mid-December to mid-January, Monday to Saturday, 10.30am to 5.00pm (4.00pm from November to March)

Admission £3.75, children £2.75

A separate establishment to Abbot Hall, but housed in its old stable block and keeping the same hours. You can buy joint tickets to save a few quid if you're visiting both. It's a small but prestigious museum that provides a wealth of material for anyone wanting to find out more about Lakeland, its people and its industries. It won the first ever Museum of the Year award in 1973, and it's still outstanding.

The re-creations of various workshops, complete with genuine, hand-worn tools and instruments, are excellent, and most of the exhibits are on open display – you can touch them, walk round them, peer under them, even sniff them if you want to. Some of the drawers are worth opening too. One of the nicest things is that many of the exhibits came from local people, and it's all so well done that it looks as though the people who used these tools have just knocked off for lunch and might be back at any minute to carry on working. Look out for the paint shop door upstairs, covered in 'stalactites' of paint where the brushes used to be worked out.

There's a replica of Arthur Ransome's study, with many of his possessions, including his desk, typewriter, pipe and slippers; a beautiful old printing press, made of cast iron and once used by the *Westmorland Gazette*; a hundred-year-old weaving loom; massive old clocks and signs; and a traditional Lakeland kitchen, bedroom and farmer's parlour, furnished as they might have been in the 18th or 19th centuries. Excellent replica of a Kendal street *c*.1900, with chemist's shop and perfumery. Loads of nostalgic old photos strewn around.

Part of the success of the displays is the minimal use of labels and text, though this has some drawbacks – quite often you find yourself wondering what on earth you're looking at. Arm yourself with the guidebook before you go in, or use the listening posts, one of which teaches you to count in Cumbrian dialect. If you're in on a Wednesday in a school holiday you might get to see a demonstration of one of the Lakeland crafts on original equipment.

★★ Kendal Museum

Opposite the station
Tel. 015397 21374 or visit *www.kendalmuseum.org.uk*

Open all year round, Thursday to Saturday, 12.00pm to 5.00pm

Admission £2.80, children free

Kendal is full of surprises. Not only does it have one of the best art galleries in the country, it also has one of its oldest museums. Kendal Museum was first opened in 1796 when a gentleman by the name of William Todhunter staged an exhibition of 'curiosities'. Admission was 'one shilling per person; children, workmen and students 6d each'. Children now go free, so that's progress.

The museum has transformed itself from a typical municipal museum of the old school into an imaginative, hands-on centre that does more than just explain what you're looking at. You can wander back in time to trace original Cumbrian Man, follow a nature trail of 520 million years of Lakeland wildlife and wonder what on earth big game were doing in the Lake District in the wildlife gallery. There's a big collection of Lake District rocks and minerals, and a display dedicated to the legendary Alfred Wainwright, who was curator here for 30 years. See his trademark pipe and (washed) walking socks in his reconstructed office. There's a fun interactive display on medieval life in Kendal Castle. The museum inherited a large collection of stuffed animals, which are interesting but don't really have much to do with the area.

The museum is run by South Lakeland District Council, which explains why opening hours have been cut to just 15 hours a week, but it's well worth fitting in a visit if you can. There's a free car park for visitors, which is a bonus in Kendal.

★ The Quaker Tapestry

Friends Meeting House, Stramongate
Tel. 015397 22975 or visit *www.quaker-tapestry.co.uk*

Open April to December, Monday to Friday except bank holiday Mondays, 10.00am to 5.00pm

Admission £4.90, children £2.00

The Quaker movement has close local connections, and this tapestry celebrates its history from 1652 in 77 hand-embroidered panels. More than 4,000 people around the world had a hand in making it, and there are some interesting scenes illustrating Quaker beliefs and practices. A short film in the exhibition centre explains more. For the first three months of each year the tapestry leaves Kendal to go out on the road, and it's so far been displayed in 150 or so venues in the UK and abroad. The tea rooms are open all year round from Monday to Friday.

Keswick

★★ Cars of the Stars

Standish Street
Tel. 017687 73757 or visit *www.carsofthestars.com*

Open in February half-term and from one week before Easter to November, daily, 10.00am to 5.00pm; December until Christmas, weekends only, 10.00am to 5.00pm

Admission £4.00, children £3.00

Another of those museums that began as a personal hobby and didn't know where to stop. Keswick dentist Peter Nelson has collected 30 or so vehicles that have appeared in TV and films, including *Chitty Chitty Bang Bang*, Lady Penelope's FAB1 pink Rolls Royce as used in *Thunderbirds*, Del Boy's Robin Reliant from *Only Fools and Horses*, Mr Bean's Mini, James Bond's Aston Martin and Harry Potter's Ford Anglia. An amazing and unique collection, mostly put together in only five years. Why did no one in America think of it? It's situated in an old garage, and the collection has to be rotated to fit it all in, but the tableaux and sound system are improving all the time. Strange copyright laws mean you're not allowed to take photos or video footage of the cars. Shop.

★★ Cumberland Pencil Museum

Southey Works, beside the river in the southwest part of town
Tel. 017687 73626 or visit *www.pencils.co.uk*

Open all year round, daily, 9.30am to 4.00pm (sometimes later in busy periods)

Admission £3.00, children £1.50

A good museum for children on a rainy day, and paradise if you happen to be a pencil freak. It proudly bills itself as the only attraction in the world devoted exclusively to the pencil. Others museums might flirt with the pencil, but this is the real thing.

The museum does a good job of charting the pencil's history from the day in the 16th century when Borrowdale shepherds stumbled across graphite. They have a re-created graphite mine so you can see where the stuff comes from, plus pencil-making machines, video displays and a children's activity area where you can scrawl away. Demonstration days too. The museum boasts the world's longest pencil at 26 feet (8 m), though nowadays it's something of a celebrity and often out and about raising money for charity, so ring in advance if you want to see it. Don't miss the very clever wartime pencils, with a secret compartment containing a compass and a map of Germany. There's a World of Colour shop where you can buy, wait for it … pencils. Ironically, all of the graphite for the pencil works now comes from abroad. Plenty of parking on site, which you'll appreciate if you've ever tried to park elsewhere in Keswick.

★★ Keswick Museum and Art Gallery

Fitz Park
Tel. 017687 73263 or visit
www.allerdale.gov.uk/keswick-museum

Open April to October, Tuesday to Saturday and bank holiday Mondays, 10.00am to 4.00pm

Admission free

Much more of an idiosyncratic collection of strange objects than a normal little municipal museum and undoubtedly one of Cumbria's oddest. Almost gets three stars, just for not trying to fit the mould, but that would be unfair on the really professional ones at Kendal and Grasmere.

On the serious side, there are excellent collections of letters and documents to do with Wordsworth, Southey, Coleridge and Walpole. Look out for an original copy of *The Three Bears*. Did you know that Southey wrote it? Bet you didn't. (In his version it's an old woman who eats their porridge – Goldilocks is a later addition.) There's some interesting stuff on the history of the town and the growth of tourism too.

Among the dafter exhibits, there's a 664-year-old mum-
mified cat, Napoleon's teacup, the skin of a giant cobra, a
mantrap and a 13 feet (4 m) scale model of the Lake District.
Where else could you find all of that under one roof? Perhaps
the best loved item in the museum is a set of 19th-century
musical stones, each giving out a different note when struck,
so musical visitors can play tunes – and are allowed to, but
using hands only, which can be very tiring. They were played
before Queen Victoria in 1848. She was not amused.

There's a small art gallery, with frequently changing
exhibitions.

★ Honister Slate Mine

Honister Pass, Borrowdale
Tel. 017687 77230 or visit *www.honister.com*

Open all year round, daily, 9.00am to 5.00pm (opens
10.00am Saturday and Sunday); tours daily at 10.30am,
12.30pm and 3.30pm

Admission to visitor centre free; tours £9.75, children £4.75

The highest tourist attraction in the Lakes. Not actually in
Keswick – in fact it's 9 miles (14.5 km) away – but that's the
nearest town. An ancient mine that is now the last working
slate mine in England. Thanks to the enterprise of Mark
Weir, whose grandfather worked in the mine, it's also transformed itself into a very professional and successful tourist
attraction. There's a visitor centre explaining more about the
history of the place, and a variety of excellent guided tours,
either on the flat around the factory or down deep into the
11 miles (17.7 km) of mine tunnels. Book in advance if you
want a tour in the school holidays.

The latest attraction is the Via Ferrata, a sort of rock
climbing trail for softies. It follows the Victorian miners'
route to work – though miners didn't have the safety harnesses
and permanent attachments to a cable that modern-day
Honister visitors have. They provide two Via Ferrata tours a
day (11.00am and 1.00pm) with all kit and instruction,
priced £19.50 or £9.50 for children.

Back at the visitor centre, you can buy slate products, or
pay £10.00 for as much green slate as you can get in your car
boot. Free tea and coffee for visitors; a nice touch.

★ Keswick Mining Museum

Otley Road
Tel. 017687 80055 or visit
www.keswickminingmuseum.co.uk

Open all year round, daily except Mondays in the winter,
10.00am to 5.00pm; winter times can changes, so check in
advance if you're making a special trip

Admission £4.00, children £1.50

This fine little museum is packed with mining memorabilia and is a good introduction to some of Cumbria's most important industries over the centuries. Keswick received miners from Germany from the 16th century, and the story of mining over the centuries is nicely laid out. There are mining uniforms and helmets, rocks and minerals, lots of photographs and a video of miners' recollections. What strikes you most of all is how terrifyingly dangerous so much of the work was.

★ The Puzzling Place

Museum Square
Tel. 017687 75102 or visit *www.puzzlingplace.co.uk*

Open all year round, daily, 10.00am to 6.00pm

Admission £3.50, children £2.75

A fairly recent and pretty, ahem, puzzling addition to Keswick's tourist attractions. Andy Wallace, a local lad, and his brother got the idea from something they saw in New Zealand. It's a bit homemade but getting increasingly professional, and it'll appeal to clever kids, old and young. Especially if it's raining. There are dozens of holograms to wonder at, plus interactive computer things, a gallery of illusions and lots of infuriating puzzles. Also sells brainteaser-type toys. Don't step into the anti-gravity room if you've had a few drinks.

Maryport

★★ Senhouse Roman Museum

The Battery, on the north side of Maryport
Tel. 01900 816168 or visit *www.senhousemuseum.co.uk*

Open April to October, daily except Mondays and Wednesdays from April to June, 10.00am to 5.00pm; November to March, Friday to Sunday, 10.30am to 4.00pm

Admission £2.50, children 75p

One of the country's oldest and most important private collections of Roman relics. It was begun in 1570 by John Senhouse, who collected bits from the old Roman Fort at Maryport, and passed them down through 12 generations of his family. It was finally opened to the public in 1990 in a converted Victorian naval battery, overlooking the town.

The big attractions are the 24 military altars, probably the best example of Roman lettering and inscriptions ever found in Britain. The museum has only a few rooms, but take them slowly if you want to savour the sexual undertones of items like the Serpent Stone, a Celtic phallus over 5 feet (1.5 m) high, or the 'Pin Up Girl', a naked girl carved in stone to welcome soldiers going on leave. There's a re-created watch-tower overlooking the Solway Firth and the earthworks, which mark where the old fort used to be. You could walk northwards to find milefort 21. The whole of this coast has its own defence system, an extension of Hadrian's Wall, with Maryport as its headquarters – hence the importance of this site.

★ Maryport Maritime Museum

Senhouse Street, close to the harbour
Tel. 01900 813738 or visit
www.allerdale.gov.uk/maryport-maritime-museum

Open all year round, Monday to Saturday, 10.00am to 4.00pm

Admission free

This neat, attractive little museum is run on a shoestring as it admirably makes no charge for admission and is supported by the local borough council – but it's nevertheless full of imagination and enthusiasm. It's devoted almost exclusively to the maritime history of Maryport, once a very important centre. Models of ships, tools and lots of photographs of old Maryport and of general maritime interest. There are also items relating to two local seafaring lads: Fletcher Christian, leader of the mutiny on the *Bounty*, and Thomas Henry Ismay, founder of the White Star Line, parent company of the *Titanic*. Much of the material was donated by a local resident, Annie Robinson, who helped to set up the museum in 1974. The museum also houses the TIC and runs several festivals in the town.

Millom

★ Millom Folk Museum

Railway station
Tel. 01229 772555 or visit *www.millomfolkmuseum.co.uk*

Open Easter to October, Tuesday to Saturday, 10.30am to 4.30pm

Admission £3.00, children 50p

Millom is a bit of a trek from the Lake District proper, but the museum is a good way to spend an hour or two if you find yourself here. It's a bit overcrowded, but visitors are encouraged to handle the exhibits by the excellent staff, who work hard to get you engaged. You'll see interesting old costumes and reconstructions of a mine cage, a mining family's kitchen and shop fronts. Puts the rise and fall of this coast's prosperity into perspective. There is also an exhibition about the life and work of Millom's most famous son, poet Norman Nicholson, and a shop.

★ RAF Millom Museum

Bank Head Estate, next to Haverigg Prison, 2 miles (3.2 km) from Millom
Tel. 01229 777444 or visit *www.rafmillom.co.uk*

Open all year round, daily, 10.30am to 5.00pm

Admission £2.00, children £1.00

A nice counterpoint to Carlisle's Solway Aviation Museum, and air enthusiasts will want to do both. This one's housed in the former RAF Millom base and focuses mostly on wartime aviation and pilots' training in nearby airfields, though it's also got some interesting stuff on the RAF's involvement in mountain rescue. More than 4,000 photographs and some medals, uniforms and bits of planes retrieved from crashes, laid out with care in different zones.

Nenthead

Nenthead Mines Heritage Centre

Nenthead, on the A689
Tel. 014343 82037 or visit *www.npht.com*

Open April to October, daily, 10.30am to 5.00pm

Admission with a mine tour £6.50, children £2.00 (without a tour £4.00, children free).

Right on the very edge of Cumbria in the north Pennines, but worth a visit if you're nearby or have a particular interest in the county's rich mining heritage. Lead and zinc were the things here, and it was a very busy mine in the 18th and 19th centuries. It's now preserved by the North Pennines Heritage Trust, which has created a good centre where you can inspect the old mine workings and learn a bit about life underground for the miners. There's a huge waterwheel you can control yourself, and kids enjoy panning for minerals. Café, shop and walking trails.

Penrith

★★ Rheged

Off the A66, 2 miles (3.2 km) southwest of Penrith
Tel. 017688 68000 or visit *www.rheged.com*

Open all year round, daily, 10.00am to 5.30pm

Admission free (varying charges apply for the cinema)

Not technically a museum – it's got elements of a shopping park, cinema and motorway service station among other things – but undoubtedly a fine tourist attraction and a nice showcase for all things Lakeland. It was built into a hill on the outskirts of Penrith and just off the M6, and its claim to fame is that it is Europe's biggest grass-covered building.

Rheged was the name for Cumbria's ancient Celtic kingdom, and it introduces the wonders of Cumbria via the more modern medium of a giant-screen cinema. There are several films a day, plus music, workshops, lectures and craft sessions. The free Discovering Cumbria exhibition, an audio-visual extravaganza, is a lively race through millions of years of local history, and there's an information centre to help plan visits elsewhere. The gallery space has some good, locally focused exhibitions. Lots of shops and eating places, though they do at least try to introduce visitors to the joys of Cumbrian food and drink.

★★ The National Mountaineering Exhibition

Rheged, off the A66 2 miles (3.2 km) southwest of Penrith
Tel. 017688 68000 or visit *www.rheged.com*

Open all year round, daily, 10.00am to 5.30pm

Admission £3.00, children £2.50

This is the closest you'll get to the fells without having to trouble yourself with any climbing. It's also the best single thing about Rheged, and distinct from the rest of it – not least because you have to pay to get in – so we've listed it separately.

It's the only permanent mountaineering exhibition in the UK and was put together by experts, including Chris Bonnington. It's world-class, telling the story of mountaineering from the very beginning with gripping stories of adventures throughout. There's lots of original equipment so you can chart how much it's changed over the years, and you can try some of it on. Photos, short films and recordings are all well arranged to take you through camps and stages over the decades. Much of the focus is on British expeditions to the Himalayas, and there's a display on Mallory, the climber who disappeared on Everest in 1924, his body not found until 1999. You can see the mitten that was on his hand, as well as his climbing kit. Of more local interest is the camera that the Abraham brothers lugged up mountains in 1897 to take their famous photos of the fells.

★ Wetheriggs

Clifton Dykes, 4 miles (6.4 km) southeast of Penrith, on the Cliburn road off the A6
Tel. 017688 92733 or visit *www.wetheriggs-pottery.co.uk*

Open all year round, daily, 10.00am to 5.30pm (4.30pm from November to Easter)

Admission free but charges for activities

Wetheriggs has been a popular, steam-powered pottery for 150 years, but it's expanded itself into a more general artists' centre lately. Artists work on site, and you can find painters, sculptors, ceramicists and glassblowers as well as potters. Much of the original equipment is still in place. The grounds are attractive, with trails and animals, and there's an excellent café called The Yam. There's a Pots of Fun centre where you can have a go at making or painting your own pottery.

Penrith Museum

Middlegate, next to the Tourist Information Centre
Tel. 017682 12228 or visit *www.eden.gov.uk.museum*

Open April to September, Monday to Saturday, 9.30am to 5.00pm, Sunday, 1.00pm to 4.45pm; October to March, Monday to Saturday, 10.00am to 4.00pm

Admission free

The building was a school for 300 years, originally a charitable foundation for poor girls, then it became the TIC. Now it also houses the town's local history museum, a modest collection of photos, documents and artefacts about Penrith's history. Of little interest to outsiders and probably pretty boring for most Penrithians, although it does have some good special events and exhibitions, and there's some interesting stuff about local legends. Free, too. There have been proposals to shift it to Rheged, no doubt jazzing it up in the process, but the district council has so far resisted.

Ravenglass

★ Ravenglass Railway Museum

Ravenglass Station
Tel. 01229 717171 or visit *www.ravenglass-railway.co.uk*

Open mid-March to October, daily, 9.00am to 5.00pm

Admission free

Tells the story of the miniature railway and its place in the valley. The route opened in the 1870s to transport haematite ore, and there's interesting material on the mining connections. There are models, posters, tickets and videos, all quite interesting, but the best exhibit is the Synolda engine – a twin of the original Ravenglass railway engine, which was built in 1815.

Seascale

★★ Sellafield Visitors Centre

Sellafield
Tel. 019467 27027 or visit *www.yottenfews.com*

Open all year round, daily, 10.00am to 4.00pm; it some-times closes for special events, so ring in advance if you're desperate to see it

Admission free

Just in case you didn't know, this is the nuclear power gener-ating and waste fuel reprocessing plant on the west Cumbrian coast. Opened in 1956 with the name Calder Hall, then rebranded as Windscale in the 1970s and Sellafield in the 1980s. What started as a small attached visitor centre has also been transformed several times – on the last occasion with help from the Science Museum in London into a whizz-bang, interactive science exploration centre. They were clearly fed up with being mocked, by this Guide in particular, for using their exhibition as an exercise in self-justification, and this latest incarnation certainly goes beyond that.

Sellafield is never likely to be many families' top choice for a day out, but they're trying hard to attract kids in partic-ular. Clever children will love it, and because it's all free it makes for a cheap day out. Now there's information on all forms of creating electricity – solar, hydro, gas, coal, wind and nuclear – so that you, the visitor, the tax payer, can try to decide which are best. It's all very high tech, lavish and interactive, with lots to press and watch, and there's loads of space as there aren't many physical objects to see. A new highlight is what they call an immersion cinema, where you can play games and control what you see. It all ends with the viewer voting for the best source of energy. The day I was there, wind won. One of the attendants said wind usually did win, unless there happened to be lots of staff watching, in which case nuclear fuel wins. There is also a centre for educational visits and – rather incongruously, you might think – a nature trail through the grounds.

Threlkeld

★★ Quarry and Mining Museum

Just south of Threlkeld, off the B5322
Tel. 017687 79747 or visit
www.threlkeldminingmuseum.co.uk

Open Easter to October, daily, 10.00am to 5.00pm

Admission to museum £3.00, children £1.50; mine tours £5.00, children £2.50

There's been a resurgence of interest in Cumbrian mining lately – and quite right too, since it played such a vital part in the area's history. Several other mines have opened up recently, but along with Honister Slate Mine, Threlkeld's is the best. It's also the biggest: a sprawling, 70 acre (28 ha) site in and around an old quarry, with a great deal to see. The excellent mining museum, formerly at Caldbeck, has been much enlarged and displays artefacts like tools and mining equipment as well as lots of minerals. You can go underground to a re-created mine and explore the quarry's railway on *Sir Tom*, a newly restored locomotive. Good shop, where you can buy books to learn more.

Ulverston

★ Laurel and Hardy Museum

Upper Brook Street, a side street between King Street and The Ghyll
Tel. 01229 582292 or visit
www.laurel-and-hardy-museum.co.uk

Open February to December, daily, 10.00am to 4.30pm
(from 10.30am on Sundays)

Admission £3.00, children £2.00

Ulverston might seem an unlikely place to find the world's largest collection of Laurel and Hardy memorabilia, but that's because you didn't know that Stan Laurel was born here. This museum was set up by the late Laurel and Hardy fanatic (and one-time mayor of Ulverston) Bill Cubin. There is a mind-boggling amount of stuff – posters, letters, portraits, possessions, clothes, hats, furniture, statues – and a small

cinema showing films and documentaries on a continuous loop. A real curiosity, and not a little bonkers, but worth seeing. If you're really keen, Stan's birthplace is on the other side of town, marked by a plaque; the staff can direct you.

Whitehaven

★★ The Beacon

West Strand, on the harbour
Tel. 01946 592302 or visit
www.thebeacon-whitehaven.co.uk

Open all year round, Tuesday to Sunday plus bank holiday Mondays, 10.00am to 4.30pm

Admission £4.60, children free

A handsome building in a great location, with four floors of material covering Whitehaven's social, maritime and industrial history. It underwent a big refurbishment in 2007, emerging as more of an interactive, audio-visual experience than a museum, and aimed squarely at families. It charts the fluctuating fortunes of Whitehaven, and there's lots of interest on how it became so prosperous from its trade links with America, and its role in slavery, mining and shipping. The very top floor is all about that Cumbrian obsession, the weather, with lots of interactive gizmos and a chance to present the weather forecast. There are regular special exhibitions, usually excellent, in the first-floor Harbour Gallery (free entry). The refurbishment has also brought an expanded shop and a restaurant and an activity room on the ground floor.

★★ The Rum Story

Lowther Street
Tel. 01946 592933 or visit *www.rumstory.co.uk*

Open all year round, daily, 10.00am to 5.00pm (4.30pm from October to March)

Admission £5.45, children £3.45

The second of Whitehaven's multimillion pound tourist attractions. This one's in the town centre, within the courtyards and cellars of a 1785 bonded warehouse. It's the world's first exhibition on the story of rum, though there can't be a lot of competition. Why isn't it in the Caribbean, you might wonder? The answer is that the town was once huge in the rum trade, so there are a lot of local artefacts and history. And to save you trailing to the West Indies when you'd much rather be in Whitehaven, they have re-created the sights and sounds of tropical rainforests and slave ships. It tells an unusual but specific story well and with imagination, and brings the slave trade vividly to life. The outside courtyard and café have an amazing kinetic rum clock, which jumps into action every half hour.

★ Haig Colliery Mining Museum

Solway Road along the cliffs
Tel. 01946 599949 or visit *www.haigpit.com*

Open all year round, daily, 9.30am to 4.30pm

Admission free

There were 1,800 men working in this pit in the 1950s, some of them 2,000 feet (610 m) down and 5 miles (8 km) out under the sea. The pit was left derelict when it finally closed in 1986, still with 14 dead miners entombed from a 1927 disaster. Since 1994 a voluntary organisation has been restoring the buildings and the machinery and engines used by the miners. Photos and recordings explain what miners did inside and outside of the pit, and there are some displays about some of the appalling accidents here and in other pits along the coast. It's quite an eerie place and gives a glimpse of the hard life of the miners. The guides are knowledgeable, and they're adding to the collection all the time.

Windermere

★★★ Blackwell

1½ miles (2.4 km) south of Bowness on the B5360
Tel. 015394 46139 or visit *www.blackwell.org.uk*

Open all year round, daily, 10.30am to 5.00pm (4.00pm from November to March)

Admission £5.45, children £2.75

The wonderful 1900 building was created by Mackay Hugh Baillie Scott in the Arts and Crafts style, and it's the best example of his work open to the public. It was built as a holiday home for a rich Manchester brewer – about as perfect an escape from grim industrial life as is possible to imagine. Restored and renovated in 2001 by the Lakeland Arts Trust (also owners of Abbot Hall in Kendal) to house exhibitions and displays and to add original furniture to bring the rooms to life. The craftwork is wonderful, with stained glass windows, exquisite patterned wall coverings and motif stone and woodwork. Lovely fireplaces and inglenooks, with window seats to enjoy the views of Windermere. It's the attention to detail in little things like the door knockers, latches and tiles that make it special. The gardens are terraced to make the most of the views, and you can sit out there with something from the upmarket caff on a nice day. The shop has crafts and books, and there's a regular programme of exhibitions. You can also pick up details of the Arts and Crafts Trail, a recommended tour of other historic and arty places in the Lakes.

★★ The World of Beatrix Potter

The Old Laundry
Tel. 015394 88444 or visit *www.hop-skip-jump.com*

Open all year round, daily, 10.00am to 5.30pm (4.30pm in winter)

Admission £6.00, children £3.00

One of Lakeland's most popular exhibitions, packing them in round the clock, round the year. The pulling power of Beatrix Potter's lovely books is old, but the re-creations of her country-side and characters are much more modern. See Peter Rabbit in his radish patch, Mrs Tiggy-Winkle in her kitchen, Jeremy Fisher in his pond. There are video introductions to Potter and her stories, and the characters will have children squealing with excitement. The crowds mean you can sometimes feels like you're being herded through, but it's all good fun. The Japanese love it, but superior Tate Gallery types without children prefer to inspect the original watercolours at the Hawkshead gallery or the Armitt Collection in Ambleside. Café and souvenir shop.

Windermere Steamboat Museum

Rayrigg Road
Tel. 015394 45565 or visit *www.steamboat.co.uk*

Currently closed; ring or check the website for details of progress

Shut at the time of writing to allow for a major overhaul of both the building and of the museum's dozen or so steamboats, led by the Lakeland Arts Trust after it won a £500,000 grant from the lottery. But it's always been a popular museum for

those disembarking from the Windermere ferries, providing a nice history of transport on the lake. Vessels include *Esperance*, the model for Captain Flint's houseboat in Arthur Ransome's *Swallows and Amazons*; *Osprey*, a fine steam launch that used to take passengers out on the lake; and *Dolly*, thought to be the oldest mechanically powered boat in the world. There are early motor boats, yachts, canoes and Beatrix Potter's rowing boat. The museum has organised exhibitions and steam enthusiasts' events in the past, and promises to do so again once it reopens. No stars as no one knows what it'll look like when it's finished, but we've given it two in the past and it should be better and more popular than ever when it's all done.

Workington

Helena Thompson Museum

Park End Road, just off the A66
Tel. 01900 606155 or visit *www.htmworkington.co.uk*

Open all year round, Tuesday to Sunday, 1.30pm to 4.00pm (from 10.30am in July and August)

Admission free

Yes, even Workington has its own little museum, set in an 18th-century house near Workington Hall. It has been here for years, but a minuscule budget means it doesn't go overboard on promotion (unlike its nuclear neighbour a few miles down the coast), and it's now run by volunteers rather than the borough council as in the past. The house was bequeathed to the people of Workington by Helena Thompson herself, and the museum shows off some of her silver and porcelain. She enjoyed costumes, so there are plenty of those, ranging from the 18th to the 20th centuries. Upstairs there's some interesting local history, charting the rise and fall of Workington as an industrial powerhouse.

CHAPTER ELEVEN

Literary Lakes

On the trail of Wordsworth and the Lake Poets, plus Beatrix Potter, John Ruskin and more literary notables

William Wordsworth

William Wordsworth gave us the Lakes and the Lakes gave us Wordsworth. No one should leave Lakeland without communing with Wordsworth, either by visiting one of his homes in person or remembering in spirit some of the things he wrote. As well as his poetry, he also wrote *A Guide to the Lakes*, a bestseller in its time and still well worth a read today. At the height of his literary fame, as a poet laureate and all that, a vicar is said to have asked him: 'Excuse me, Mr Wordsworth, have you written anything else, apart from your Guidebook?'

It is possible today to put together a very good tour of the Lakes following Wordsworth's life biographically, and plenty of people, including American and Japanese scholars, do so. Here are some of the places most closely associated with him, arranged in chronological order.

★★ Wordsworth House

Main Street, Cockermouth
Tel. 01900 824805 or visit *www.wordsworthhouse.org.uk*

Open Easter to October, daily except Sunday, 11.00am to 4.30pm

Admission by timed ticket £4.90, children £2.60

Wordsworth was born here in 1770, the second of five children of a lawyer who was an agent for the Lowther family. The house, which went with the job, is still the handsomest in Cockermouth. Wordsworth wrote about it in his autobiographical poem *The Prelude*, bathing naked in the local river and chasing butterflies with his beloved sister Dorothy. The house and fine garden are structurally as they were, and after recent research and restoration by the National Trust the interior is presented as it would have looked for the family. There's a working Georgian kitchen, costumed 'servants' and a Discovery Room, with exhibits about the great man. Small shop.

Penrith

Both of Wordsworth's parents came from Penrith, and he spent some time there as a young boy. But his days were not happy: his mother died when he was eight and his father when he was 13. There was no money, as it turned out the Lowther family had not paid his father's wages. His guardians did not like him, considering him wild and unruly, and they separated him from his sister Dorothy. She was sent to live with relations, while William went to board at a little grammar school on the other side of the Lake District.

Nothing Wordsworthian can be seen in Penrith today, though you can climb the Beacon, a hill just outside the town, mentioned in *The Prelude*, which has good views of the Lake District. St Michael's Church in Barton, just before you

Mrs. W. Wordsworth.

reach Pooley Bridge from Penrith, has his grandfather's grave. His grandparents' home is now Arnisons, a magnificently old-fashioned outfitters on Market Square.

★★ Hawkshead Grammar School

No longer a school but open as a museum. The desks and books are laid out just as they were in Wordsworth's time (see Chapter 10).

★★ St Michael and All Angels' Church

Hawkshead

Wordsworth described it as snow white, but it has now been un-whitewashed. The location, perched over the village, is superb, and the interior is varied and interesting.

Ann Tyson's Cottage

Hawkshead
Tel. 015394 36405 or visit *www.anntysons.co.uk*

Wordsworth boarded here with a 'dame' (landlady), who became a substitute mother. You can stay there too, since it's now a smartly converted guesthouse called Ann Tyson's House. Apart from changing its name to Wordsworth Street, the street it's on hasn't changed much – but it's probably a bit more comfy than in his day. Wordsworth also lodged for a while in an unknown building in Colthouse, just outside the village.

Keswick

Wordsworth lived at Old Windebrowe for a short time in 1794 after he had been to Cambridge and France. (He had an illegitimate daughter by a French girl, a fact that was kept secret in his own lifetime.) This was William and Dorothy's first home in the Lakes since their childhood. Here, William nursed his friend Raisley Calvert, who subsequently died, leaving William enough money to be able to concentrate on a career as a poet. The premises are now used by the Calvert Trust, an organisation providing outdoor activities for the disabled, and the Wordsworth room is not usually open to the public. Contact them for access if you're really keen to see it (tel. 017687 72255 or visit *www.calvert-trust.org.uk*). There is a small plaque outside the Robin Hood Inn in King Street, Penrith, where Raisley Calvert died.

★★★ Dove Cottage

Town End, Grasmere
Tel. 015394 35544 or visit *www.wordsworth.org.uk*

Open daily except early January to early February, 9.30am to 5.30pm

Admission to house and museum £6.50, children £4.10

This is the Wordsworth shrine and the main pilgrimage centre for tourists and scholars alike. It has come to symbolise Wordsworth's philosophy of 'plain living and high thinking'. He lived longer at Rydal Mount, but by that time he was past his best as a poet. It was at Dove Cottage that his greatest works were written.

Wordsworth spotted the cottage while he was out on a walk with Samuel Taylor Coleridge. He moved in at Christmastime 1799, with his sister Dorothy. Later he married Mary Hutchinson, and three of their children were born here. He was also joined by Sarah Hutchinson, his wife's sister. Add to that a frequent flow of friends staying at this tiny, seven-roomed house, and things became pretty crowded. They moved out in 1808 to a much larger house, Allan Bank, across the valley but still in Grasmere.

Dove Cottage is much as it was in William and Dorothy's day and is very lovingly cared for by the Wordsworth Trust. The garden has been restored and even the old summerhouse rebuilt. Except during the height of summer, log fires are usually kept burning in the grates, and visitors are offered a chatty and well-informed guided tour. Inside, most of the furniture is Wordsworth's, and the general aim is to keep it the way it was when he lived there. The only jarring note is from a few items that belonged to Wordsworth later in his life but that Dove Cottage got to first. The rivalry between the Wordsworth places can be fierce.

Next to the Cottage is the excellent Wordsworth Museum. Go there first, if you can, because the background to his life will help you get more out of the house tour. During the summer it's best to visit the Cottage early in the day as it gets very, very crowded (though even then you might run into the early-morning coach parties, fresh from their hotels and wanting to blast round the cottage before heading off to Gretna Green). It gets busy on wet days during the school holidays too, as families look for something to do away from

the fells. But if you get the chance to wander around on your own, it's easy to imagine what it must have been like to have lived there.

The adjacent Jerwood Centre, a magnificent Lakeland stone building opened in 2005 by Seamus Heaney, hosts a steady flow of Wordsworth scholars, and there's a shop and restaurant too. It's worth checking for events, because there are frequent author readings and special exhibitions at the museum.

Neither of Wordsworth's other homes in Grasmere is open to the public. Allan Bank can easily be seen from down by the lake as it is above the village, directly under Helm Crag. It is owned by the National Trust but rented privately. The chimneys at Allan Bank smoked too much and Wordsworth fell out with the landlord, so he moved in 1811 to the Old Rectory, opposite St Oswald's Church. It was a cold, damp house, and by 1813 two of William's children had died there, so he and Mary decided to quite Grasmere Vale altogether and move to Rydal.

The vale seethes with Wordsworth associations. William, Mary and Dorothy are buried in St Oswald's churchyard, and they also left some of their 'pet' names on the surrounding landscape. On the road above Town End, walking towards White Moss, there is a field gate that Wordsworth used to call the 'wishing gate', now unromantically covered in barbed wire. Behind the Swan Hotel at the foot of the Dunmail Raise is Greenhead Ghyll, the setting for Wordsworth's poem 'Michael'. Down in the village is the Wordsworth Hotel, emblazoned with a facsimile of his signature and featuring such horrors as the Prelude restaurant and the Dove and Olive Branch bar. (Dove Cottage was originally an inn called the Dove and Olive Bough.) The hotel has no connection of any sort with the poet, and that whirring noise you can sometimes hear in Grasmere churchyard is Wordsworth spinning in his grave.

★★★ Rydal Mount

Rydal, on the A591 between Grasmere and Ambleside
Tel. 015394 33002 or visit *www.rydalmount.co.uk*

Open March to October, daily, 9.30am to 5.00pm;
November to February, daily except Tuesdays, 10.00am to 4.00pm; closed for most of January

Admission £5.00, children £2.00; gardens only £2.50 for adults

Rydal Mount was William's final home until his death in 1850. In his own lifetime it became a poetical shrine to his fans – he would sometimes receive as many as a hundred visitors a day, flocking to the gate in the hope of a glimpse of the great man. He became poet laureate in 1843 and would issue great pronouncements on the purpose and structure of poetry, though he has the distinction of never writing a line of official verse during his laureateship. Rydal Mount is a somewhat grander house than their previous homes, and William and Dorothy both thought they had gone up in the world when they moved in. Once something of a rebel, by now William was a staunch supporter of the old order and had moved well beyond the 'plain living' of Dove Cottage.

Originally a 16th-century farmhouse, Rydal Mount is still owned and lived in by descendants of William. Rather unimpressive from the outside, it is set in beautiful grounds, originally landscaped by William with fine terraces, and a riot of colour in the spring. The house itself contains a lot of his furniture, manuscripts and possessions, and the rooms are nicely restored. When William died, most of the effects were sold off and bought by local people. Over the years, many have gradually been returned to their former homes.

On a fine day Rydal Mount can be lovely, and the magnificent view from the garden has hardly altered since William last saw it. There's more space inside than there is at Dove Cottage, and visitors are fewer, so you get more of a chance to imagine Wordsworth at home and at work. The house hosts regular readings and other events, and there's a shop for your Wordsworth books and souvenirs.

At the bottom of the lane to Rydal Mount, just behind the church, is an area of land called Dora's Field. It was given by William to his daughter, and when Dora died in 1847 he planted daffodils on it in her memory. But these aren't the notorious daffodils that inspired Wordsworth's best known poem – those are to be found in Gowbarrow Park on the west side of Ullswater, through which William and Dorothy passed in 1802. Dora's Field and Gowbarrow Park are both now owned by the National Trust and are freely accessible.

The Lake Poets

Wordsworth gathered about himself quite a circle of other literary notables of the period. They became known as the Lake Poets, though in style there was little connection between them.

Samuel Taylor Coleridge (1772–1834) was the first. As soon as the Wordsworths were installed in Dove Cottage, he moved up to Greta Hall in Keswick, just to be near them. He would often walk over to Dove Cottage for the evening, sometimes coming via Helvellyn. Coleridge was a notable walker and toured the Lakes extensively, often with Wordsworth. In 1802 he made the first recorded crossing of Broad Stand between Scafell and Scafell Pike, a walk that has since become too dangerous to follow without ropes. It makes him Lakeland's first ever recreational rock climber, albeit an unwilling and unwitting one.

Greta Hall was part of Keswick School and is now a privately owned house offering self-catering accommodation (tel. 017687 75980 or visit *www.gretahall.net*). Details of Coleridge's life and work can be found in the nearby Keswick

Museum in Fitz Park. He eventually left his family, took to drugs, lived abroad and then moved to London, where he died in 1834.

In 1803 **Robert Southey** (1774–1843) joined Coleridge at Greta Hall. They were brothers-in-law, and Southey eventually ended up supporting Sarah Hutchinson (Wordsworth's sister-in-law), which perhaps explains his frequent visits to Dove Cottage. Southey hardly wrote any verse directly connected with the area, but he wrote the original version of the Three Bears, a good piece of children's verse about the Lodore Falls and a fine biography of Nelson. He also wrote the first official history of Brazil, and the government of that country paid for the memorial to him that is now in St Kentigern's churchyard in Crosthwaite, Keswick. Southey spent almost all his adult life in the Lakes and, with Wordsworth, made it the centre of English poetry for several decades. He became poet laureate in 1813, replaced by Wordsworth when he died at home in Keswick in 1843.

Thomas de Quincey (1785–1859) is now most famous for writing *Confessions of an English Opium-Eater*, but he also wrote a wonderful book of gossip and memories of Wordsworth, Coleridge and Southey called *Recollections of the Lakes and Lake Poets*. He was an early fan of Wordsworth – although the great man treated him rather badly later in life – and he made three separate attempts to visit his hero at Dove Cottage, coming up all the way from Oxford. Each time his nerve failed him, and he retreated. He finally got there in 1807 and eventually took over the lease on the house when Wordsworth and family moved out. Dorothy made him some curtains and was amazed at the huge quantities of books he installed in the house. He upset the family almost at once by knocking down their summerhouse and cutting down the orchard to let more light into the cottage. Dorothy refused to speak to him after that. The Wordsworths snubbed him further when he began an affair with a local farmer's daughter, whom he eventually married. She came from Nab Cottage, beside the A591 overlooking Rydal Water, and De Quincey moved in in 1829, though he retained Dove Cottage to house all the books. The house is now, rather oddly, a residential English language school.

De Quincey became the second editor of the *Westmorland Gazette*, but got the sack for not going to the office. He was a tenant of Dove Cottage for 27 years, though he only lived there for 15, and the house has several items of interest, including his opium balance (he wrote *Confessions* while he was there) and some fascinating portraits. The house is described very well in *Recollections of the Lakes and Lake Poets*.

John Ruskin

Writer, philosopher, artist, critic, conservationist and champion of many social causes, John Ruskin (1819–1900) first came to the Lakes as a young boy in 1824. Rather precociously, he wrote his first poem about the area, a 2,000-line epic, at the age of 11, and returned often, but it wasn't until 1871, at the age of 52, that he decided to settle in the Lake District. Coniston village has a Ruskin Museum with interesting memorabilia, and there's a monument to him at Friar's Crag on Derwentwater, which bears his quote: 'The first thing which I remember as an event in life was being taken by my nurse to the brow of Friar's Crag on Derwentwater.' His tombstone is in St Andrew's churchyard in Coniston. But the main stop on a Lakeland Ruskin tour is …

★★★ Brantwood

2 miles (3.2 km) southeast of Coniston on the eastern shore of the lake
Tel. 015394 41396 or visit *www.brantwood.org.uk*

Open daily from mid-March to mid-November, 11.00am to 5.30pm; otherwise Wednesday to Sunday, 11.00am to 4.30pm

Admission £5.95, children £1.20; gardens only £4, children £1.20

Ruskin bought Brantwood on the shores of Coniston for £1,500, without even first seeing it. 'Any place opposite Coniston Old Man *must* be beautiful,' he reasoned. What he actually got was 'a mere shed of rotten timbers and loose stone', but he soon transformed it into a beautiful home, stocked with art treasures (particularly the paintings of Turner, of whom he was an early champion) and with magnificent gardens, and he lived there for the last 30 years of his life.

Brantwood is today open to the public in accordance with Ruskin's original wish, and it's is an excellent museum and country house, rivalling other literary Lake District big guns, such as Dove Cottage and Hill Top. The house contains many of Ruskin's paintings and possessions; look out for the Ruskin-designed wallpaper downstairs. There's a video about his life on show that conveys his political messages; he fought hard against the worst aspects of Victorian society and values.

Brantwood's estate of 250 acres (100 ha) has been revived in the spirit of Ruskin, and there are now eight separate gardens as well as trails through pastures and woods. There is a jetty to bring people across the lake to Brantwood by the National Trust's steam yacht *Gondola*, while the Coniston Launch calls in on its cruise of various points around the lake. Brantwood has tea rooms called The Jumping Jenny (named after Ruskin's boat), a good bookshop and the Coach House arts and crafts gallery. There's a year-round programme of guided walks, concerts, talks, readings, exhibitions, craft demonstrations and outdoor plays.

Beatrix Potter

Like a lot of Lakeland 'off-comers', Beatrix Potter was a Londoner, born there in 1866. Her family had connections with Lancashire cotton, and she spent her holidays from the age of 16 in the Lake District, in rented but rather grand houses, around Windermere and Derwentwater. Her parents were genteel, upper middle class Edwardians, and she was educated at home and expected to devote her life to her parents or get married. She found an outlet for her artistic talents in drawing and painting 'little books for children', and encouraged by the family's Lakeland friend, Canon Rawnsley, her first book, *The Tale of Peter Rabbit*, was published in 1901.

Over the next eight years she wrote another 13 tales, mostly while in the Lake District. She bought Hill Top Farm at Near Sawrey in 1905, and in 1913 married William Heelis, a local solicitor. After that, she devoted her life to an increasing number of farms bought with her book royalties and to the preservation of the countryside. She did a great deal to help the work of the National Trust, again with the encouragement of Canon Rawnsley, one of its co-founders.

Beatrix Potter died in 1943. All her property – 15 farms with their Herdwick flocks, many cottages and 4,000 acres (1,620 ha) of land – came to the National Trust. She asked that the Herdwicks, her favourite sheep, should continue to be bred, and that both farms and cottages should have local, reliable tenants. Potter has been the cause of millions of pounds worth of tourism since her death, and interest in her Lake District connections has rocketed again since a film of her life was released in 2006. Yew Tree Farm at Coniston became Hill Top for the purposes of *Miss Potter*, which has some fine shots of the Lake District if you can put up with the Hollywood schmaltz.

★★ Beatrix Potter Gallery

Hawkshead

Contains many of her original paintings (see Chapter 10).

★★★ Hill Top

Near Sawrey
Tel. 015394 36269 or visit *www.nationaltrust.org.uk*

Open Easter to October, daily except Thursday and Friday,
10.30am to 4.30pm

Admission by timed ticket £5.40, children £2.70; entry to
the garden and shop is free when the house is closed on
Thursdays and Fridays; shop and garden open daily from
Easter to Christmas

Beatrix Potter built an extension on the house for her tenant
farmer, but kept the original 17th-century building for her
own use. She wrote many of her books there and sometimes
stayed a few nights, but at no time did she actually live there.
Nearby Castle Cottage became her home after she married
William Heelis.

Hill Top, which contains Beatrix Potter's furniture, is
small and very popular, with about 65,000 people passing
through each year and coaches winding their way up the
narrow lanes. The National Trust tries to protect the building
against erosion from the sheer number of visitors, restricting
opening hours and timing admissions to prevent overcrowd-
ing. It must be one of the very few houses open to the public
where they go to such lengths to restrict visitors. Best to go
early in the morning.

The house is interesting enough, and the cottage garden
is worth inspecting too. There are other Potter-related sights
nearby, including the Tower Bank Arms, which looks pretty
much as it was when she drew it in *The Tale of Jemima
Puddle-Duck*, and the National Trust sometimes runs themed
walks to link them together. You can park at Hill Top, but the
best approach is from Bowness via the Windermere ferry and
the summer shuttle bus service.

James Spedding and Mirehouse

The final major literary home in the Lakes is Mirehouse. It
was once the home of James Spedding, a noted literary figure
of the 19th century and the author of a 14-volume biography
of Francis Bacon. One of his more notable visitors at
Mirehouse was Tennyson, who stayed there while working
on his version of the Arthurian legend. Thomas Carlyle, a
frequent visitor, said it was 'beautiful and so were the ways
of it ... not to speak of Skiddaw and the finest mountains
on earth'.

Spedding's family had other literary connections: his father,
John, spent six years in the same class as William Wordsworth
at Hawkshead Grammar School. Some of Wordsworth's
letters, along with those of Robert Southey and Hartley
Coleridge, can be seen at Mirehouse.

★★ Mirehouse

Near Bassenthwaite Lake, off the A591 4 miles (6.4 km) north of Keswick
Tel. 017687 72287 or visit *www.mirehouse.com*

Open Easter to October, Wednesdays and Sundays, plus Fridays in August, 2.00pm to 5.00pm; gardens, walk and tea room open daily Easter to October, 10.00am to 5.30pm

Admission £4.80, children £2.40; gardens only £2.60, children £1.30

Still in the Spedding family, Mirehouse today is the epitome of the English country manor house. The rooms are delightful, the house historic, and the setting majestic. Very often a pianist is playing, and children are actively encouraged. The Speddings are likely to be on hand to welcome visitors – if so, ask them to let you hear their Tennyson recording – the poet himself reciting 'The Charge of the Light Brigade'. There's all sorts of interesting family memorabilia, and manuscripts, portraits, letters and books show off the literary links.

There's a signposted walk through the gardens and woodlands and by the lake shore. Altogether a house not to miss. The excellent Old Sawmill Tea Rooms are opposite the entrance by the car park.

Ten more literary connections in Lakeland

Most of the key writers of the 19th century seem to have visited the Lake District, and many took on holiday homes or settled there. If you want to explore the connections in more detail, an excellent companion is Grevel Lindop's *A Literary Guide to the Lake District* (Sigma Press).

W.G. Collingwood, writer, artist and archaeologist, lived at Lanehead near Coniston, moving there to be closer to his great friend John Ruskin. He was also friendly with Arthur Ransome, and the house became a location in *Swallows and Amazons*. It's now an outdoor education centre.

Charles Dickens and **Wilkie Collins** toured the Lake District in 1857, describing their travels in *The Lazy Tour of Two Idle Apprentices* (republished by the Echo Library and well worth a read if you can find a copy). They stayed at the Queen's Head Inn at Hesket Newmarket (now called Dickens House and privately owned) and went on an ill-advised expedition to climb Carrock Fell, getting caught in rain and mist. 'Drenched and panting, [he] stands up with his back to the wind, ascertains distinctly that this is the top at last, looks round with all the little curiosity that is left in him, and gets in return a magnificent view of – Nothing!'

The journalist and critic **William Hazlitt** visited Southey at Greta Hall but left in a rush, pursued by visitors, having got himself rather too involved with one of the local girls.

The Liverpool-born poet **Felicia Hemens** lived at Doves Nest in Ambleside. She's not very famous today, but she wrote 'Casablanca', known for its first line, 'The boy stood on the burning deck', which spawned a host of parodies.

The poet **John Keats** came to the area in 1818, visited Rydal Mount to see Wordsworth and climbed up to the waterfalls at Stock Ghyll in Ambleside. He also climbed Skiddaw and described Castlerigg Stone Circle in 'Hyperion II'.

Harriet Martineau, journalist, philosopher and feminist, built The Knoll at Ambleside and lived there for 30 years. She wrote *The Complete Guide to the English Lakes* (but didn't give star ratings to anything). She was a friend of the Wordsworths, and her visitors included Charlotte Brontë, George Eliot and Matthew Arnold.

Norman Nicholson, perhaps the best known writer of the western side of Cumbria, lived all his life in the house where he was born in Millom. His poems, many of them in local

HUGH WALPOLE & HIS DOG BINGO

dialect, and his essays on Cumbria's industries, traditions and people are well worth seeking out. He is buried in St Andrew's churchyard in Millom, and his old house on St George's Terrace is marked by a plaque.

Arthur Ransome went to school in Windermere and the Winster Valley and lived as an adult near Coniston. He based his famous children's stories on local places, and *Swallows and Amazons* amalgamates the lakes of Windermere and Coniston. The Coniston Launch runs a themed cruise of some of the locations.

A frequent visitor to the Lakes, **Sir Walter Scott** was a friend of the Lake Poets. He first came as a guest of Wordsworth and stayed with him at Dove Cottage, but was soon put off by the diet of three meagre meals a day – 'two of which were porridge' – that William thought was in keeping with his ideal of 'plain living'. So he used to climb out of his bedroom window every morning and sneak off to the nearby Swan Inn for a proper breakfast, before returning and getting back into bed as if nothing had happened. Scott used Castle Rock in St John's-in-the-Vale as the setting for his verse romance 'The Bridal of Triermain'.

The novelist **Sir Hugh Walpole** lived at Brackenburn, a house above the southwest shore of Derwentwater on the slopes of Cat Bells. His four famous Herries novels were set in Borrowdale, and the home of Judith Paris can be seen at Watendlath, beside the tarn. Brackenburn is now privately owned.

It's worth noting that not all of the literary visitors to the Lake District liked it. **Daniel Defoe** passed through on a tour of Britain in 1724 and wrote: 'Westmorland is a country eminent only for being the wildest, most barren and frightful of any that I have passed over in England, or even in Wales. Nor were these hills high and formidable only, but they had a kind of unhospitable terror in them … all barren and wild, of no use or advantage either to man or beast.' Tsk.

Literary events and festivals

The Lake District's literary tradition continues, and there's a healthy crop of events through the year, including these.

Words by the Water
This is the biggest of Cumbria's literary festivals, an excellent ten-day long celebration of reading and writing hosted by the Theatre by the Lake in Keswick on the shores of Derwentwater in February and March. There are workshops and exhibitions too (tel. 017687 74411 or visit *www.wayswithwords.co.uk/cumbria*).

Kendal Mountain Book Festival
Part of the town's Mountain Festival, this stages talks by literary climbers, mountaineers and adventurers. It's held

each November (tel. 015397 25133 or visit *www.mountain-film.co.uk*).

Lakeland Festival of Storytelling
Run in Staveley and Ings, in late September in odd-numbered years, by legendary Lakeland storyteller Taffy Thomas (visit *www.taffythomas.co.uk*).

Word Market Festival
Held in Ulverston in the first half of February. The organisation runs workshops and events for south Cumbria all year round (visit *www.word-market.org.uk*).

Wordsworth Trust
The Trust has organised annual winter conferences, summer schools and books festivals at and around Dove Cottage in Grasmere, though the future of these is currently under review. For up to date details, as well as news about the ongoing programme of readings and other events, tel. 015394 35544 or visit *www.wordsworth.org.uk*.

Sedbergh Festival of Books and Drama
The festival, which is held in late August and early September, attracts some big names as well as lesser known local authors. Although it's the wrong side of the M6 for the Lake District proper, Sedbergh is well worth a visit all year round, as it's England's only book town and has plenty of good second-hand bookshops (tel. 015396 20125 or visit *www.sedbergh.org.uk*).

Literary Lunch
This annual event, open to the public, is held to present prizes for the Lakeland Book of the Year. Details from Cumbria Tourism (tel. 015398 22222 or visit *www.cumbriatourism.org*).

CHAPTER TWELVE

Animal Attractions

*Animal parks and the best places to meet
Lakeland's farmyard friends*

Well, if Literary Lakeland can have a whole chapter to itself, why not Animal Lakeland? Assorted animal and fishy attractions are now one of Lakeland's growth industries, so here's our choice of the best places to enjoy real, live animals. You could, of course, wander on the fells and see sheep and rabbits for free, but come on – farmers and conservationists have to make a living somehow. Especially since the foot and mouth crisis of 2001, which prompted many farms to find new ways of bringing in the public to make a few quid.

Many of these places are outside the main tourist areas – a definite advantage when the central Lake District is stuffed to bursting point. Several are open all year too (well, you can't close animals for the winter).

Animal parks

★★★ Lakeland Sheep and Wool Centre

Egremont Road, 1 mile (1.6 km) south of Cockermouth
Tel. 01900 822673 or visit *www.sheep-woolcentre.co.uk*

Open all year round, daily, 9.00am to 5.30pm; four shows
daily from March to October except Friday and Saturday,
at 10.30am, 12.00pm, 2.00pm and 3.30pm

Admission to show £4.50, children £3.50; general
admission to centre free

It's an ugly-looking modern building on the A66 outside
Cockermouth, but rather plush inside. The centre is a mini-
empire with a decent shop, a fairly charmless restaurant
(which seems more like a motorway caff), a reasonably priced
hotel … and an astounding live show. Four times a day in a
300-seat theatre, pedigree sheep and cows strut their stuff on
stage. There are sheepdog, shearing and milking demonstrations, and spectators are invited up on to the stage to meet
the stars afterwards. Hugely entertaining and surprisingly
educational. Don't be put off by the pong. The animals have
a rest on Fridays and Saturdays, though the centre is still
open and you can watch the highlights on video.

★★ Aquarium of the Lakes

Lakeside, Newby Bridge
Tel. 015395 30153 or visit *www.aquariumofthelakes.co.uk*

Open all year round, daily, 9.00am to 6.00pm (5.00pm
from November to March)

Admission £7.50, children £5.00

A specially built water wonderland right by the shore of
Windermere. The idea is to take you on a journey down a
Lakeland river from the mountains to the sea at Morecambe
Bay, showing you lots of fish along the way including
pike, shark and Lakeland's speciality, the charr. There are
more than 30 themed habitats in all, and you dip under
Windermere along the way. Staff are very helpful, and there
are daily talks and a quiz trail for kids. Jolly educational. Café
and shop. You can arrive by boat from Bowness or Ambleside
– buy a combined ticket as you embark – or by steam train
from Haverthwaite.

★★ Lake District Coast Aquarium

South Quay of the harbour, Maryport
Tel. 01900 817760 or visit
www.lakedistrict-coastaquarium.co.uk

Open all year round, daily, 10.00am to 5.00pm

Admission £5.00, children £3.25

Not to be confused with the one at Lakeside, which is a bit more educational. But Maryport's version has a wide range of fish – 2,000, from 200 species, housed in 45 themed displays – and lots of family fun. You can even stroke the bigger fish in the Ray Pool and watch different varieties being fed (four demonstrations daily). There are also a remote control boating pool, outside adventure playground, mini-golf course, café and shop. Unlike Newby Bridge, it has also been featured in a novel, *John Dory*, by John Murray (Flambard Press), about a man who falls in love with one of the fish.

★★ South Lakes Wild Animal Park

Just outside Dalton-in-Furness (follow the brown elephant signs)
Tel. 01229 466086 or visit *www.wildanimalpark.co.uk*

Open all year round, daily, 10.00am to 5.00pm (4.30pm from November to March)

Admission £10.50, children £7.00

Lakeland's only zoo covers just 14 acres (5.6 ha), but it contains well over a hundred different species, many of them walking around naturally on the same paths as you. Well, as naturally as can be expected if you're a lemur living in Cumbria. You'll probably see the giraffes from the main road as you approach – they've given plenty of drivers a shock. There are Sumatran tigers, rhinos, bears and monkeys, among others. It prides itself on being friendly to the animals as well as to the public, and it supports projects around the world to protect endangered species. Before each of the several daily feeding sessions, wardens will talk about conservation and animal treatment. For a suitable donation to the supported projects you can join the staff as a keeper for the day, and the 50p fare for a ride on a miniature train around the site also goes to the adopted projects. Souvenir shop, café and picnic facilities.

★ Eden Ostrich World

Langwathby Hall Farm, Langwathby, 5 miles (8 km) northeast of Penrith on the A686
Tel. 017688 81771 or visit *www.ostrich-world.com*

Open March to October, daily, 10.00am to 5.00pm;
November to mid-February, daily except Tuesdays, 10.00am to 5.00pm

Admission £4.95, children £3.95

On a real farm, which means you can also see sheep, cattle and pigs, plus some rare and exotic breeds. But the big attraction are the ostriches, especially if you can catch chicks hatching. There's a good riverside walk, tea room, picnic area, maze, children's play area and gift shop. No dogs allowed inside, though they helpfully provide kennels in the car park. A nice way to get there is via the Settle to Carlisle train line; Langwathby station is a five-minute walk away.

★ Lake District Osprey Project

Dodd Wood Viewpoint, overlooking Bassenthwaite Lake
Tel. 017687 78469 or visit *www.ospreywatch.co.uk*

Open all year round at any time; ospreys are usually seen only from mid-April to August, when staff are usually on hand daily, 10.00am to 5.00pm

Admission free

After much hard work to coax them in, ospreys have been breeding in the forests around Bassenthwaite lake since 2001. There's no guarantee that they'll be there, but they've been back every year since, usually successfully rearing chicks. The viewpoint at Dodd Wood is hosted by the Lake District National Park Authority, the Forestry Commission and the RSPB, and it's a good spot to watch the ospreys swooping over the lake for fish. If you're in luck and get a good view, the sight is breathtaking. There are high-powered telescopes and helpful staff to tell you all about the birds. A live webcam feed from the nest is relayed to screens at the Whinlatter Visitor Centre.

★ Lakeland Bird of Prey Centre

Within the Lowther estate just outside Askham, 5 miles (8 km) south of Penrith
Tel. 01931 712746

Open April to October, daily, 11.00am to 5.00pm

Admission £6.00

Situated in the walled garden of Lowther Park, with over 150 birds of prey including hawks, eagles, falcons, buzzards and owls. There are flying displays at 1.00pm and 3.00pm, and you can see the birds at other times in their aviaries. Tea room and shop attached.

★ Lakeland Heavy Horse Centre

Dearham, between Cockermouth and Maryport
Tel. 01900 818023 or visit *www.lakesheavyhorses.co.uk*

Open April to October, daily, 10.00am to 4.00pm
(closed Mondays from mid-September to end-October)

Admission £5.45, children £3.45

The visitor centre on a working farm, which shows off some rare breeds of horses, opened with support from DeFRA in 2006. There are demonstrations twice a day, cart and trap rides and an exhibition explaining more about the animals and their role in farming. A Pets Corner offers interaction with other farm animals. Café, children's play area, walking trails and shop.

★ Lakeland Wildlife Oasis

Hale, on the A6 2 miles (3.2 km) south of Milnthorpe
Tel. 015395 63027 or visit *www.wildlifeoasis.co.uk*

Open all year round, daily, 10.00am to 5.00pm

Admission £6.00, children £4.00

This bills itself as 'the Northwest's Favourite Little Zoo', though South Lakes Wild Animal Park might have something to say about that. But it's well worth battling through the school parties to get in. There's a good mixture of live animals and hands-on evolutionary story, with lots of buttons to press. It's good for a wet day because a lot is under cover, including tropical and butterfly halls. It's well set out, despite looking uninspiring from the outside. There's a wild animal area in the grounds.

Like its rival at Dalton, this place is big on conservation and looks after some endangered species as part of international breeding programmes. Friendly staff run regular 'meet the animals' sessions, and for £75 you can shadow them as a keeper for the day. Highlights include giant millipedes, the pygmy marmoset (the world's smallest monkey) and, outside, the 'observation bubble' in the meercat enclosure. Small café and gift shop.

★ The Owl Centre, Muncaster Castle

1 mile (1.6 km) east of Ravenglass on the A595
Tel. 01229 717393 or visit *www.owls.org* and
www.muncaster.co.uk

Open daily except January, 10.30am to 6.00pm or dusk if
earlier

Admission to owl centre, gardens and maze £7.00, children
£5.00; with castle too £9.50, children £6.50

Just one of Muncaster Castle's attractions (see Chapter 13).
The Owl Centre is the headquarters of the World Owl Trust,
a charity promoting owl conservation. It is a breeding centre
and has more than a hundred owls from 50 species, making
it one of the biggest collections in the world, ranging from
the European Eagle Owl, the biggest owl in the world, to the
tiny Pygmy Owl. There's a Meet the Birds display and photo
opportunity every day at 2.30pm, and Heron Happy Hour at
4.30pm. Café and accommodation.

The Alpaca Centre

Snuff Mill Lane, Stainton, Penrith
Tel. 017688 91440 or visit *www.thealpacacentre.co.uk*

Open all year round, daily, 10.00am to 5.00pm

Admission free

Said to be the UK's first alpaca centre, rearing and breeding
these llama-like creatures. Their soft but hard-wearing fleeces
make nice jumpers. You can watch the alpacas from the visitor centre and learn about their history (and how they ended
up in a field in Cumbria). Guided tours are available. Shop,
tea room and gallery.

Open farms and working farms

This is a growth industry in the Lake District, with more and
more farms realising that there's money to be made by opening
their doors to families. They're usually at their best in spring,
when you can see the young animals.

You can also stay on an increasing number of farms in
the Lake District, and many of them will be pleased to show
you around. Bring your wellies and you can probably muck
in with the farmer. See Chapter 4 for some of the best farms
to stay.

★★ Trotters World of Animals

Coalbeck Farm, near Armathwaite Hall at the north end of
Bassenthwaite
Tel. 017687 76239 or visit *www.trottersworld.com*

Open all year round, daily, 10.00am to 5.30pm or dusk if earlier

Admission £6.50, children £4.80

Once a working farm and now an ambitious animal park that has expanded its collection well beyond the usual farm suspects to take in lemurs, monkeys, meercats, zebra, eagles and hundreds more. There are feeding and flying demonstrations and opportunities to get up close to the animals. Even the snakes. Most of the animals have been given names: Charlie the mandrill, Rosie and Hutch the otters and, inevitably, Monty the python.

There's lamb and chick feeding in spring, pony and tractor rides, hawk flying displays and a programme of special events throughout the year, including candlelit evenings in December. It's well managed and big on conservation and advancing people's understanding of the animal kingdom. Tea room, indoor soft play centre, gift shop. Nearby Armathwaite Hall offers plush country house accommodation.

★ Ducky's Park Farm

Flookburgh
Tel. 015395 59293 or visit *www.duckysparkfarm.co.uk*

Closed at the time of writing for refurbishment but due to reopen in 2008; ring or check the website for details of hours and prices

The visitor centre is targeted firmly at children, with plenty of chances to meet the animals. It also aims to educate people about farming methods. They let you get up close to most of the breeds, and children can bottle-feed the young in the spring. Café by the name of Daffy's Diner, picnic and soft play areas.

★ The Gincase Farm Park

Silloth-on-Solway
Tel. 016973 32020 or visit *www.gincase.co.uk*

Open all year round, daily, 10.30am to 4.30pm (closed Mondays from November to Easter)

Admission to farm park £2.50, children £1.50

A big collection of the usual and more unusual farm breeds, all in paddocks to view. It's great for children, who get to feed the lambs and hold the rabbits. Playground. There is also free admission to the craft gallery and very good tea room.

Holme Open Farm

Sedbergh
Tel. 015396 20654 or visit *www.holmeopenfarm.co.uk*

Open by arrangement; telephone to discuss visits

This working farm on the Dales side of Cumbria has lots of different breeds of sheep and cattle, plus goat, ducks, geese and pigs. They specialise in educational visits, explaining about the workings of the farm and encouraging children to hold and feed the animals. Nature trail.

Low Sizergh Barn

Sizergh, near Kendal
Tel. 015395 60426 or visit *www.lowsizerghbarn.co.uk*

Open all year round, daily, 9.00am to 5.30pm
(5.00pm from January to Easter)

Admission free

More of a farm shop and craft gallery than a place to see animals, but there's a 1½ miles (2.4 km) farm trail and the chance to watch the cows being milked from the excellent tea room.

Natland Millbeck Farm

Natland Millbeck Lane, accessed opposite Asda in Kendal
Tel. 015397 31141

Open all year round, daily, 9.30am to 5.30pm

Admission free

A working dairy farm with Holstein Friesians milked twice a day. The big selling point is that they turn the milk into very good ice cream, which is served at a parlour on the farm. Good farm shop too.

Nature reserves

Cumbria Wildlife Trust looks after the county's wildlife in town and country. It manages about 40 nature reserves in Cumbria, from ancient woodlands to pristine coastal areas to peat bogs. South Walney Nature Reserve, which has 30,000 nesting gulls, one of the largest number in Europe, has a visitor kiosk in the summer. For more information on its work and nature reserves tel. 015398 16300 or visit *www.cumbria-wildlifetrust.org.uk*. The trust is also very active in helping to protect the red squirrel, fast disappearing but better protected in Cumbria than just about anywhere. There's a SoS (Save Our Squirrels) campaign going on; add your support and report sightings at *www.saveoursquirrels.org*.

The job of looking after Cumbria's 25 designated National Nature Reserves is done by Natural England (tel. 08456 003078 or visit *www.naturalengland.org.uk*). Bassenthwaite Lake is the most noteworthy of its sites.

CHAPTER THIRTEEN

Homes and Gardens

*Your guide to the best stately homes,
castles, churches, old mills, ancient monuments
and gardens*

Cumbria has plenty of stately and historic delights. As elsewhere in Britain, financial necessity means that many owners
of grand houses have had to open up in recent years and let
the rest of us come in and gape, or have handed them over to
public or other bodies that now care for them. Here are the
best of them.

Homes

★★★ Dalemain

On the A592 south of Penrith towards Pooley Bridge
Tel. 017684 86450 or visit *www.dalemain.com*

Open April to October, Sunday to Thursday, 11.00am to
4.00pm; gardens also open the same days and hours at other
times, except from Christmas to early February

Admission £6.50, children free; gardens only £4.50,
children free

A large, Georgian-fronted house with extensive grounds.
The house itself is medieval, Elizabethan and early Georgian,
added to continuously over the centuries. Fascinating architecturally, it contains family portraits of the Hasells, who
have lived there since 1665. The servants' quarters offer an
idea of life if you weren't born a Hasell. Probably *the* best
house to see in the northern lakes, if you've only got time for
one. There are guided tours of the house in the mornings, and
you're left to roam where you like in the afternoons.

The magnificent garden is famous for its rare trees, shrubs and roses and is especially pretty in late spring or early summer. There's a small museum of agricultural bits and pieces, like turnip bashers, in the 16th-century barn. There's a tea room in the baronial hall. The TV adaptation of *Jane Eyre* in the late 1990s was shot here (in the house and grounds, that is, not the tea room).

★★★ Levens Hall

5 miles (8 km) south of Kendal off the A6
Tel. 015395 60321 or visit *www.levenshall.co.uk*

Open April to early October, Sunday to Thursday, 12.00pm to 4.30pm; gardens and tea room open 10.00am to 5.00pm

Admission £9.50, children £4.50; gardens only £6.50, children £3.50

If Dalemain is the top house in the north Lakes, this is the pick of the south. A magnificent Elizabethan mansion, although it originally began as a Norman pele tower. Some fine paintings, Jacobean furniture and plaster-work to be seen. There's a fascinating fireplace in the south drawing room with carvings depicting the four seasons, the four elements and the five senses. Levens Hall is owned, lived in and run by the Bagot family. It tries hard to be a family attraction, providing lots for kids, including a steam ride on Sundays and bank holidays, and it can be a bit commercial for some tastes, but at least they're trying. Look out for the fabulous wood carving in many rooms, and the collection of bits and pieces owned by the Duke of Wellington and Napoleon Bonaparte.

The stunning topiary gardens were first laid out in 1694 by the French gardener to King James II, Guillaume Beaumont. As well as the magnificent topiary there are all sorts of treats, including a herb and rose garden and a water garden, built to mark the 300th anniversary of Beaumont's original work. There are excellent occasional guided tours; check for times. There's also a gift shop, plant centre and tea room. Look out for Levens' Morocco Ale, brewed to the house's secret recipe since Elizabethan times.

★★★ Muncaster Castle

1 mile (1.6 km) south of Ravenglass on the A595
Tel. 01229 71614 or visit *www.muncaster.co.uk*

Open daily mid-February to early November, 12.00pm to 5.00pm; gardens, maze and owl centre open daily, 10.30am to 6.00pm or dusk if earlier

Admission £9.50, children £6.50; without house £7.00, children £5.00

It may seem strange to have a castle in this section – but blame the Scots, who are indirectly responsible for the architecture of many of Cumbria's historic homes. Like many others, Muncaster is based on a defensive pele tower, built in 1235 to keep them at bay. In the 1860s the fourth Lord Muncaster had it rebuilt into a tasteful mansion, and it's been the ancestral home of the Pennington family for 800 years now. The current generation have contributed to an entertaining audio guide to listen to as you wander round.

The house contains interesting furniture, tapestries and paintings, including some by Reynolds and Gainsborough, and a 6,000-book library. The 77 acres (31 ha) of gardens are magnificent in early summer, when the rhododendrons and azaleas are at their best, especially viewed against the backdrop of the rugged Lakeland fells. One of the finest displays in Europe. There are several marked trails around the grounds. Muncaster is the headquarters of the World Owl Trust and home to its Owl Centre. It's also got a vole maze, shop and tea rooms. A great day out, all in all, and you can even stay over in the former coachman's quarters or nearby self-catering accommodation if you haven't got round everything.

The house is closed in the winter, but the grounds, owl centre and maze remain open, and the castle puts on Darkest Muncaster walks. It prides itself on being one of the most haunted houses in Britain and runs all-night Ghost Sits in the Tapestry Room for private parties.

★★ Conishead Priory

Priory Road, 2 miles (3.2 km) from Ulverston on the A5087 Tel. 01229 584029 or visit *www.conisheadpriory.org*

Open Easter to October, weekends and bank holiday Mondays by guided tour at 2.15pm or 3.30pm only; gardens open daily all year round from dawn to dusk; everything closed for festivals in the last two weeks of May and from mid-July to mid-August

Admission £2.50, children £1.50; grounds and temple free

A 19th-century Gothic priory on the site of a 12th-century Augustinian priory. Since 1976 it has been the home of a Buddhist monastery, lived in by about a hundred members of the Manjushri Mahayana community. The Priory was derelict when they took it over, having been at various times a hotel and then a convalescent home for Durham miners, but they have restored it nicely to its former glory. It's an amazing house, one of the most spectacular in Cumbria, with 100 feet (30 m) octagonal turrets and spires, cloisters, massive stained glass windows in the great hall, and wood panelling. The 70 acres (28 ha) of wooded grounds go down to the shore of Morecambe Bay and house the World Peace Temple, based on a traditional Buddhist design. The Buddhists are very welcoming to visitors and will tell you lots about their way of life. Tasteful, ever so healthy café (open weekends and bank holiday Mondays from 2.00pm to

5.00pm, Easter to October) and small souvenir shop, strong on Buddhist gifts. The centre hosts festivals and courses on Buddhism and meditation; visit *www.manjushri.org* for details.

★★ Holker Hall

Cark-in-Cartmel, on the B5278
Tel. 015395 58328 or visit *www.holker-hall.co.uk*

Open daily except Saturday from April to October, 12.00pm to 4.00pm; gardens 10.30am to 5.30pm

Admission £9.25, children £5.00; gardens only £5.95, children £3.00

An outstanding country house dating back to the 17th century, though largely rebuilt in 1871 after a devastating fire. The site itself used to belong to Cartmel Priory. The house contains some beautiful examples of panelling and wood carving and some rare paintings, including works by Joshua Reynolds and Anthony Van Dyck. It is a magnificent stately home, owned and lived in by Lord and Lady Cavendish but with few of the ropes and restrictions that you usually expect at places like this. The gardens are wonderful, at their best in early summer, and contain what is said to be the oldest monkey puzzle tree in the country.

There's a lot going on at Holker, which can sometimes put you off because it sounds more like a country fair than a stately home. There's a garden festival in May or June, plus Halloween trails, spring and Christmas markets and the like. The café, food hall, gift shop, picnic area and playground either add further to the experience or distract from the house, depending on your viewpoint. If you want to see the house and grounds at their best without the crowds, plan a visit outside the special events.

★★ Hutton-in-the-Forest

Just off the B5305 between Penrith and Wigton
Tel. 017684 84449 or visit *www.hutton-in-the-forest.co.uk*

Open May to September on Wednesdays, Thursdays, Sundays and bank holiday Mondays, 12.30pm to 4.00pm; grounds open daily except Saturdays from April to October, 11.00am to 5.00pm

Admission £6.00, children £3.50; gardens only £3.50, children £1.00

Originally a 14th-century pele tower with 17th-, 18th- and 19th-century additions. It is the home of Lord and Lady Inglewood, and you get the distinct feeling that the occupants are around, which they usually are. Very satisfying architecturally, it is like visiting three stately homes in one. Good gardens with some excellent tree specimens and a very good tea room. The gardens are open most of the year, but the house has some peculiar opening times, and you have to be smart to catch it open. Every late July the grounds host Potfest in the Park, a festival of the work of a hundred or so potters, and there's occasional open-air Shakespeare. There are also regular Gamekeepers' Walks through the grounds.

★★ Sizergh Castle

3 miles (4.8 km) south of Kendal, off the A591
Tel. 015395 60951 or visit *www.nationaltrust.org.uk*

Open April to October, Sunday to Thursday, 1.00pm to 5.00pm; gardens open 11.00am to 5.00pm

Admission £6.70, children £3.30; gardens only £4.50, children £2.20

Home of the Strickland family for 700 years and handed over to the National Trust for safe keeping in 1950. There was an original house on the site, but as the Scots came marauding it was replaced in 1340 with a pele tower, the largest tower in Cumbria still standing. The great hall was added in 1450, and some very fine panelling and carving – some of the best in the country – were added in Elizabethan times. A lovely house. The 1,600 acre (647 ha) estate is crossed by public footpaths, so it's a good place to combine with a walk. The gardens date from the 18th century and include two lakes and a rock garden. The National Trust has inevitably added a shop and tea rooms. A good farm shop, Low Sizergh Barn, and pub, the Strickland Arms, are close by.

★★ Townend

Troutbeck, 3 miles (4.8 km) north of Windermere
Tel. 015394 32628 or visit *www.nationaltrust.org.uk*

Open April to October, Wednesday to Sunday and bank holiday Mondays, 1.00pm to 5.00pm

Admission £3.80, children £1.90

This is a 1626 statesman farmer's home – rather more prosperous than your average farmhouse, though less grand than some of the piles featured here – in an interesting, unspoilt hamlet. Very typical of its period and a nice example of Lake District vernacular architecture. A dark little place (no lights and it sometimes closes early if it's really dark), it has original and surprisingly elaborate furniture and panelling, plus books and papers accumulated over the centuries by the Browne family, who lived here over four centuries until 1943. A real fire burns most days. The small garden is laid out to resemble a photograph of Townend from the late 19th century.

★ Swarthmoor Hall

Swarthmoor Hall Lane, Ulverston
Tel. 01229 583204 or visit *www.swarthmoorhall.co.uk*

Open mid-March to mid-October, Tuesday to Friday at 2.30pm for guided tours; other times by arrangement if staff are available; gardens always open

Admission £3.50, children £2.50

Elizabethan manor house built around 1586. George Fox, principal founder of the Quakers, first came to preach here in 1652 and later married Margaret Fell, whose house it was. The house became the powerhouse of the Quaker movement (Swarthmoor in the USA is named after it). It was bought by the Religious Society of Friends (the Quakers) in 1954 and used for educational and residential purposes. Six rooms can be seen, containing furniture and books – including a 1451 Tudor bible – belonging to Fox and the Quaker movement.

There are also several grand houses with literary connections that are well worth a visit: **Wordsworth House** in Cockermouth, **Rydal Mount** in Rydal, **Mirehouse** near Keswick and **Brantwood** near Coniston. See Chapter 11 for more about these. **Blackwell**, the arts and crafts house near Bowness, is another architectural highlight (see Chapter 10).

Gardens

Most of the above-mentioned homes – notably Dalemain and Levens – have fine gardens that are open to the public, and you can usually get admission to them without having to pay for the house. Details above. Don't miss the gardens at Brantwood and Mirehouse either. But here are several more worth seeing in their own right, even if they don't have a stately home attached.

★★★ Holehird Gardens

1 mile (1.6 km) north of Windermere on the A592

Open daily all year round, from dawn to dusk

Admission free, but donations welcome

The Lakeland Horticultural Society's 10 acres (4 ha) of hillside gardens, lovingly tended to by volunteers since the society bought a plot of land from the Holehird house. There's a vast range of plants, alpines in a glasshouse, herbaceous borders and big rock and heather gardens. National collections of astilbes, hydrangeas and polystichum ferns, if you know what they are. A real gardeners' garden. Society wardens are on hand to guide from Easter to October.

★★ Acorn Bank

Temple Sowerby, 6 miles (9.7 km) north of Penrith on the A66
Tel. 017683 61893 or visit *www.nationaltrust.org.uk*

Open late March to October, Wednesday to Sunday and bank holiday Mondays, 10.00am to 5.00pm

Admission £3.40, children £1.70

Shrubs, roses and an outstanding collection of 250 culinary and medicinal herbs in this small, walled garden, part of the Acorn Bank manor house (not open to the public). Traditional fruit varieties grow in the orchards. There are walks through the gardens to a partially restored watermill. Excellent spring display and occasional events, including a June Newt Watch. Shop and tea room.

★★ Copt Howe

Chapel Stile, Great Langdale
Tel. 015394 37685

Open on selected days from April to July; phone for details of hours and prices

A small but delightful mountain garden crammed with azaleas, rare shrubs, conifers and plantations, plus some unusual plants retrieved from mountain expeditions around the world. It's something of a wildlife sanctuary, and there are stunning views along the valley and up to the Langdale Pikes. Visiting feels like a great adventure, since you have to ring a message line for details of the limited opening times and hope that you're in luck.

★★ Fell Foot Park

Near Newby Bridge at the southern end of Windermere
Tel. 015395 31273 or visit *www.nationaltrust.org.uk*

Open daily all year round, 9.00am to 5.00pm, or dusk if earlier

Admission free (car park charge)

A smashing location with lovely views of the fells and lake frontage. The National Trust has restored the grounds towards their Victorian splendour, and there are displays of daffodils and rhododendrons in spring. It's a good picnic spot, and you can hire boats to take out on the lake, but it can get busy in the summer. There was once a grand house here, but it's long gone. There are a shop and tea room (open mid-March to October, 11.00am to 5.00pm).

★★ Graythwaite Hall

4 miles (6.4 km) north of Newby Bridge along the western shore of Windermere
Tel. 015395 31333 or visit *www.graythwaitehall.co.uk*

Open April to August, daily, 10.00am to 6.00pm

Admission £3.00, children free

There are 12 acres (4.8 ha) of garden, landscaped in 1896 by Thomas Mawson. Marvellous for rhododendrons and azaleas, and there are a Dutch garden and rose garden. Look out for the dogs' cemetery.

★★ Rydal Hall

Rydal, between Ambleside and Grasmere
Tel. 015394 32050 or visit *www.rydalhall.org*

Open daily all year round, 10.00am to 4.00pm

Admission free, but donations welcome in an honesty box by the entrance

The hall itself is mainly Georgian, though parts go back to before 1600. It is now owned by the Diocese of Carlisle, and it is used for conferences and retreats and is not generally open to the public. But there is free access to the gardens, completely rebuilt in 1909 by Thomas Mawson. Visit the waterfalls, much painted by the Early Tourists, and the nearby Grotto, a summerhouse once regularly visited by William Wordsworth. The gardens also have a nice fountain and splendid views over Rydal to the lake. Regular tours are led by the head gardener. There's an ongoing project to restore the landscape to Mawson's original vision and to turn the present tea rooms (also open daily) into a larger visitor centre. The gardens at nearby Rydal Mount, originally landscaped by the greenfingered Wordsworth, are also worth a visit (tel. 015394 33002 or visit *www.rydalmount.co.uk*).

★ Stagshaw Gardens

½ mile (800 m) south of Ambleside on the A591
Tel. 015394 46027 or visit *www.nationaltrust.org.uk*

Open daily April to June, 10.00am to 6.30pm; also open July to October by appointment; send your request and an sae to Property Office, St Catherine's, Patterdale Road, Windermere LA23 1NH

Admission £2.00 by honesty box at the entrance

Rhododendrons, camellias and azaleas, all in 8 acres (3.2 ha) of woodlands. Thoughtfully open to the public when they're at their best in spring. They were set up by Cuthbert Acland, a regional agent for the National Trust, and are maintained as a memorial to him. There are some good walks in Skelghyll Woods next to the gardens. There's very limited parking; instead, park at Waterhead and walk ½ mile (800 m) back.

★ Winderwath Gardens

Temple Sowerby, 5 miles (8 km) east of Penrith on the A66
Tel. 017688 88250

Open March to October, Monday to Friday, 10.00am to 4.00pm, Saturdays, 9.00am to 12.00pm

Admission £3.00, children free

Here are 4 acres (1.6 ha) of private gardens with lots of alpine and Himalayan plants. There are also a vegetable garden, pond area and picnic spot, and second-hand gardening tools for sale.

Other gardens

Another way of seeing well laid-out formal gardens is to visit some of the larger former country houses. **Brockhole**, for instance, has 30 acres (12 ha) of terraced garden and grounds laid out by Thomas Mawson, which can be accessed for free via the Lake District National Park Visitor Centre. There are also some good grounds adjacent to some of the grander hotels: at the **Langdale Chase Hotel** between Windermere and Ambleside and the **Storrs Hall Hotel**, 3 miles (4.8 km) south of Bowness.

Another good way of visiting lots of gardens not normally open to the public is provided by the National Gardens Scheme. Each year it publishes a brochure of gardens open on selected days, with comprehensive details of dates, charges, what you can see and whether you can get a cup of tea. Money raised on these days goes to various good causes, and 50 or so gardens take part. The brochure is available from gardens, garden centres and TICs or from the NGS direct (tel. 01483 211535 or visit *www.ngs.org.uk*).

There are several big gardening events in the Lake District calendar. The Ambleside Daffodil and Spring Flower Show in late March; the Holker Hall garden festival in late May or early June; the Lakeland Rose Show in Kendal in mid-July; and the Westmorland Horticultural Society's summer and autumn shows in Kendal in July and September are among the highlights.

Castles

There are quite a few castles dotted about the Lake District, many of them designed to repel the onslaughts of the marauding Scots. Some are little more than pele towers, others are follies or neo-Gothic mansions, and many are romantic ruins. Admission is free and access available at any time unless otherwise stated, usually because there's not much left to see.

★★★ Carlisle Castle

Tel. 01228 591922 or visit *www.english-heritage.org.uk*

Open April to September, daily, 9.30am to 5.00pm, October to March, daily, 10.00am to 4.00pm

Admission £4.20, children £2.10

Carlisle is Cumbria's best castle by far, looking dark, grim and foreboding like a castle should – not like your soft and fancy turreted southern castles. It has a stirring history, with Mary Queen of Scots and Bonnie Prince Charlie connections. Visit the prison rooms to find the graffiti and the licking stones where prisoners desperate for moisture licked the walls. It also houses the excellent Border Regiment Museum (admission free with castle ticket).

★★ Brougham Castle

1 mile (1.6 km) southeast of Penrith on the A66
Tel. 017688 62488 or visit *www.english-heritage.org.uk*

Open April to September, daily, 10.00am to 5.00pm

Admission £3.00, children £1.50

A well-preserved ruin of an important castle built within the ramparts of a Roman fort. It's one of the many castles restored by Lady Anne Clifford and the place where she died in 1676. You can climb the keep, but it's steep. There's a good introductory exhibition. The best of Cumbria's many ruined castles.

★ Brougham Hall

1 mile (1.6 km) south of Penrith, just off the A6
Tel. 017688 68184 or visit *www.broughamhall.co.uk*

Open daily all year round, 9.00am to 6.00pm, or dusk if earlier

Admission free, but donations welcome (they suggest £3.00 or £1.50 for children)

Looks like a castle, feels like a castle, but really a stately home. It dates back 500 years and was once the home of Lord Brougham, Lord Chancellor. He received so many royal visitors over the years that it was known to Victorians as the Windsor of the North. It now houses various small craft-type businesses and a small museum while it is restored by an enthusiastic and hard-working charity.

★ Wray Castle

2 miles (3.2 km) south of Ambleside on the B5286

Future opening hours to be confirmed; contact the National Trust for up-to-date details (tel. 015394 35599 or visit *www.nationaltrust.org.uk*)

Not really a castle, but a Victorian folly that is now owned by the National Trust. The grounds have been open to the public for a while, but the house had been closed for years until the ground floor was opened up in summer 2007. Beatrix Potter stayed here on her first visit to the Lake District at the age of 16, and she later bought most of the land surrounding the building, though she never owned the castle itself. The grounds are very pleasant; look out for the mulberry tree planted by Wordsworth. There are delightful lakeside walks with spectacular views.

Brough Castle

8 miles (13 km) southeast of Appleby off the A66

The Normans and Romans both built defences here. It was restored by Lady Anne Clifford but fell into disrepair after her death, and is now a ruin, though the keep, gatehouse and tower are reasonably well preserved.

Cockermouth Castle

Part ruined, part lived in and very rarely open to the public, except occasionally during the Cockermouth festival. There's a good view of the walls from beside the river.

Dalton Castle

Market Place, Dalton-in-Furness
Tel. 01524 701178 or visit *www.nationaltrust.org.uk*

Open Saturdays, Easter to September, 2.00pm to 5.00pm

Admission free, but donations welcome

The pele tower was built by the monks of Furness Abbey as protection against the Scots. Now it's looked after for the National Trust by the Friends of Dalton Castle. Displays of armour and painter George Romney inside.

Egremont Castle

Not far from the main street and on top of a mound with views over the town. There's some stylish herringbone masonry on what's left of it. The keep is 12th century.

Kendal Castle

The ruin is perched in the park on a hill above the eastern side of the town. It's an impressive stone-built affair and 800 years old. Once home to Catherine Parr, the last wife of Henry VIII. There are great views across Kendal.

Kirkoswald Castle

7 miles (11.3 km) north of Penrith on the B6413

The ruined tower is in a farm field to the southeast of the village. One of a group of castles built to deter the Scots from penetrating south and east through Millerstang and Stainmore. You can glimpse it from nearby footpaths, but access is prohibited because it's in a dangerous condition.

Lowther Castle

South of Penrith off the A6
Tel. 01931 712577 or visit *www.lowther.co.uk*

No public access, but you glimpse it as you drive through
Lowther Park between Lowther and Askham. Built in the early
19th century but dismantled in the 1950s after the Lowthers
moved out. It is now a shell, but there are ambitious plans to
eventually restore it to former glories.

Pendragon Castle

4 miles (6.4 km) south of Kirkby Stephen on the B6259

There are Arthurian connections all over Cumbria, and
Pendragon was reputedly founded by Arthur's father. Rebuilt
in the 14th and 17th centuries, it's now a ruin. The landowner
allows access, but take care exploring because it's in poor
condition.

Penrith Castle

Open daily, all year round, 7.30am to 9.00pm
(4.30pm in winter)

The ruins are opposite the railway station in the public park.
A favourite dwelling of Richard III when he was Warden of
the West Marches. The sandstone ruins give off a fine glow as
the sun goes down.

Piel Castle

Piel Island, off the coast by Barrow-in-Furness

Originally built by the monks of Furness Abbey to protect their harbour from the Scots. The ruins are impressive, especially when viewed from the mainland. Access is only restricted by whether you can get to the island. Boats go there from Roa Island during the summer, subject to tides and weather. Contact John Cleasby on 01229 475770 or 07798 794550 for details of his services.

See also **Sizergh Castle** and **Muncaster Castle** in this chapter's section on stately homes – because that's what we think they are.

Mills

There seems to be a little growth industry in Cumbrian mills, with several being renovated and reopened in the last few years, either as museums or working mills following centuries-old systems. They're great to look at and listen to, and best of all for families, many of them do first-class teas and cakes. Here are a few of the best mills open to the public, each offering more than just a glimpse of a turning wheel or two.

★ Eskdale Mill

Boot, Eskdale
Tel. 019467 23335

Usually open April to September, 11.30am to 5.30pm, but may be closed on Mondays; ring in advance if you're planning a special visit

Admission £1.50, children 75p

This water-powered mill is in a fantastic setting, close to the Eskdale end of the Ravenglass railway. Owned for a while by Cumbria County Council, it's now looked after by the Eskdale Mill and Heritage Trust. Two watermills and their wooden machinery run most days, and there are displays to tell you what's going on. Enthusiastic volunteers are often on hand to tell you about the mill too. It's awaiting a licence to run on a commercial basis.

★ Gleaston Watermill

Off the A5087 south of Ulverston
Tel. 01229 869244 or visit *www.watermill.co.uk*

Open all year round, Tuesday to Sunday and bank holiday Mondays, 10.30am to 5.00pm

Admission £2.50, children £1.50

There have been watermills here for 600 years, though the present building dates from 1774. It's one of three mills that served the now ruined Gleaston Castle. Commercial milling stopped in 1948, but the 18 foot (5.5 m) wheel has been lovingly restored over 16 years by Mike and Vicky Brereton. If the interpretation displays seem a bit worthy, remember that she was a maths teacher, he a computer consultant. Shop, excellent traditional tea room called Dusty Miller's, and you can stay over in a converted pig sty; they say it retains many original features.

★ Little Salked Watermill

1 mile (1.6 km) from Langwathby off the A686
Tel. 017688 81523 or visit *www.organicmill.co.uk*

The mill centre is open daily all year round except January, 10.30am to 5.00pm; tours of the mill are held at 12.00pm, 2.00pm and 3.30pm daily except Wednesdays and Saturdays

Admission by guided tour £3.50, children £1.50

An 18th-century, water-powered corn mill, fully working and producing a large and increasingly famous range of organic stone-ground flour. They do guided tours, run cookery courses and sell terrific homemade food in the shop.

Heron Corn Mill

Beetham, off the A6
Tel. 015395 65027 or visit *www.heronmill.org*

Ring or check website for opening hours and admission prices

There was a mill on this site as far back as 1220, grinding corn for Conishead Priory, and as recently as the 1950s. Today it's looked after by a working charity that runs a local arts programme. The mill was closed to visits for major refurbishment in 2007, funded by the lottery among others, but is due to open again to the public in 2008.

The Watermill Café, Priest's Mill

Caldbeck
Tel. 016974 78267 or visit *www.watermillcafe.co.uk*

Open all year except early January to mid-February, daily, 9.00am to 5.00pm (4.30pm from November to early January)

Priest's Mill was built by a Caldbeck vicar in 1702 and was used to grind corn for more than 230 years. It was then used as a sawmill in a workshop until floods wrecked it in 1965. A restoration project in the 1980s involved returning the 14 foot (4 m) wheel to working order, and it now gives its name to a very good and popular upmarket café in the main building.

Churches

Cumbria has one cathedral, several abbeys in various states of repair and a host of interesting churches. They tend not to be as ornate or rich as southern churches, either outside or in. Many of them, especially near the border, were semi-fortified to repel raiders, but they are all rich in history and archaeological interest. Listing all of them would take up the rest of the book, so here are ten of the most famous and interesting. Unless opening times are given, access is usually daily during daylight hours and free, though donations are always welcomed.

★★★ Carlisle Cathedral

Tel. 01228 548151 or visit *www.carlislecathedral.org.uk*

Open all year round, daily, 7.30am to 6.15pm
(5.00pm on Sundays)

Begun as an Augustinian church in the early 12th century and promoted to the ranks of cathedrals in 1133 – the only Augustinian house in England to achieve this. It's also one of the country's smallest cathedrals, but it has a magnificent east window, one of the best in England. The west end and transepts are the earliest parts. Most of the decorative features were rebuilt following a fire in 1292. The Civil War took some toll on the structure, and it had to wait until Victorian times for a decent restoration. Don't miss the 15th-century paintings behind the choir stalls, or the carved altarpiece, the Brougham Triptych. Shop. Opposite the main entrance is the Prior's Kitchen in the monks' old dining hall, and a good bookshop is attached.

★★ Cartmel Priory

Visit *www.cartmelpriory.org.uk*

Open all year round, daily, 9.00am to 5.30pm (3.30pm in winter)

Founded by William Marshall, the baron of Cartmel, in the late 12th century. There's now nothing remaining of the priory except the gatehouse, which is looked after by the National Trust (see Chapter 10), and the church, which has been restored several times. As a result, it's a collection of styles, but no less enchanting for that. The east window is 15th century, and the best feature is the carved oak miserichords, with some delightful mermaids, apes, elephants and uni-corns. A very quiet, impressive church.

★★ Furness Abbey

Between Barrow-in-Furness and Dalton-in-Furness, close to the hospital

Tel. 01229 823420 or visit *www.english-heritage.co.uk*

Open April to September, daily, 10.00am to 5.00pm;
October to March, Thursday to Sunday, 10.00am to
4.00pm

Admission £3.50, children £1.80

Mentioned by Wordsworth in *The Prelude*, but now a ruin in
the care of English Heritage. The remains are very impressive,
some parts almost at their original height. It dates from around
1127, and the layout can be clearly seen in sections. The
walls rear overhead, and you get a powerful feeling of the
monastery's size and influence. There's a visitor centre, and
audio guides are available on request.

★★ Lanercost Priory

2 miles (3.2 km) northeast of Brampton
Tel. 01697 73030 or visit *www.english-heritage.org.uk*

Open April to September, daily, 10.00am to 5.00pm;
October to March, Saturday and Sunday, 10.00am to
4.00pm

Admission £3.00, children £1.50

Sandwiched between Brampton and Hadrian's Wall, this was
an easy target for the Scots (more so than for the tourist).
Edward I called in quite often. The nave is now used as the
parish church, and the ruins are surprisingly intact, almost
as impressive as Furness.

★ Mosedale Quaker Meeting House

Visit *www.northcumbria.quaker.eu.org*

The Quakers have strong roots in Cumbria, dating back to
George Fox's early years (see the entry on Swarthmoor Hall
in this chapter). In 1653 he came to preach at Mosedale, a
tiny hamlet south of Caldbeck, and later a Meeting House
was built there, which still stands today. It's been exquisitely
restored, and although small and humble with just one room,
it's well worth stopping for – especially during July and
August, when volunteers serve rather nice teas.

★ Shap Abbey

1 mile (1.6 km) west of Shap
Visit *www.english-heritage.org.uk*

Founded in 1180. One of the few Premonstratensian abbeys
standing. In a nice setting, you come across it unexpectedly.
The tower is the only part relatively intact, though you can
still see the layout. It's looked after by English Heritage,
which allows free access at any time. If you want to see some
of the stones that were once part of the abbey, look closely at
Lowther Castle.

★ St Bega's

Bassenthwaite, just off the A591
Visit *www.stbega.org.uk*

In a stunning location by the lake, with Skiddaw looming. It dates back to 950, and the font is thought to be 14th century, though much of the church was rebuilt in the 1870s. There are plenty of literary links thanks to Mirehouse, a short walk away.

★ St Mary's

Wreay, 5 miles (8 km) south of Carlisle
Visit *www.stmaryswreay.org*

This is worth visiting to wonder at its incongruity. Built in the 1840s, it was designed by Sarah Losh as a memorial to her parents and sister. Because they had enjoyed travelling in Italy, she based it on a Roman basilica, full of columns, ornaments and religious symbolism.

★ St Olaf's

Wasdale Head

It has a few rivals laying claim to the title, but this is certainly one of the smallest churches in England, with six pews down each side. It's also one of the best located, sheltered by trees in one of the most beautiful valleys in the Lake District, with fells rising steeply all around. The church is probably 16th or 17th century, but the roof is thought to have been made from a Viking longship. There's a window honouring the war dead of the Fell and Rock Climbing Club, and the graveyard has bodies of climbers killed on the fells.

Holme Cultram Abbey

Abbeytown, just east of Silloth on the B5302

Not currently open to the public

The little hamlet on the west coast gets its name from the abbey, and the houses got their stone from its remains. Founded in 1150 by Cistercian monks from Melrose Abbey, it was largely destroyed by the dreaded Scots, most notably and comprehensively by Robert the Bruce. The remains have served in recent times as the parish church, but a fire started by an arsonist destroyed the roof and devastated much of the interior in 2006. A major restoration is planned, and a big fund-raising campaign is under way.

Other churches

Almost every town or village in the Lakes has a church of some interest, although some are little more than a stone cabin. Some are very remote, while others in the towns provide perfect escapes from the noise and bustle on busy days. Except for in Grasmere, where everyone is searching for the Wordsworth graves, their churchyards are usually completely ignored. Here are some more of our favourite parish churches and churchyards.

St Mary's, **Ambleside**: interesting memorabilia on Wordsworth, Matthew Arnold and W. Forstep

St Martin's, **Bowness**: excellent stained glass window

St Martin's, **Brampton**: windows by Edward Burne-Jones and William Morris

St James's, **Buttermere**: plaque to Wainwright within sight of his beloved Haystacks

St Anthony's, **Cartmel Fell**: marvellous isolation

All Saint's, **Cockermouth**: large, Victorian sandstone and a Wordsworth window

St Andrew's, **Dacre**: four amazing bears at each corner of the churchyard

St Catherine's, **Eskdale**: lovely riverside location

St Oswald's, **Grasmere**: follow the crowds to THE grave

St Michael and All Angels', **Hawkshead**: brilliant views

St Michael's, **Isel**: perfect little Norman church

Holy and Undivided Trinity, **Kendal**: a wide, spacious church with a 13th-century nave; usually known more simply as the parish church

St John's, **Keswick**: lovely views

St Kentigern's, Crosthwaite, **Keswick**: the graves of Robert Southey and Canon Rawnsley

St Michael's, **Lowther**: a fine spot in the Lowther estate and memorials to several generations of the family

St Mary's, **Rydal**: Wordsworth was churchwarden here for a while

St James', **Whitehaven**: a spectacular Georgian interior

Ancient monuments

There are loads of good archaeological sites in Cumbria, but for many you'd need a magnifying glass and a portable archaeologist to get anything out of them. Here are the monuments and stone circles where you can actually see something. All are openly accessible unless otherwise stated.

★★★ Bewcastle Stone Cross

One of the oldest and most magnificent crosses in Europe, even if it's lost its head. In the churchyard of the village (north of Hadrian's Wall and only just in Cumbria), it is a beautifully carved sandstone cross, 1,300 years old and over 13 feet (3.9 m) high. Covered with incredible carvings. Amazing that it is still left outside, exposed to all weathers, and not indoors at the British Museum. The cross and the church of St Cuthbert's stand within the ramparts of a Roman fort.

★★★ Birdoswald Roman Fort

7 miles (11.3 km) east of Brampton, off the B6318
Tel. 016977 47602 or visit *www.english-heritage.org.uk*

Open April to October, daily, 10.00am to 5.30pm (4.00pm
in October)

Admission £4.10, children £2.10

The best Roman site in Cumbria, with decent remains to be
seen in situ. There's the fort itself, where 1,000 or so Roman
soldiers might once have been based, and good chunks of
Hadrian's Wall, which is now a World Heritage Site. Looked
after by English Heritage, which also provides a visitor centre
with some of the findings from excavations, and a café and
shop. It's a good point to join Hadrian's Wall for a walk.

★★ Castlerigg Stone Circle

Just off the A591 before you reach Keswick from the south

A fantastic, atmospheric setting, surrounded by high fells,
though the stones themselves are not very impressive: 38 of
them in a circle, roughly 90 feet (27 m) across. Thought to be
3,000 to 4,000 years old. Like the economy, no one can
explain it.

★★ Gosforth Cross

Another sandstone cross, this one Viking and over 12 feet
(3.7 m) high. Tall and slender, it looks frighteningly fragile
and is covered with mythological heroes and Viking legends.
It was probably carved in the 10th century. Situated in St
Mary's churchyard at Gosforth, on the west coast by Wasdale.

★★ Hardknott Roman Fort

Near the top of the Hardknott Pass, on the left as you go up
from Eskdale

You can easily miss the fort from the road. There's not a lot to
see compared to Birdoswald, but it's a dramatic site guarding
the road between the Galava and Glannaventa (Ravenglass)
forts. The parade ground is fascinating and the views fantastic.
The walls still stand, though not very high. The Roman name
was Mediobogdum, and it gives a wonderful idea of why the
Romans came to a grinding halt in these far-flung places. It's
looked after by English Heritage, but access is free at any time.

★★ Long Meg and Her Daughters

½ mile (800 m) from Little Salked, just north of Penrith

Long Meg is the tallest of the 68 stones, about 10 feet (3 m)
high and covered with mysterious symbols. The circle of
other stones – her Daughters – is huge, nearly 300 feet (90 m)

wide. It probably dates from around 1500 BC. Off the beaten track, but an incredible place. Wordsworth was impressed:

> *A weight of awe, not easy to be borne*
> *Fell suddenly upon my spirit – cast*
> *From the dread bosom of the unknown past*
> *When first I saw that family forlorn.*

★ Galava Roman Fort

The remains of a Roman fort at Waterhead, just south of Ambleside. The old local name is Borrans Fort. The foundations remain and the original fort probably dates from around AD 79. To get a really good view of the layout, climb Todd's Crag on Loughrigg and look down on it. Ambleside's Armitt Collection (see Chapter 10) has some of the findings from excavations.

★ Irton Cross

A near perfect cross, 10 feet (3 m) high and more than a thousand years old. Intricately decorated with Runic inscriptions and patterns. It stands in the churchyard of St Paul's in Irton, just north of Ravenglass near Santon Bridge.

★ Mayburgh Henge

Just off the A6 1 mile (1.6 km) south of Penrith

A circular bank up to 20 feet (6 m) high and 300 feet (90 m) across, with a single monolith about 10 feet (3 m) high perched in the middle. Probably built around 2000 BC and most mysterious.

★ Roman Bath House, Ravenglass

Tucked away down a leafy track from the village, this is a real surprise – the walls still stand 13 feet (4 m) high. Now that's some bathroom. Very little remains of the substantial fort it served. There's an excellent Roman museum further up the coast at Maryport (see Chapter 10).

Finally, an oddity. ★★ **The Bowder Stone** is one of Lakeland's most famous features – an isolated rock, 30 feet (9 m) high and weighing a couple of thousand tonnes. It appears to be balanced precariously, away from the rock face, overlooking the valley. How it got there, no one knows. A ladder allows you to walk to the top. It is perfectly safe, but just try walking under the overhanging sides – quite unnerving. Located in the Borrowdale Valley along the B5289, with a nearby car park and well-marked footpath to it.

CHAPTER FOURTEEN

People, Customs and Phrases

Famous residents and visitors, some Cumbrian curiosities and how to understand the natives

Residents and visitors

Apart from all those Big Literary Names, from Wordsworth to Potter, who will forever be associated with the Lake District, there are quite a few more from different walks of life whose names you might come across while you're exploring Cumbria. Here's a brief selection.

Joe Bowman

The huntsman of the Ullswater hounds from 1879 to 1924, he died in 1940, aged 90. Smart hunting folks maintain that he was a better breeder than John Peel, though he is remembered only in local Cumbrian hunting circles.

Mary of Buttermere

Or the Maid of Buttermere. Mary Robinson, the beautiful daughter of an inn-keeper, was wronged by a blackguard who bigamously married her in 1802. Her case became the talk of the nation, was turned into a West End melodrama and was mentioned by Wordsworth in *The Prelude*. She is buried in Caldbeck Church. Also celebrated in a novel by Melvyn Bragg: *The Maid of Buttermere* (Sceptre).

Lady Anne Clifford

High Sheriffess of the County of Westmorland, Lady Anne (1590–1676) owned vast estates, including the castles of Appleby, Brougham and Pendragon, and she was responsible for restoring many of them. She also founded hospitals and charities, and is now seen as an early feminist heroine. There's a trail around Yorkshire and Cumbria in her honour (see Chapter 9).

The Lowthers

Cumbria's ruling family. For 400 years they have been the most dominant, wealthiest and most innovative family in the whole region, though their ancestral home, Lowther Castle near Askham, is now empty, a romantic ruin. At one time they were like feudal kings in Cumbria, lords of all they surveyed. Wordsworth's father worked for them, and Wordsworth himself, having started off hating them, became very keen to have their patronage and friendship. They were behind the industrial mining and shipping development of West Cumbria from the 18th century. Throughout Cumbria today you will see references to the Lowther family, in street names, shops, cinemas and now in horse trials and a country park. The fifth earl, an eccentric spendthrift, was passionate about sport and gave his name to the famous Lonsdale Belt for boxing. He was also passionate about the colour yellow and made all his servants wear yellow livery. The Automobile Association, for whom he was first president, took their colour from him. To this day Cumbrian Tories at election time always sport yellow, not blue as elsewhere in the land. The seventh earl, James Lowther, died in 2006. His eldest son, Hugh, inherited his title as the eighth earl but got none of the family fortune, his father having apparently struck him out of his will in later life. The Lowther estate and fortune, thought to be worth more than £300 million, is now the subject of some complex litigation.

Joss Naylor

This Wastwater farmer and fell-runner extraordinaire set and still holds many unbelievable records for stamina, including a little jaunt to celebrate his 60th birthday: non-stop over

60 summits, each over 2,500 feet (762 m), 100 miles (160 km) with 40,000 feet (12,192 m) of ascent.

John Peel

Huntsman and a legend in his lifetime, if only a local one, for his passion for the hounds, John Peel (1777–1854) was born and lived in the Caldbeck area. He devoted all his energies to his hounds, often at the expense of his own family. A much more selfish, unattractive figure than his legend might suggest, though he has been adopted as a hero of those who opposed the recent ban on fox hunting. The famous song that commemorates him – now a sort of unofficial Cumbrian national anthem – was never heard by Peel himself, since the words were put to the present tune 15 years after his death. He died in 1854 and is buried in Caldbeck churchyard.

Canon Rawnsley

Of Crosthwaite Church, Keswick. Canon Rawnsley (1851–1920) was a founder of the National Trust and one of Lakeland's great activists and preservationists. He was a friend of Beatrix Potter and loved bonfires and hated rude postcards.

Will Ritson

An innkeeper at Wasdale Head, Will Ritson (1808–90) claimed to be a personal friend of Wordsworth and De Quincey. He was also renowned as the biggest liar in England. An annual competition is still held in West Cumbria to find the biggest liar of the year (see Chapter 15).

Wonderful Walker

The Rev. Robert Walker (1709–1802), curate of Seathwaite in the Duddon Valley, was known throughout Lakeland for his care and kindness. Despite living on a pittance all his life, he gave endlessly to the poor. He was written about by Wordsworth in his Duddon sonnets.

And here's a roll-call of more people who were born, died or lived for some time in the Lake District …

Robert of Eaglesfield (near Cockermouth): the founder of Queen's College, Oxford, 1340

Sir George Downing: the MP for Carlisle, 1656, gave his name to Downing Street

Catherine Parr: the sixth wife of Henry VIII lived in Kendal, 1512

Thomas Lawson (1630–91): a Westmerian Quaker, teacher and botanist

George Fox: the founder of the Quakers, lived in Ulverston, 1670–75

George Romney (1734–1802): the artist was born in Dalton-in-Furness and died in Kendal; he was buried in Dalton

Sir John Barrow: the explorer and founder of the Royal Geographical Society was born in Ulverston in 1764

Fletcher Christian: the *Bounty* mutineer was born in Cockermouth in 1764

John Dalton: the atom theorist was born in Eaglesfield, Cockermouth, in 1766

James Boswell: the biographer of Dr Johnson was Recorder of Carlisle, 1788–90

William Wordsworth (1770–1850): the poet was born in Cockermouth and died in Rydal

Samuel Taylor Coleridge: the poet lived in Keswick, 1800–10

Robert Southey: the poet lived in Keswick, 1803–43

Thomas De Quincey: the writer lived in Grasmere, 1803–30

William Wilberforce: the abolitionist lived in Windermere, 1780–88

John Peel (1776–1854): the huntsman was born and died in Caldbeck

John Wilson: alias Christopher North, writer, lived in Windermere, 1807–15

Percy Bysshe Shelley: the poet lived in Keswick, 1811–12

Dr Thomas Arnold: the headmaster retired to Ambleside, 1834–42

Samuel Plimsoll: MP and creator of the Plimsoll line on ships was born in 1824 and brought up in Penrith

Matthew Arnold: the poet (son of Thomas) lived in Ambleside, 1834–42.

Harriet Martineau: the writer lived in Ambleside, 1844–76

W.E. Forster: the educational reformer lived in Ambleside, 1850

John Ruskin: writer, artist and much more lived in Coniston, 1871–1900

Sir Arthur Eddington: the first public supporter of Einstein's theory of relativity was born in Kendal in 1882

Stan Laurel: the comedian and one half of Laurel and Hardy was born in Ulverston in 1890

Beatrix Potter: the children's writer lived in Sawrey, 1906–43

Ben and **Winifred Nicholson:** the artists lived in Brampton in the 1920s

Arthur Ransome: the children's writer lived in Coniston, 1930–67

Sir Hugh Walpole: the novelist lived by Derwentwater, 1932–41

Lord (Norman) Birkett: the judge was born in Ulverston in 1883

Kurt Schwitters: the German artist lived in Ambleside and died in Kendal in 1948

Kathleen Ferrier (1912–53): the singer lived in Silloth and Carlisle

Norman Nicholson (1914–87): the poet was born, lived and died in Millom

George MacDonald Fraser: the writer was born in Carlisle in 1925

Lord (Willie) Whitelaw (1918–99): the Conservative politician lived near Penrith

Ken Russell (b. 1927): the film director had a home in Borrowdale

A. Wainwright: the one and only lived in Kendal, 1941–91

Lord Hoyle: the scientist lived near Ullswater in the 1970s and 1980s

Margaret Forster: the writer was born in Carlisle in 1938

Melvyn Bragg: the author and broadcaster was born in Wigton in 1939

Chris Bonnington: the mountaineer has lived in Caldbeck since 1974

Doug Scott: the mountaineer has lived near Carlisle since 1982

Anna Ford: the broadcaster was brought up in Wigton and Brampton

Desmond Bagley: the thriller writer was born in Kendal

Geoffrey Kendal: the Shakespearean actor and father of Felicity was born in Kendal and changed his name to his place of birth

Jancis Robinson: the wine buff was educated in Carlisle

Eddie Stobart: the nation's greatest, best dressed transport firm is based in Carlisle

… and some famous people who have dropped in over the centuries.

Agricola: the Roman governor led a campaign in Cumbria in AD 79

St Cuthbert: the bishop and missionary visited Carlisle and district in 685

David I, king of Scotland: died in Carlisle in 1153

Edward I, the Hammer of the Scots: died in Burgh-by-Sands in 1307

Robert the Bruce: plundered Cumbria in 1314

Mary Queen of Scots: was imprisoned in Carlisle Castle in 1568

Celia Fiennes: the traveller visited the Lakes in 1698

Daniel Defoe: toured Cumbria in 1724

Bonnie Prince Charlie: was captured in Carlisle in 1745 and marched through Cumbria

John Wesley: the evangelist toured the Lakes in 1759

Thomas Gray: the poet and travel writer toured in 1767 and 1769

Benjamin Franklin: the US statesman stayed near Derwentwater in 1772

J.M.W. Turner: the painter toured the south Lakes in 1797 and 1816

Charles Lamb: the writer stayed in Keswick in 1802

John Paul Jones: the American sailor raided Whitehaven in 1778

William Hazlitt: the writer and critic stayed in Keswick in 1803

Sir Walter Scott: the Scottish writer was a regular visitor to Lakes from 1805 to 1825

Sir Humphrey Davy: the scientist stayed in Grasmere in 1805

John Constable: the painter spent two months in the Lakes in 1806

George Canning: the statesman visited in 1817

Robert Owen: the reformer visited in 1817

John Keats: the poet visited the Lakes and climbed Skiddaw in 1818

Ralph Waldo Emerson: the American essayist visited in 1833

John Stuart Mill: the philosopher stayed in Keswick in 1833

Lord Tennyson: the poet stayed at Bassenthwaite in 1835 and spent his honeymoon there in 1850

Branwell Brontë: worked as tutor in Broughton-in-Furness in 1840

Thomas Carlyle: the historian and essayist visited Bassenthwaite from the 1840s to the 1870s

Charlotte Brontë: the writer stayed in Ambleside in 1849 and 1850

Mrs Gaskell: the writer and biographer of Charlotte Brontë stayed in Ambleside in 1850

Charles Dickens and **Wilkie Collins:** the writers toured the Lakes together and climbed Carrock Fell in 1857

Woodrow Wilson: the 28th US president visited Grasmere in 1895 and later visited Carlisle, where his mother lived

Donald Campbell: the racing driver was killed on Coniston in 1967

Bill Clinton: the 42nd US president proposed to his wife, Hillary, by Ennerdale in 1973

Sting: the singer has a holiday home in Grasmere

Some customs and curiosities

The Buttermere Round

A coach trip in the olden days from Keswick down Borrowdale and over Honister to Buttermere, then over Newlands back to Keswick. Passengers had to get off and walk up all the steep hills. References can still be seen in old Lakeland engravings and writings.

Charr

A species of fish unique to Windermere. It's a form of trout, a very ancient fish, which is thought to have been left behind after the Ice Age and got stuck, unable to migrate. Potted charr and charr pies were considered a great delicacy in the last century and were exported to London (see Chapter 5).

Dry stone walls

Walls without mortar or cement are put together by hand from natural stones and slates. It's a much harder art than it appears. Between 1750 and 1850 most of the open fells were enclosed or divided by these walls, even up to the mountain tops. It was an enormous undertaking, and despite the inhospitable conditions many of them still stand intact to this day. A survey in 1996 estimated there were more than 9,000 miles (14,484 km) of walls across Cumbria, enough to stretch from England to Australia. The National Park Authority runs events at which you can try your hand at dry stone walling, and there are competitions at which people who have turned up to watch end up having a go.

Fell ponies

A distinctive feature of the northern and eastern fells, fell ponies are mostly black, brown or bay, and they roam wild in groups around the open fellside and commons. In bad weather they gather near villages or on minor roads. They appear to be completely wild and are allowed to breed and wander freely, but they do have owners, so don't try to steal any. Formerly they pulled small farm carts or worked down the mines. Now they are very popular as children's ponies.

Gurning

A traditional event going back 700 years, which is held annually at the Egremont Crab Fair. Competitors have to put on a horse collar and make the most ridiculous or ugly face they can (see Chapter 15).

Hodden grey

A type of undyed, grey cloth, which is very hard wearing and was mentioned in the John Peel song, 'coat so grey'.

Merry Neet

A merry night, Cumbrian style, with singing and entertainment, traditionally held after fox hunting.

Rushbearing

An annual ceremony at churches in Grasmere and elsewhere to commemorate the renewal of rushes, which were laid on the bare church floor every August, then taken up in the spring (see Chapter 15).

Spinning galleries

Wooden balconies on farm buildings where the wool was spun. The best known example – see all those postcards – is Yew Tree Farm near Coniston.

Statesmen

The ancient name of yeoman farmers, independent small farmers, with perhaps no more than 50–100 acres (20–40 ha). They still make up most of the central farming community.

Words and phrases

They all speak English, so in theory you should not have too many problems. But here's a little phrasebook to help you out when you're talking to the locals. Their accents and place-names often betray the influence of earlier settlers, especially Norse, and it is as well when map-reading to know the meaning of the more common words that are peculiar to Cumbria.

Beck: stream

Blea: blue

Fell: mountain, open hill slopes

Force: waterfall

Garth: enclosure, field

Ghyll or gill: narrow ravine, usually with a stream

Grange: outlying farm belonging to a monastery

Hause: narrow pass

Holm: island

How: small hill, mound

Intake: land enclosed from waste

Kirk: church

Mere: lake, pool

Nab: projecting spur

Nes: headland, promontory

Pike: sharp summit, peak

Scree: loose stones, debris

Scarth: gap in a ridge

Tarn: small mountain lake

Thwaite: clearing in a forest

Place-names and their meanings

Most of the lakes, fells, towns and villages have an interesting story behind their name, with roots in Old Norse, Old English or Celtic languages. Here are 25 of the most interesting translations or stories behind the names.

Ambleside: pastures by the river sandbanks

Bassenthwaite Lake: lake by Bastun's clearing

Blencathra: the chair-shaped mountain (it looks like that if you see it from the right angle)

Bowness: the bull's headland

Buttermere: the lake by the grazing pastures

Coniston Water: from *cyning tun*, meaning 'king' and 'settlement'

Ennerdale Water: from the valley of a Viking bigwig called Anund or something similar

Glenridding: the valley full of bracken

Great Cockup: disappointingly not named after a walker's misadventures, but from the woodcock that were found there

Hardknott: rough, craggy fell

Haweswater: Hafr's lake

Hawkshead: the abode of Haukr, or someone similarly called

Keswick: the cheese farm

Kirk Fell: the mountain above the church

Loweswater: the leafy lake

Raise: from the Old Norse dialect for pile of stones

Robinson: named after a local landowner, Richard Robinson

Rydal: the valley of the rye

Sawrey: muddy places

Scafell Pike: the fell with the bare summit

Staveley: clearing where staves are found

Thirlmere: the lake with a gap or narrowing (it had a narrow middle section until it was turned into a reservoir

Troutbeck: the trout stream

Wetherlam: home of the castrated ram

Windermere: the lake of Vinandr, or someone with a similar name

Sheep names

The local names for the ages and sex of sheep also betray their Norse origins and are still in common use. *Yow* means ewe; *gimmer* means a yearling; *tup* means a male; *hogg* is last year's lamb; *twinter* is a two year-old; *trinter* is a three year-old.

When Cumbrian farmers count their sheep they use an ancient Celtic form of counting. Even non-farming Cumbrians, in the big smoke like Carlisle, say *yan* for one and *yance* for once. Counting up to twenty sheep goes something like this:

1 = yan,
2 = tan,
3 = tether,
4 = mether,
5 = pimp,
6 = teezar,
7 = leezar,
8 = catterah,
9 = horna,
10 = dick,
11 = yan-dick,
12 = tan-dick,
13 = tether-dick,
14 = mether-dick,
15 = bumpit,
16 = yan-a-bumpit,
17 = tan-a-bumpit,
18 = tedera-bumpit,
19 = medera-bumpit,
20 = giggot.

Now you can go anywhere.

CHAPTER FIFTEEN

Sports and Entertainments

A guide to Lakeland's pastimes, festivals, shows and quirky events, and where to get your sporting and cultural fixes

The native sports are what make Cumbrian gatherings so unusual. You will see sports that exist nowhere else in the world. They are fascinating to watch, even if you have no idea what is going on.

After the spectator events in this chapter come the do-it-yourself activities, from fishing and riding to climbing and sailing, and numerous interesting oddities in between. Then finally, some of the entertainments for more cultural types that are on offer in Cumbria, notably theatre, music and cinema. Yes, the National Park does have cinemas.

Cumbrian sports

Cumberland and Westmorland Wrestling

Probably the most famous of the Lake District's native sports, and you can see it practised at all the main sporting events. It began with Norsemen and at one time was widespread across the country. Today Cumbria is one of its last strongholds (pun intended), and it's an important feature of many of the annual sports and agricultural shows. It looks like a trial of strength but is actually quite technical. The best wrestlers usually follow in the family tradition and seem to be practically bred for it. Just like the best animals.

Two men face each other in a small arena, watched by two judges and a referee. The wrestlers are usually dressed in costumes that resemble combinations and embroidered bathing trunks, though the dress code has been relaxed lately to encourage more youngsters to take part without fear of ridicule from their mates. After shaking hands, the two men 'tak hod' – that is, lock arms behind each other's back. The aim is to try to topple the other fellow to the ground and break his hold. If both fall, the one on top is the winner. The secret lies in tempting your opponent into a position of apparent security and then quickly overbalancing him. To the casual spectator the technical subtleties are often not very obvious, but the events usually have a sense of atmosphere and tradition that makes them well worth attending.

Fell-running

One of the principal attractions of a Lake District sports day. Races consist of a race to the top of the nearest fell, often a gruelling struggle of 1,500 feet (460 m) or more, round a flag at the summit, then back down into the arena in a breakneck dash. A straightforward but torturous race. The best of all is the 150-year-old Grasmere guides' race, which can be quite spectacular and very exciting to watch (though nothing to do with boy scouts and brownies).

The Lake District is Britain's unofficial fell-running capital and is home to numerous races, where contestants set themselves seemingly impossible tasks to achieve in as short a time as possible. The ultimate challenge is the Bob Graham Round, a circuit of 72 miles (116 km) and 42 peaks with 27,000 feet (8,230 m) of ascent that must be completed within 24 hours. Bob Graham was a runner and Keswick guesthouse owner who first did the route, wearing tennis shoes and eating boiled eggs to keep him going. The Bob Graham 24 Hour Club now has more than 1,200 members who have emulated the great man, though many more have seen their efforts end in painful failure. Naturally, runners have tried to make the round harder for themselves over the years – by doing it in midwinter, for instance, or doing clockwise and anticlockwise rounds back to back. The fastest ever round was done by fell-running legend Billy Bland, who got home in less than 14 hours. Superhuman. For a good account of fell-running by someone who's done it, read Richard Askwith's *Feet in the Clouds* (Aurum Press).

Hound trailing

A popular sport in Cumbria for well over a century, hound trailing probably originally derived from the method used by huntsmen to train fox hounds. It's effectively fox hunting without the fox, and it can be great fun to watch, even if you only get to see the action at the very start and finish. From a starting point, a trail is set down by dragging an aniseed-soaked cloth over the fellside, making the course as difficult as possible by including fences, hedges, walls and a variety of terrain. For a fully grown dog, the trail can be up to 10 miles (16 km) long and can take 25–45 minutes to complete.

After the scent has been laid, the hounds are released by their owners. They pick up the scent and rush off into the hills. They'll be out of sight until the finish, when they follow the trail back and the owners shout, whistle and wave to coax their animals over the line. The end can be quite exciting, but for most serious spectators the attraction lies in betting on which hound will win. The local Cumbrian bookies, who appear at most big sports, are a feature in themselves.

Trailing is held throughout Cumbria from April to October. The *Whitehaven News* is the hound trailer's bible and carries details of venues and times for the area, though tracking down some locations can be tricky; ask your friendly TIC. Hound trailing is also an important part of many of the shows and sports days.

Sheep dog trials

Nowadays these take place all over the country and are well known through the *One Man and His Dog* TV series that ran for many years. But they began in the north of England. The first took place in Northumberland in 1876 and the following year sheep dog trials were being held on Belle Isle, Windermere. In 1891 the Lake District Sheep Dog Trials Association was formed.

Five sheep are released at one end of the arena, up to ¼ mile (400 m) away. The shepherd has to remain at his post while his dog – usually a Border Collie – gathers the sheep and brings them back to the shepherd through a series of obstacles. The final and most difficult part is to coax the sheep into a pen,

and it is only at this stage that the shepherd is able to assist, other than by whistling and calling.

Towards the end, the tension can build up quite rapidly, and there is often a sense of magic about the way the shepherds control their dogs. These events are very popular, and when they are set against the Lakeland fells on a fine, summer day you are seeing them at their best. They often form a part of an agricultural or sports show, but see them at the Rydal or Patterdale Sheep Dog Trials for the greatest sense of atmosphere.

A Cumbrian sport now consigned to history is **fox hunting**. It wasn't ever unique to Lakeland, of course, though its most famous exponent, John Peel, is buried in Caldbeck churchyard. Fox hunting on the fells was always radically different from the polite social occasions of the south, since the Lakeland farmer hunted primarily to kill foxes and keep down their numbers and did so on foot. The ban on fox hunting, introduced in 2005, caused a huge stir in Cumbria, and campaigns continue to have it repealed. The most famous hunting pack, the Blencathra Foxhounds, also known as the John Peel Hunt, still meets regularly.

Sporting shows

There are several dozen sporting and farming shows held every year in the various Cumbrian towns and villages, all worth going to, and most of them include native Cumbrian sports. Keep an eye on local papers or notice boards for the smaller village shows, for they have a flavour of their own, but the two Big Sports Days are held at Grasmere and Ambleside. Try to fit in one of them if your time in the Lakes coincides.

See Chapter 1 for a calendar of shows and contact nearby TICs for more details nearer the day. Note that shows can be cancelled or curtailed at short notice if there's any local crisis, like an outbreak of foot and mouth disease – as happened in 2001 and, to a lesser extent, in 2007. But that's about the only thing that will stop these annual get-togethers. A bit of bad weather certainly won't.

★★★ Ambleside Sports

Last Thursday in July

Held in Rydal Park, just north of Ambleside. It can chart its history back some 200 years, and it's now one of the biggest events of its kind in the Lake District, with fell races, wrestling, hound trailing and bike races. There are lots of add-ons – food and craft stalls, a beer tent and plenty to keep kids entertained. An exciting event in a lovely fellside setting. There's quite a rivalry between Ambleside and Grasmere these days for the title of best show.

★★★ Grasmere Sports

Third or fourth Sunday in August
Visit *www.grasmeresportsandshow.co.uk*

A major Lakeland sporting event, whose continuous records date back to 1852. It attracts up to 10,000 spectators and is held in The Ring – the field just outside Grasmere, across the A591 from Town End and Dove Cottage. It's a brilliant location with all the usual running, throwing and cycling events, attracting professionals and amateurs from all over the country, along with the best of the traditional, local events, like Cumberland and Westmorland wrestling (there's a contest for the best costume worn by the wrestlers too). Also the famous guides' fell race and hound trailing. It gets very crowded, so go early – otherwise about the only place to park is Keswick. Full of atmosphere and excitement. Despite its size and fame, this remains a local show, unique to the area and still administered mainly by Grasmere people. It has come in for a bit of criticism recently for trying to widen its appeal by increasing inflatable this, bouncy that. Ignore the sideshows and support the real events.

★★ Cartmel Races

Meetings on the late May bank holiday weekend, mid-July and August bank holiday weekend
Visit *www.cartmel-steeplechases.co.uk*

Probably the smallest of the National Hunt courses, set at the opposite end of the village to the Priory. Apart from horse racing there is usually a small fairground, along with stalls and refreshment tents. It's not worth families spending the whole day there, as it can get very crowded, but perhaps worth using as a base for a day out exploring Cartmel itself and the surrounding area.

★★ Lowther Horse Driving Trials and Country Fair

First or second weekend in August
Visit *www.lowther.co.uk*

Held on the Lowther Estate near Penrith, this is the largest established occasion of its kind and one of the county's leading sporting events. As well as the horse driving trials (in which Prince Philip has been known to take part), there are plenty of supporting attractions like riding demonstrations. The country fair itself has a wide range of stalls and events.

Agricultural shows

The distinction between sporting shows and agricultural shows can get a bit blurred in the Lake District, with many of the farming and country events attracting people who have come to watch the sheep dog trials, hound trails or wrestling.

Though the farming community turns out in force, nearly all the shows are intended for the general visitor too, so are well worth seeking out if they coincide with your holiday. Here are a dozen of the best.

★★★ Wasdale Shepherds' Meet and Show

Second Saturday in October

Well worth going out of your way for. With a superb setting at Wasdale Head, this is one of the best sheep shows in Cumbria, with lots of classes for breeds, sheep dogs, shepherds' crooks and even their boots. There are also tug-of-war events, fell races, hound trails and competitions for tractors. Very good.

★★★ Westmorland County Show

Second Thursday in September
Visit *www.westmorland-county-show.co.uk*

Held at Crooklands outside Kendal and one of the best one-day shows in Cumbria. It's better than the Cumberland Show, or so Westmerians like to believe. All kinds of agricultural competitions and displays, dog shows, Cumberland and Westmorland wrestling, show jumping, horse-drawn carriage driving and a silage competition (one for the professionals only, perhaps). Pulls in 25,000 to 30,000 people. A shuttle bus takes people to and from Kendal for free, which saves on nightmarish car park queues.

★★ Appleby Horse Fair

Runs until the second Wednesday in June, usually from the preceding weekend

Not really an agricultural show, but set up by a charter of 1685 as a fair for horse trading. Today it is world-famous, the largest event of its kind anywhere, and attracts a huge gypsy gathering. Well worth going to if it coincides with your visit for the sheer spectacle and bustle. Great if the weather is good. People arrive and camp out in the area up to a week before the day of the sales.

★★ Borrowdale Shepherds' Meet and Show

Third Sunday in September
Visit *www.borrowdaleshow.org.uk*

Held at Rosthwaite in the beautiful Borrowdale Valley. It's a big day out for local farmers, but it offers the full Lakeland works for the general visitor too: sheepdog trials, hound trailing, fell-running, wrestling, tug-of-war, dry stone walling demonstrations and much more. Lots for the kids. Get there early as the roads get clogged.

★★ Cumberland Show

Penultimate Saturday in July
Visit *www.cumberlandshow.co.uk*

Held in Rickerby Park, Carlisle, and for many years it's has been the largest of the agricultural shows in Cumbria. Lots of traditional and modern events staged to make it a whole day's entertainment.

★★ Ennerdale Show

Last Wednesday in August

Held at Bowness Knott, Ennerdale. What began as a small flower show has evolved into a delightful agricultural and horticultural show, with hound trails, fell-racing, sheep dog trials and gymkhana. It all ends with a dance in the evening. About the only time of year this pretty valley is anything like busy.

★★ Keswick Show

August bank holiday Monday

An important agricultural show with more general appeal than most, thanks to all the hound trails, Cumberland and Westmorland wrestling competitions, sheepdog trials and the like. Held at Crossings Field, it often pulls in 10,000 people or more.

★★ Loweswater Show

First Sunday in September

Thought by many to be the nicest small show of them all.

★★ Skelton Show

Third Saturday in August
Visit *www.skeltonshow.com*

Formerly a little local show, in recent years this has exploded in size, content and enterprise, and it now bills itself as the biggest village show in Cumbria, with more animals on show than many of its rivals. Held in Old Park at Hutton-in-the-Forest near Penrith.

★ Eskdale Show

Last Saturday in September
Visit *www.eskdale.info*

Primarily a sheep show – it's the big day out for Herdwicks – but also including fell races, hound trailing, children's sports and singing and horn-blowing competitions. A good mix of locals and tourists. Held on the field by the King George IV pub. The mountains provide a superb backdrop.

★ Gosforth Show

Third Wednesday in August

Another traditional Cumbrian agricultural show, with additional entertainments in the form of terrier racing and a gymkhana. Along with the Eskdale and Hawkshead shows, this tends to be a mainly agricultural affair which is probably more fun for locals than visitors, but it's worth taking in if you happen to be in the area at the time. Or you could plan a day's outing around it and explore the area.

★ Hawkshead Show

Penultimate Tuesday in August
Visit *www.hawksheadshow.co.uk*

Along the same lines as Gosforth, but with its own specialisms, like fell ponies and competitions for best shepherds' sticks.

Sheep dog trials

In addition to the trials that can be found at some of the agricultural shows, there are several Lakeland events where the dogs take centre stage. Here are the best three.

★★ Rydal

Second Thursday after first Monday in August

Held in Rydal Hall grounds, just outside Ambleside on the A591

This attracts a big crowd as it's in the middle of the summer holidays. It's the best of the sheep dog events because it's fun and doesn't take itself too seriously.

★ Patterdale Dog Day

August bank holiday Saturday.

Held in the King George V playing fields
Visit *www.patterdaledogday.co.uk*

Now well into its second century and still very much a farmers' rather than tourists' event. But there's plenty to entertain, including fell races, hound trails and sheep shearing demonstrations.

★ Threlkeld

Third Wednesday in August

In Burns Field, Threlkeld, near Keswick

Has plenty of side events like children's sports and pet competitions.

Rushbearing ceremonies

Rushbearing is one of the Lake District's longest surviving customs, dating from the time when the old earth floors of churches would be covered with rushes, which were changed once a year amid great celebration. The practice largely died out when floors became paved over, but it is still held in affection in the Lakes. These days the 'rushbearing' is a cross made of rushes and flowers and carried by the children of the parish. A procession is led by a band, followed by the clergy and then the children of the village, carrying the bearings. The procession usually goes around the town or village and ends at the church with hymns and prayers.

There are five rushbearing ceremonies remaining in the Lake District, any one of which is worth going along to watch. The children of Ambleside and Grasmere are traditionally given a piece of Grasmere gingerbread if they have carried one of the rushes. Well worth a morning's work. Warcop is probably the most interesting spectacle of the five and is accompanied by children's sports and a military band.

St Mary's Church, **Ambleside** – first Saturday in July
St Oswald's Church, **Grasmere** – Saturday nearest St Oswald's day (5 August)
St Theobald's Church, **Great Musgrave** – first Saturday in July
St Mary and St Michael's Church, **Urswick** – Sunday nearest St Michael's day (29 September)
St Columba's Church, **Warcop** – St Peter's day (29 June), unless it falls on a Sunday, in which case it moves to the previous Saturday (the 28th)

Miscellaneous events

Now we come to seven things that aren't quite sports and aren't quite agricultural or traditional but that are nonetheless becoming a fixed part of the Lakeland calendar.

★★ The Biggest Liar in the World Competition

Third Thursday in November
Tel. 01946 514960 or visit *www.santonbridgeinn.com/liar*

An eccentric little competition that takes place every year at the Santon Bridge Inn between Eskdale and Wasdale. It's in honour of Will Ritson, a 19th-century publican at the Wasdale Head Inn. 'Auld Will' was a genuine and sincere man who nevertheless lied constantly; one tale was that turnips in Wasdale grew so big that the dalesfolk quarried into them for their Sunday lunch and then used them as sheds for the Herdwick sheep. (Nowadays, so the joke goes, people live in turnips because they are natural features of the landscape and they do not need planning permission from the National Park Authority.)

In 1974, Tom Purdham won the contest by telling a visiting BBC TV team – which had turned up to film the winner – that he wasn't taking part in the contest. The team were convinced and went home without filming him. Other winning lies have included some nonsense about Halley's Comet really being an everlasting carpet woven from Herdwick sheep wool; a story about floating hotels on the lakes; and the theory that farting sheep were causing global warming. The contest is strictly for amateurs, and politicians, journalists and lawyers are barred from entry – because they'd win every time. The competition is organised by the pub with help from Copeland District Council and sponsorship from Jennings. Tickets to the event include a tatie pot supper. Hard to believe, but it's a good night out.

★★ Egremont Crab Fair and Sports

Third Saturday in September
Visit *www.egremontcrabfair.org.uk*

One of Cumbria's oldest and oddest annual events. Dating back to 1267, the fair begins with the parade of an apple cart, from which apples are thrown to the crowds along Main Street, and the erection of a greasy pole with a prize at the top for anyone who can reach it – in the past a side of mutton or a top hat, but these days more likely to be hard cash. There are track and field events and hound trails during the day. In the evening there is a pipe-smoking contest and the event for which the fair is famous: the World Gurning Championships. The entrants to this revered competition put their heads through a horse collar and grin or 'gurn' – the object being to pull the most revolting expression; the most grotesque wins. Entrants with dentures tend to have an advantage here, though it is said that one year the contest was won by a sympathetic onlooker who was just watching.

★★ Ulverston Lantern Procession

Mid- to late September
Tel. 01229 581127 or visit *www.lanternhouse.org*

Established in the 1980s by Welfare State International, an Ulverston creative group now known as Lanternhouse International. Homemade lanterns are accompanied by bands as they are paraded through the streets to Ford Park, where there's some sort of themed concluding event. Gets up to 10,000 people and can be quite a sight.

★ Cumbria Steam Gathering

Last weekend in July
Visit *www.steamgathering.org.uk*

An impressive gathering of old steam cars, traction engines and commercial vehicles. There's also a fairground, arena displays and market. Held on Cark airfield near Flookburgh, it usually gets well over a thousand exhibits. Noisy.

★ Kendal Torchlight Carnival

Second Friday in September
Visit *www.kendaltorchlightcarnival.co.uk*

Has grown out of the Kendal Gathering, a sort of mini-festival in and around Kendal, and it's timed to follow the Westmorland County Show. Hundreds of people join in a procession route, lit by torches and candles, which winds through the town on the final evening of the Gathering. There's a different theme each year and always a great carnival atmosphere. Get there early because the police close the town to traffic.

★ Lakeland Rose Show

Second weekend in July
Visit *www.lakelandroseshow.co.uk*

Like a lot of things in life this show got great ideas, began to take itself terribly seriously and forget its original purpose. Then crashed. Now resurrected in a much smaller and nicer way in Crooklands Show Field near Kendal. Lots of different classes for judging, plus a big craft fair and craft demonstrations.

FRED

Late September and early October
Visit *www.fredsblog.co.uk*

A new, fortnight-long 'Art Invasion Across Cumbria'. The idea is to take art out into the countryside via installations and other creative 'happenings' by dozens of artists. Weird but occasionally wonderful. Claims to be the biggest event of its kind in Europe.

Outdoor recreations

Having described the spectator sports and where you can go and see them happening, we now come to the do-it-yourself sports and activities. The range and eccentricity of what's available seems to be increasing all the time.

Ballooning

You can take a trip over the Lake District in a hot air balloon – and a real one at that, not one of those tethered things that you queue for hours to get to at local shows. High Adventure operates from Bowness but launches from different spots and takes different routes according to wind conditions. You travel about 10 miles (16 km) in a one-hour flight, which usually leave in the morning or evening. The cost is £185 per person, but once you're up there, wow, it's a different world (tel. 015394 47599 or visit *www.high-adventure.co.uk*).

Canoeing and kayaking

If you are a self-sufficient canoeist there are lots of lakes and rivers to paddle on, but check access first (see Chapter 7 for lakes information). The British Canoe Union updates and coordinates the latest info, and runs courses in the Lakes (tel. 0845 370 9500 or visit *www.bcu.org.uk*). Several specialist outdoor activity companies provide canoe hire and tuition; try Windermere Canoe and Kayak (tel. 015394 44451 or visit *www.windermerecanoekayak.com*) or Lakes Canoe and Kayak (tel. 01228 521276 or visit *www.lakescanoeandkayak.co.uk*).

Caving

Well, if people try to get as high as they can in the Lakes, why not go as deep down as possible too? The old mines offer some great exploration, but you'll need expert guidance. Instructors and guides include High Points (tel. 07799 694128 or visit *www.highpoints.co.uk*). Or get some advice from the British Caving Association (visit *www.british-caving.org.uk*).

Climbing

Rock climbing was virtually invented in the Lake District by a group of climbers basing themselves at Wasdale Head. Nowadays if you're out on any of the fells that has a suitable rock face nearby you'll probably see little figures moving slowly across it, strung together with gaily coloured ropes. Not something for the novice to try without proper instruction or equipment.

A number of guidebooks to the crags are available, many of them published by the tireless Fell and Rock Climbing Club of the Lake District (visit *www.frcc.co.uk*). A good way of getting started in the area, and for making contact with clubs or like-minded individuals, is to visit one of the outdoor adventure and clothing shops; see Chapter 16 for some of the best. They usually keep up-to-date lists of instructors, sometimes acting as booking agencies for freelance guides. A couple of the many instruction agencies worth trying are Capricorn Mountaineering (tel. 015394 44925 or visit *www.rock-climbing-courses.co.uk*) and Climb 365 (tel. 015394 48046 or visit *www.climb365.net*).

If you enjoy 'virtual reality' climbing – all the adrenaline buzz without the hassle of wet rock – try a climbing wall. There are good ones in Keswick (tel. 017687 72000 or visit *www.keswickclimbingwall.co.uk*) and Kendal (tel. 015397 21766 or visit *www.kendalwall.co.uk*).

Cycling

The Lake District has some brilliant cycling, as long as you don't mind lots of ups and downs. See Chapter 3 for the long-distance trails in the area. A few companies offer biking holidays: try Holiday Lakeland Cycling Tours, which offers trips on long-distance cycle paths or a Nine Lakes Tour (tel. 016973 71871 or visit *www.holiday-lakeland.co.uk*); or Country Lanes, which does day trips to long tours (tel. 015394 44544 or visit *www.countrylanes.co.uk*). There are some good mountain bike trails in Grizedale and Whinlatter forests. Cycling up and down fells is also becoming more popular, to the fury of walking purists. Cumbria Tourism has a website full of useful resources at *www.cyclingcumbria.co.uk*.

Diving

Ever wanted to see what's beneath the surface? Divers have always flocked to the lakes, even if some of them are very murky. Haweswater, with the village of Mardale submerged in it, is particularly popular. But the lakes can be dangerous, so get expert guidance. Permission is often needed too. A good resource is *www.freshwaterdiver.com*.

Fishing

As you'd imagine with so much water around, the Lake District is great for fishing. Every angler must hold a Rod Fishing Licence, and in many places you'll also need a permit, since most patches of water seem to be either owned or let to clubs, associations or some other body. See Chapter 7 for general lake-by-lake guidance. Note that some lakes and tarns have rare fish, like schelly and vendace, which it is illegal to take. Charr is unique to Windermere and rare, but not yet endangered.

There are a few well-established fisheries in the National Park. Esthwaite Water Trout Fishery offers a good way to get out on to a pretty lake, and it does hire, tuition and fish sales (tel. 015394 36541 or visit *www.hawksheadtrout.com*). There are also plenty of fishing tackle shops around Cumbria, and they can usually sort out permits and licences for you. Those handy for the National Park include Carlson's Fishing Tackle on Kirkland in Kendal (tel. 015397 24867); The Fishing Hut on Windermere Road in Grange-over-Sands (tel. 015395 32854); Go Fishing on Glebe Road in Bowness (tel. 015394 47086); and the outstandingly named Rods 'n' Sods on The Gill in Ulverston (tel. 01229 582367).

If you'd like to get regularly involved in fishing in the Lakes, the biggest club is the Windermere, Ambleside and District Angling Association. They have stacks of resources and advice (tel. 015395 35630 or visit *www.lakedistrictfishing.net*). If you want a guide or instructor, the *Westmorland Gazette*'s fishing columnist Patrick Arnold is your man (tel. 01229 889792 or visit *www.englishlakesflyfishing.co.uk*).

Golf

Some of Cumbria's most testing courses are on the windswept extremities of the county, like Seascale and Silloth-on-Solway. But there are some courses inside the National Park, which win the best scenery awards. Try these four.

Cockermouth Golf Club
Embleton, north of Bassenthwaite Lake
Tel. 017687 76223 or visit *www.cockermouthgolf.co.uk*

Eskdale Golf Course
Ravenglass
Tel. 01229 717680 or visit *www.eskdalegolf.co.uk*

Keswick Golf Club
Threlkeld Hall, Threlkeld
Tel. 017687 79324 or visit *www.keswickgolfclub.com*

Windermere Golf Club
Cleabarrow, Windermere
Tel. 015394 43123 or visit *www.windermeregolfclub.net*

High wire

In which you move from high-level point to point by edging over rope bridges, swinging from the trees like Tarzan or zooming down zip slides. It's great fun, especially for kids and companies wanting to do some team bonding. Grizedale Forest has a course run by Go Ape, which is open most of the year round, though closed in December and January. Prices are £25 for 'Gorillas' (adults) and £20 for 'Baboons' (children). They even claim to have cured some peoples' fear of heights (tel. 0870 45 9189 or visit *www.goape.co.uk*).

Offroad driving

No matter how wild the terrain, someone will eventually try to drive a car over it. It appals some walkers, and they can create a racket, but most agencies are fairly responsible and stick to their set trails. Windermere-based Kankku provides 4×4 high thrills, and they're particularly popular with corporate types (tel. 015394 47414 or visit *www.kankku.co.uk*).

Parachuting

For the really adventurous. The North West Parachute Centre is based at Cark Airfield near Flookburgh, Grange-over-Sands, and does tandem skydives, where you don't have to worry about opening the parachute (but do have to worry about falling 2 miles or 3.2 km) for £190 (tel. 015395 58672 or visit *www.hollywinds.com*). If you prefer to spectate, Humphrey Head – the headland near Grange-over-Sands – has a grandstand view.

Paragliding

The sort where you struggle to a high lump of land and hurl yourself off, then float gracefully down, courtesy of a mini-parachute. You can get tuition with Air Ventures (tel. 07830 281986 or visit *www.airventures.co.uk*) or Sunsoar Paragliding (tel. 0870 199 7343 or visit *www.sunsoar-paragliding.com*). If you get a taste for it, you could join the Cumbria Soaring Club (tel. 015395 61969 or visit *www.cumbriasoaringclub.co.uk*).

Photography

Not quite as energetic as paragliding, but there can be few better places to learn or practice. Residential courses are run by renowned Lake District photographer and writer Bill Birkett (tel. 015394 37420 or visit *www.billbirkett.co.uk*) and Lakeland Photographic Holidays (tel. 017687 78459 or visit *www.lakelandphotohols.com*).

Riding

Very popular in the Lakes, and several companies specialise in guided trips, from an hour's ride to a weekend-long trek.

Bigland Hall Equestrian
Haverthwaite
Tel. 015395 30333 or visit *www.biglandhall.com*

Classic Hackers
Hawkshead
Tel. 015394 45124 or visit *www.classic-hackers.co.uk*

Cumbrian Heavy Horses
Whicham Valley
Tel. 01229 777764 or visit *www.cumbrianheavyhorses.com*

Hipshow Riding Stables
Near Kendal
Tel. 015397 28221 or visit *www.horseridingholidays.co.uk*

Holmescales Riding Centre
Near Kendal
Tel. 015397 29388 or visit
www.holmescalesridingcentre.co.uk

Murthwaite Green Trekking Centre
Millom
Tel. 01229 770876 or visit *www.murthwaitegreen.co.uk*

Park Foot Pony Trekking Centre
Pooley Bridge, Ullswater
Tel. 017684 86696 or visit
www.parkfootponytrekking.co.uk

Rookin House Equestrian
Troutbeck, Ullswater
Tel. 017684 83561 or visit *www.rookinhouse.co.uk*

Sailing and windsurfing

There are more opportunities for courses and holidays than
ever, especially since the 10mph (16kph) speed limit forced
water skiers to get their lake thrills in gentler ways. The standard of tuition and equipment is usually excellent, and prices
are competitive. Windermere, Derwentwater, Coniston or
Ullswater are your best places to learn. For tuition by the
hour or day you could try:

Coniston Boating Centre
Coniston
Tel. 015394 41366 or visit *www.lake-district.gov.uk*

Run by the National Park people. Good, thorough weekend-
long courses.

Derwentwater Marina
Tel. 017687 72912 or visit *www.derwentwatermarina.co.uk*

Lessons, hire and sales, based near Keswick.

Glenridding Sailing School
Ullswater
Tel. 017684 82541 or visit *www.lakesail.co.uk*

A long-established place catering for all abilities.

Lakes Leisure Windermere
Rayrigg Road
Tel. 015394 47183 or visit
www.lakesleisure.org.uk/windermere

The only place of its kind that is financed by a district council – good for them. Very reasonably priced. Also have wind-surfers and canoes for tuition.

The Low Wood Watersports and Activity Centre
Windermere
Tel. 015394 39441 or visit *www.elh.co.uk/watersports*

This has diversified into a wide range of activities since the speed limit, and offers courses tailored to abilities.

Nichol End Marine
Derwentwater
Tel. 017687 73082 or visit *www.nicholendmarine.co.uk*

A friendly, family-run place offering windsurfing, sailing, canoeing and kayaking lessons or hire.

River Deep Mountain High
Tel. 015395 31116 or visit
www.riverdeepmountainhigh.co.uk.

Standard courses or tailored tuition on Coniston and Windermere. Worth mentioning for the name alone.

Skiing and snowboarding

Cross-country skiing is popular in the Lake District: it suits the uncertain conditions and the terrain, and it's sometimes the only way to get around. Those who prefer downhill skiing will need the Lake District Ski Club. They ski on the back of Helvellyn, at Raise, complete with proper tows and club hut. An elusive bunch to get hold of, they will nevertheless welcome you if you choose to walk up to their club. They certainly should. It'll take you about 1½ hours, carrying all your gear. Insurance regulations mean you now have to be a member to ski, but fees are quite modest. Visit *www.ldscsnowski.co.uk* for more details.

Further north in the county at Yad Moss near Alston is the longest ski lift in England, looked after by the Carlisle Ski Club (tel. 01228 561634 or visit *www.thepriceofcheese.com* – don't ask).

For the uninitiated, snowboarding is where you whiz down a slope of snow on something resembling a shed door. The dry slope at Kendal does sessions (tel. 08456 345 173 or visit *www.kendalski.co.uk*).

Swimming

Until August and September the lakes can be very cold, at which time they become just cold. There are occasional organised swims for charity or just for fun, especially on Windermere. The British Long Distance Swimming Association collates event information (visit *www.bldsa.org.uk*). Holiday company Swimtrek offers Lakes Weekenders, stringing together swims in several lakes, presumably with some hot drinks in between (tel. 0208 696 6220 or visit *www.swimtrek.com*).

If you are feeling cowardly there are plenty of indoor pools around.

Park Leisure Centre, Greengate Street, **Barrow-in-Furness** (tel. 01229 871146)
The Pools Swimming and Health Centre, James Street, **Carlisle** (tel. 01228 625777)
Leisure Centre and Pools, Castlegate Drive, **Cockermouth** (tel. 01900 823596)
Dalton Leisure Centre, Chapel Street, **Dalton-in-Furness** (tel. 01229 463125)
Lakes Leisure, Burton Road, **Kendal** (tel. 015397 29777)
Leisure Pool, Station Road, **Keswick** (tel. 017687 72760)
Leisure Centre, Southend Road, **Penrith** (tel. 017688 63450)
Lakes Leisure, Priory Road, **Ulverston** (tel. 01229 584110)
Wigton Baths, **Wigton** (tel. 016973 42412)
Troutbeck Bridge Swimming Pool, **Windermere** (tel. 015394 43243)
Leisure Centre and Pool, Moorclose, **Workington** (tel. 01900 61771)

Water skiing

There's not much of this since the 10mph (16kph) speed limit came into force on Windermere – water skiing isn't exactly high adrenaline at 9mph (14kph) – but beginners better suited to that pace can still learn on the lake. Try the Low Wood Watersports and Activity Centre (tel. 015394 39441 or visit *www.elh.co.uk/watersports*). You can get up more speed on the purpose-built lake at Port Haverigg Watersports near Millom (tel. 01229 772880 or visit *www.phwater-sports.moonfruits.com*). The seagulls don't mind the noise.

Theatre and music

The Lake District isn't exactly bursting with drama and music venues, but those that do exist are very good. They all host a variety of events – concerts, plays, lectures, recitals – and most tend to be one- or two-night occasions; the advantage is that these centres sometimes attract some of the best touring companies in the country. Here are the best of them.

★★★ Theatre by the Lake

Lakeside, Keswick
Tel. 017687 74411 or visit *www.theatrebythelake.co.uk*

One of Lakeland's – nay, the north's – biggest cultural successes. A vibrant and architecturally wonderful theatre, right by the edge of Derwentwater. The summer season is always excellent, but there are also popular plays in repertory in the Main House theatre from May to October, plus a bit more experimental stuff in the Studio. The theatre is alive all year round with music, exhibitions, talks and workshops. Good caff. Ample parking.

★★ Brewery Arts Centre

Highgate, Kendal
Tel. 015397 25133 or visit *www.breweryarts.co.uk*

An active arts centre in a restored brewery building. It has become the cultural heart of Kendal and puts on a very good range of plays, concerts, films and special events throughout the year. There is a good bar and restaurant, and it has exhibition and workshop space. It hosts Kendal's Mountain Festival each November and, recently, a Women's Arts Festival. This is really a community arts centre run on very professional lines, though it has had to cut back on programming lately because of funding difficulties. Elsewhere in Kendal the leisure centre has a growing and somewhat surprising reputation as a venue for cultural performances (tel. 015397 29511 or visit *www.lakesleisure.org.uk*).

★★ The Old Laundry Theatre

Bowness
Tel. 015394 88444 or visit *www.oldlaundrytheatre.com*

A theatre in the round, holding up to 300 people, which was built as part of the World of Beatrix Potter complex. It launched in 1982 with a play by Alan Ayckbourn, who continues to be involved as a trustee. It has an ambitious annual festival of theatre and film over October and November, now into its second decade and building a good reputation. The Old Laundry Bistro does good meals.

★★ Rosehill Theatre

Moresby, near Whitehaven
Tel. 01946 692422 or visit *www.rosehilltheatre.co.uk*

Rather a trek from the central Lakes, but another very good arts centre that puts on a range of concerts, films and plays throughout the year. Dazzling bright red everywhere in the theatre. It's particularly good for folk music, put on every other Friday. There are regular workshops and an adjoining bistro. Approaching its 50th birthday.

★ The Kirkgate Centre

Kirkgate, Cockermouth
Tel. 01900 826448 or visit *www.thekirkgate.com*

Not quite on the scale of the above centres, but it's getting there. Once a Victorian school, in one of Cockermouth's nicest streets. There's a regular programme of films, plays and concerts in a 125-seat auditorium, plus exhibitions. Particularly good for art house films and jazz. All looked after by volunteers.

★ Penrith Playhouse

Auction Mart Lane
Tel. 017688 65557 or visit *www.penrithplayers.co.uk*

Looked after by the Penrith Players, an enthusiastic team of volunteers who do everything from starring on stage to running the bar. They produce about half a dozen plays a year, and there's a good live music programme too.

★ The Sands Centre

The Sands, Carlisle
Tel. 01228 625222 or visit *www.thesandscentre.co.uk*

Cumbria's biggest entertainment venue attracts some big names and big touring productions. Big doesn't always mean best, of course, but it does turn its 1,300-seat auditorium over to local drama, music and dance groups for their productions.

Coronation Hall

Country Square, Ulverston
Tel. 01229 587140 or visit *www.corohall.co.uk*

Goes by the unlovely name of 'The Coro', but it has built up a good range of concerts, plays and ballets under the auspices of South Lakeland District Council, which has even splashed out on a bit of refurbishment. Big community centre too.

For many people the highlight of the Lake District's music calendar is the ★★ **Lake District Summer Musical Festival** (tel. 08456 442505 or visit *www.ldsm.org.uk*). Held in the first fortnight of August, it's becoming increasingly well known and always attracts some excellent musicians and orchestras to the area. Concerts are held in venues across the Lake District and, increasingly, Cumbria, although Ambleside remains the focal point. Many of the performances come from people on the International Summer School at the college in the town.

Cinemas

The National Park contains only three public cinemas.

★★ Zeffirelli's Cinema

Compston Road, Ambleside
Tel. 015394 33845 or visit *www.zeffirellis.com*

A very good and popular cinema, with some nice decorative touches. There are two screens in the main building, and another couple in a nicely converted school building next to St Mary's Church, a short stroll away. Always a good mix of blockbuster and arty films, and their enthusiasm for film shines through. Also home to a large and good vegetarian Italian restaurant. They offer a two-course meal and film ticket for £15.95. The centre's good for jazz too.

★ Lonsdale Alhambra Cinema

St John's Street, Keswick
Tel. 017687 72195 or visit
www.lonsdalealhambrakeswick.co.uk

A very smart and welcoming 270-seat cinema. Keswick Film Club – Film Society of the Year in 2006, no less – meets there every Sunday.

★ Royalty Cinema

Lake Road, Bowness
Tel. 015394 43364 or visit *www.nm-cinemas.co.uk*

This small but quite good cinema can sometimes get big feature releases surprisingly quickly, especially during the summer. There are three screens so lots of choice, even if your sitting room at home is larger.

Other cinemas

There are, of course, a lot more cinemas around the outskirts of the Lakes, especially in the larger Cumbrian towns. They include:

Apollo Cinema, Abbey Road, **Barrow** (tel. 0871 220 6000 or visit *www.apollocinemas.co.uk*)
Vue Carlisle, Botchergate, **Carlisle** (tel. 0871 240240 or visit *www.myvue.com*)
Lonsdale Alhambra Cinema, Middlegate, **Penrith** (tel. 017688 62400 or visit *www.lonsdalealhambrapenrith.co.uk*)
Rheged (tel. 017688 68000 or visit *www.rheged.com*)
Roxy Cinema, Brogden Street, **Ulverston** (tel. 01229 582340 or visit *www.nm-cinemas.co.uk*)
Plaza Cinemas, Dunmail Park, **Workington** (tel. 01900 870001 or visit *www.workington-plaza.co.uk*)

You can also see films at many of the venues in the theatres section.

CHAPTER SIXTEEN

Shopping

The best places to buy Lakeland crafts, books, antiques and walking gear, and some advice on buying houses

Yes, we know you haven't come to the Lakes to shop, or so you think. But just look at all those crowds on the pavements of Bowness and Keswick. Where do they all come from? Here are four types of shops – for antiques, books, crafts and outdoor gear – that visitors, and residents, might well want to use at some time.

Antique shops

Cartmel

Anthemion, Derbyshire Square (tel. 015395 36295)

Cockermouth

Antique Market, Cocker Bridge, Main Street (tel. 01900 824346)
Cockermouth Antiques, Station Street (tel. 01900 826746)

Keswick

John Young and Son, Main Street (tel. 017687 73434)

Kirkby Stephen

Haughey Antiques, Market Street (tel. 017683 71302)

Newby Bridge

Townhead Antiques, Newby Bridge Road (tel. 015395 31321)

Windermere

Bird Cage Antiques, College Road (tel. 015394 45063)

Bookshops

Well, you might want to buy more copies of *The Good Guide to the Lakes*. Go on, spoil the friends back home. Lakeland bookshops are terribly good on Lakeland books and maps, though not so hot on the latest sensitive novel from London. All shops that stock this book are, of course, excellent, but here's a selection. Those that sell second-hand or antiquarian books are indicated; these places can be great for a trawl of forgotten Lakeland gems, but it's often best to phone in advance because opening hours can be erratic.

Ambleside

Fred Holdsworth, Central Buildings (tel. 015394 33388)
The Good Book Place (second hand), Kelsick Court
(tel. 015394 33598)
Henry Roberts, Market Place (tel. 015394 33264)
Novel Café, Artists' Courtyard (tel. 015394 34096)
Wearings Bookshop, Lake Road (tel. 015394 32312)

Bowness

Cumbria Books, Lake Road (tel. 015394 47200)

Brough

The Book House (second-hand), Main Street
(tel. 017683 42748)

Carlisle

Bookcase (second-hand), Castle Street (tel. 01228 544560)
Bookends, Castle Street (tel. 01228 529067)
Waterstone's, Scotch Street, Tel. 01228 542300)

Cartmel

Norman Kerr Antiquarian Booksellers (second-hand),
The Square (tel. 015395 36247)

Cockermouth

The New Bookshop, Main Street (tel. 01900 822062)
Winkworth Antiquarian Books at The Printing House
(second-hand), Main Street (tel. 01900 824984)

Grange-over-Sands

Over Sands Books (second-hand), Railway station platform
(tel. 015395 36969)

Grasmere

Sam Read, Broadgate (tel. 015394 35374)

Hawkshead

Henry Roberts, The Square (tel. 015394 36650)

Kendal

Kirkland Books (second-hand), Kirkland
(tel. 015397 33220)
Waterstone's, Westmorland Shopping Centre
(tel. 015397 41771)

Keswick

Bookends, Main Street (tel. 017687 75277)
Keswick Bookshop (second-hand), Station Street
(tel. 017687 75535)

Kirkby Stephen

The Bookshop, Market Street (tel. 017683 71804)

Penrith

Bluebell Bookshop, Angel Square (tel. 017688 66660)

Ulverston

The Bookshop at the Tinners' Rabbit, Market Street
(tel. 01229 588858)

Whitehaven

Michael Moon (second-hand), Lowther Street
(tel. 01946 599010)

Windermere

Fireside Bookshop (second-hand), Victoria Street
(tel. 015394 45855)

Workington

Derwent Bookshop, Finkle Street (tel. 0845 803 8263)

For real bookworms, **Sedbergh** on the edge of the Lakes
is well worth a visit. It's England's first and only book town
and is building a reputation to rival Hay-on-Wye. There are
several second-hand shops there, including **Westwood Books**
on Long Lane (tel. 015396 21233), a vast place that claims
to be the biggest shop of its kind in the northwest. Try also

R.F.G. Hollett & Son on Finkle Street (tel. 015396 20298). But start your visit at the Book Town's HQ at the **Dales and Lakes Book Centre** on Main Street (tel. 015396 20125). Alternatively, visit *www.sedbergh.org.uk* for more info.

Some of the literary tourist attractions have good bookshops too. For anything Wordsworthy, the obvious place is the **Dove Cottage Shop** (tel. 015394 35544). John Ruskin's house at **Brantwood** has an excellent range (tel. 015394 41164). The Lake District Visitor Centre at **Brockhole** (tel. 015394 46601) and larger TICs have good local-interest books.

If you want to order Lake District books like this one from afar, a good place to start is the online shop of Bookends and Bookcase in Carlisle. They specialise in Cumbrian books and have lots of good reviews and guidance (visit *www.bookscumbria.com*).

Craft shops and galleries

These places come and go quite frequently, but the trend has been upwards in the last few years. Some are resurrecting old industries, proudly showing off their traditional methods, while others are realising that Britain's number one pastime – shopping – is good news for them, especially if combined with free parking and a café. Here's a selection of the best places. Not mentioned here are the shops and galleries that are part of larger attractions like stately homes or museums. Look out for the 'Made in Cumbria' logo; the same agency produces a useful Craft Map, available from TICs.

Ambleside

Old Courthouse Gallery
Market Place
Tel. 015394 32022

Paintings, ceramics, glassware, sculptures, textiles from a couple of hundred artists and craft-makers, many of them local.

The Rock Shop
North Road
Tel. 015394 31923

The realisation of one man's dream to put on display his considerable collection of rocks, minerals and fossils. Now has branches in Bowness and Keswick too.

Broughton-in-Furness

The Broughton Craft Shop
Griffin Street
Tel. 01229 716413

The shop specialises in jewellery. You can see the maker at work. Ring for opening times.

Caldbeck

The Wool Clip
Priest's Mill
Tel. 016974 78707

A cooperative of 15 farmers and craftspeople producing jumpers, rugs, fleece and more from local sheep's wool. They also do workshops. Closed from January to mid-February.

Carlisle

Linton Tweeds Visitor Centre
Shaddongate
Tel. 01228 527567

Based in a weaving business, set up in Carlisle in 1912 by William Linton. Through his Paris connections it began selling to Coco Chanel, whose couture house is still a customer. The looms are on display, and you can have a go yourself. There's a fabric and clothes shop, and a café.

Cartmel

Fieldhead Crafts
Devonshire Square. Tel. 015395 58651. Good initiative selling crafts produced by various local people, including some nice wooden toys. Closed Mondays to Wednesdays from January to March, otherwise open daily.

Grasmere

Heaton Cooper Studio
Opposite the green
Tel. 015394 35280

An exhibition of paintings by four generations of Lakeland's most famous painting family, plus lots of materials for artists to buy.

Lindal-in-Furness

Colony Candles
Tel. 01229 461102

Europe's largest producer of scented candles. Mainly automated now, so there's not much to watch, but there's all the candles you could ever need, plus accessories and home decor. Chandlers Country Café is next door.

Low Newton

Yew Tree Barn
Near Grange-over-Sands
Tel. 015395 31498

Lots of work by Cumbrian artists and crafters, and you can see some of them in action. Very good café.

Penrith

Rheged
Redhills
Tel. 017688 95598

An excellent showcase for dozens of Cumbrian crafters, including things in glass, wood and ceramics. Handy for souvenirs on your way back to the M6.

Sedbergh

Fairfield Mill
Garsdale Road
Tel. 015396 21958

Arts and crafts galleries, resident artists' studios and original machinery and craft tools on display. Nice tea room by the river.

Thornthwaite

Thornthwaite Galleries
Tel. 017687 78248

A contemporary gallery showcasing the work of about 130 artists, plus crafts, gifts and tea room. Ring to check opening hours; it usually cuts back to weekends in the winter and closes from mid-December to mid-February.

Ulverston

Lakes Glass Centre
Oubas Hill
Tel. 01229 581121

Features two manufacturers, Cumbria Crystal and Heron Glass. You can watch the glass making processes and the workers are friendly and informative. Two shops.

Walkers' shops

Importing, making and selling outdoor gear must rank as a mini-boom area for Cumbria. There are stacks of shops specialising in the great outdoors, supplying gear for walkers and climbers and becoming part of the landscape of the Lake District. Invaluable for guidebooks, maps and expert advice as well as wet-weather and walking clothes. Ambleside is probably the capital of the industry in the south Lakes, and it can seem as if every other shop is selling cagoules and boots. Keswick, the outdoor HQ of the northern half of the Lakes, isn't far behind. Larger shops are good sources of information on walking and climbing activities generally, and they carry notices of talks, lectures and local instructors. Some hire equipment as well as sell it. Here are some recommendations of places with knowledgeable staff and good ranges of gear.

Ambleside

The Climbers' Shop
Compston Road
Tel. 015394 32297

A good specialist shop, established since 1959. Friendly, expert staff. They hire boots.

Gaynor Sports
Market Cross
Tel. 015394 33305

Not really a specialist, but they stock a huge range of outdoor clothing. One of the biggest such shops in the country.

Lakes Climber and Runner
Cheapside
Tel. 015394 33660

Good for specialist climbing equipment and booking guides.

Stewart R. Cunningham
Rydal Road
Tel. 015394 32636

Tends to be expensive, but carries a good range of extras not available elsewhere.

Bowness

Stuart's Sports
Lake Road
Tel. 015394 43001

A good reputation for selling top stuff at less than top prices. Looks a bit cramped but search around and you'll find what you need. It's been under the same ownership for 30 years.

Coniston

Coniston Outdoors
Lake Road
Tel. 015394 41733

A comprehensive range with all the usual brands.

Keswick

George Fisher
Borrowdale Road
Tel. 017687 72178

THE classic outdoor shop, beautifully restored. Expert advice, weather forecasts and Abraham's Tea Room upstairs if you decide you'd rather eat than walk.

Needle Sports
Main Street
Tel. 017687 72227

Good for proper mountaineering and climbing kit.

The Sick and the Wrong
Southey Street
Tel. 017687 80297

Specialist in snowboarding and paragliding with a workshop to repair kit.

Wasdale Head

The Barn Door Shop
next to the Wasdale Head Inn
Tel. 019467 26384

Neat little climbing shop in the headquarters of rock climbing. Good for advice and weather forecasts.

Windermere

The Outdoor Warehouse
Victoria Street
Tel. 015394 44876

Has been selling walking, climbing and skiing gear since 1975 and is particularly good on clothing. Experienced staff.

Market days and early closing

Market days are worth noting. They are often in covered market halls, selling mainly local vegetables and produce, clothes and domestic stuff. They are often very colourful and full of country folk. See also Chapter 5 for details of all the brilliant farmers' markets around the county.

Ambleside – Wednesday
Appleby – Friday
Barrow-in-Furness – Monday, Wednesday, Friday and Saturday
Broughton-in-Furness – Tuesday
Carlisle – Monday to Saturday
Egremont – Friday
Kendal – Wednesday and Saturday
Keswick – Saturday
Kirkby Lonsdale – Thursday
Kirkby Stephen – Monday
Maryport – Friday
Milnthorpe – Friday
Penrith – Tuesday and Saturday

Sedbergh – Wednesday

Shap – Monday

Silloth – Thursday and Sunday

Ulverston – Thursday and Saturday

Whitehaven – Thursday and Saturday

Wigton – Tuesday

Workington – Wednesday and Saturday

Unlike London and most southern towns, some Lake District shopkeepers still often have one half day off every week when they close at lunchtime. There is no geographical consistency, though the favourite half day tends to be Thursdays. It doesn't mean that every shop in that town or village will be closed, and many of the big ones and chain stores stay open. But you have been warned.

Buying a house in the Lake District

For the last 200 years millions of people who have visited the Lakes have come away with the same fantasy: of finding a nice little cottage and settling down here for good. It's not easy. Wordsworth had a hell of a problem doing so. He never owned his own house – both Dove Cottage and Rydal Mount were rented – and it took him years of begging letters to influential friends to get himself a nice local job as Distributor of Stamps for Westmorland. With property prices what they are, it's harder to achieve now than ever, but it can be done.

One of the best ways of getting a foothold in Cumbria is to look around the fringes of the county. Or, if you have a good idea, plus a bit of talent and energy, you could even start your own business in Lakeland. The founders of Sharrow Bay started from scratch, and the Mountain Goat tour company was begun by an off-comer. It is very often the outsiders who bring new life and new vitality, but there are problems peculiar to the Lake District, due to the fact that it's a National Park. Your chances of being allowed to open a hamburger joint on the top of Skiddaw are a bit slim, for instance.

Where to settle?

As a general rule, the southern half of the Lakes is more expensive than the north, thanks to the better road and rail links. Folks from Liverpool and Manchester tend to settle round the southern Lakes, while people from Newcastle aim for the northern bits. Grasmere, despite the crowds, is still considered a very desirable place to live, especially near the lake. Ambleside and Coniston are also expensive. Windermere and Bowness are equally expensive, but thought a bit flash. Borrowdale is smart, but Keswick is bourgeois. Furness has some discriminating fans, while the Caldbeck fells are an acquired taste.

Just outside the National Park boundaries there are smart fringes and not so smart fringes. No one wants to live amid the industrial deadliness of west Cumbria, unless they have no alternative, so avoid Workington, Cleator Moor, Frizington and Distington. Barrow has few fans outside Barrow. Whitehaven is on the way up. Nicest of all along the western fringe is to look for somewhere near Cockermouth. The eastern side of the Lakes is where the landed gentry seem to have ended up – the Lowthers and other landed nobs are near

Penrith, and some of the biggest and nicest houses of all are in the Eden Valley.

House hunting and prices

Local papers are the best starting point when house hunting. The *Westmorland Gazette* is best for the south and central Lakes, while the *Cumberland News* or *Keswick Reminder* cover the north. The *Cumberland and Westmorland Herald* is best for the east. Most local papers offer subscriptions by post, which is the best way of staying in touch with the market from outside. See Chapter 1 for website details.

Now we come to the tough bit. It's tough to generalise about prices, and even tougher when you realise just how much you will have to spend to get that really desirable cottage – the one everyone wants, with the cosy porch, the nice view of the lake and the pretty fell behind. But from the bottom of the price range upwards, this is what you might expect to pay:

- An undesirable terrace house in a place like Workington or the slummier parts of Carlisle: £50,000
- A remote cottage, in rotten condition, near the Scottish border or on the Pennines: £100,000
- A better situated but unconverted cottage, on the pleasant fringes of the National Park, such as around Cockermouth, Penrith, Kendal or Furness: £140,000
- A small terraced house in one of the National Park towns, like Windermere: £180,000
- An unconverted cottage on the fringes, like Caldbeck: £210,000
- A village house with no views: £250,000
- Your dream cottage in a desirable situation and fully modernised: from £450,000
- A big detached house with lake frontage: not much change from £1 million.

Time sharing

This is the system whereby you acquire a share in a property for up to 80 years ahead, buying only the week or weeks of the year in which you take your holiday. For those weeks the place is yours to do with as you like – you can rent it, lend it to friends, holiday in it yourself or even swap it with other timeshare places elsewhere in Britain or abroad. The advantage is that for the rest of the year you have no worries about the property or its maintenance. And the standard of these places can be very high indeed, with facilities like swimming pools and bars on site. The disadvantages are that you can use the place only for the week or weeks you have bought, unless you do a swap, and that it never quite feels yours. There can also be quite hefty maintenance expenses, which can go up all the time. Prices vary according to which part of the year you prefer – they're higher in the summer and at Christmas and lower at the start of the year. School holidays are always expensive, and October can offer good value.

Timeshare developments in the Lake District have mostly been well received, with none of the bad publicity or dodgy selling methods of the Mediterranean. Here are some we think are among the best.

The Lakeland Village
Newby Bridge
Tel. 015395 31144 or visit *www.lakeland-village.co.uk*

A prestigious development on the banks of the River Leven in what used to be a textile mill. The timeshare accommodation consists of traditionally built Lakeland stone cottages, all finished to a very high standard. Pride and joy of the development is the leisure centre (called Cascades – they all have to have twee names), with swimming pool, jacuzzi, squash court, gym and health spa.

The Langdale Estate
Great Langdale
Tel. 015394 38016 or visit *www.langdale.co.uk*

The first of the Lake District's timeshare establishments, opened in 1982, and it remains the most successful. Built on the old Langdale gunpowder works, it now offers a range of accommodation on a landscaped estate. There are loads of facilities – health spa, leisure club, restaurant – and even a pub, Wainwrights' Inn.

Underscar
Near Keswick
Tel. 017687 75577 or visit *www.underscar.com*

A brilliant setting under Skiddaw and overlooking Derwent-water. It's a very high-class development of 25 homes with spa and restaurant set in 40 acres (16 ha).

Windermere Marina Village
Bowness
Tel. 015394 46551 or visit *www.wmv.co.uk*

Built on a privately owned marina and all frightfully nautical. The purpose-built cottages are neat and homely, and if you own a boat you can moor it alongside for the duration of your stay. In the evening you can sit on your balcony and watch the sun go down over a forest of masts. Could be deafening if they don't all tie their halyards down. The Spinnaker Club has a pool, spas, sauna, gym and bar.

Lake District Trivia

*Statistics, surveys, fascinating facts
and a Lakeland quiz*

Statistics and surveys

Tourist numbers

About 27 per cent of Cumbria's tourism revenue is generated
in July and August, and about 56 per cent of the year's total
is generated within the National Park.

> Annual number of visitors to Cumbria: 15.2 million
> Days spent by visitors: 27.5 million
> Average length of stay by non-day-trippers: 6.1 days
> Money spent by visitors: £1,074 million
> Number of overseas visitors: 210,000
> Jobs supported by tourism: 36,674

The most popular country for overseas visitors is Australia – it
must be all the backpackers. They're followed by Americans,
Germans, Canadians and Japanese.

Why people visit the National Park

The reasons, given in percentages, cited by people for a visit
in a LDNPA survey (they could cite more than one).

> Scenery/landscape: 62
> Enjoyed a previous visit: 34
> Peace and quiet: 26
> Outdoor activity: 22
> Come every year: 19
> Easy to get to: 17
> Specific attraction or event: 16
> Never been before: 14
> Own accommodation: 10

When people come to the Lakes

August is still the most popular time for a Lakeland holiday, but these days people come all year round. Cumbria Tourism conducts a survey of room and self-catering occupancy from month to month; here are its 2006 findings.

	Percentage of serviced rooms occupied	Percentage of self-catering units occupied
January	33	27
February	45	38
March	44	36
April	58	63
May	59	58
June	63	66
July	68	75
August	71	90
September	69	74
October	63	65
November	45	35
December	41	40

Where people go

This breakdown of where tourist days' are spent shows that the south Lakes gets more than a third of the visits. Allerdale gets one in five, largely because its patch includes Keswick. But the spread of tourists over the six district councils within Cumbria is fairly even. Even Barrow gets one in 12 visitors. The figures are percentages.

South Lakes: 35.8
Allerdale: 19.3
Eden: 14.6
Carlisle: 11.7
Copeland: 10.2
Barrow: 8.4

Accommodation

There are more than 100,000 beds to sleep in across Cumbria, about half of them within the National Park. Nearly 2,000 different places offer rooms for the night. The number of beds in the different sectors is as follows.

Serviced (hotels, B&Bs, guesthouses, etc.): 30,682
Non-serviced (houses, cottages, flats, chalets, etc.): 27,824
Camping and caravanning (beds or tent pitches): 43,956
Alternative (camping barns, youth hostels, etc.): 4,516

Population

The Lake District National Park is the permanent home of 41,831 people, and its population has increased by barely a thousand in the last 50 years. The county of Cumbria houses 498,900 people. Of this lot, only 17 per cent are aged under 14, and 25 per cent are aged over 60. So we're all getting older, and the number of elderly people in the Lakes is steadily rising. Will the Lake District become a museum – the people and not just the exhibits?

Most popular tourist attractions

This list is compiled by Cumbria Tourism. Some figures are estimates, and some places aren't included because they have no way of collecting data. But it's an interesting list nonetheless. Figures are for 2006.

1. Windermere Lake Cruises: 1,267,066
2. Rheged: 463,708
3. Tullie House Museum and Art Gallery, Carlisle: 270,766
4. Grizedale Forest Park: 250,000
5. Ullswater Steamers: 187,656
6. Whinlatter Forest Park: 180,985
7. Carlisle Castle: 149,762
8. Ravenglass and Eskdale Railway: 118,517
9. Lake District Visitor Centre, Brockhole: 91,715
10. Cumberland Pencil Museum, Keswick: 83,400
11. Muncaster Castle: 82,639
12. The Dock Museum, Barrow: 79,415
13. The Homes of Football, Ambleside: 68,000
14. Dove Cottage, Grasmere: 66,094
15. Sizergh Castle and Garden, Kendal: 65,062
16. Hill Top, Sawrey: 64,584
17. The Teapottery, Allerdale: 62,854
18. Northern Lights Gallery, Keswick: 60,000
19. Wetheriggs County Pottery, Penrith: 50,000
20. Lake District Coast Aquarium, Maryport: 47,464

Things people have asked

Here are some of the questions that have been put to the various Tourist Information Centres in the Lake District. Now that you know so much about Lakeland, you will, of course, be able to laugh along at their daftness.

Can you direct me to the Beatrix Potteries?

How do you fill up the lakes?

What time do the Windermere boats leave for the Isle of Man?

When is high tide on the lakes?

Can we visit the glass factory at Ravenglass?

Where's the Rhinocerous Pass?

Which mine does all the mint cake come from?

Have you got this week's Dorothy's Journals?

Where are the mountain goats?

Where are the kilt factories?

Where can I see dryrot fencing?

Where can I swim with the dolphins?

Does it ever stop raining? (OK. This one's not so daft.)

15 things you didn't know about Kendal mint cake

1. Kendal mint cake was created in 1869 in a confectionary shop and factory on Stricklandgate in Kendal.
2. One theory is that it was all a mistake. A recipe for glacier mint sweets went wrong, a pan boiled over, the contents spilt on the floor and quickly hardened, someone tasted it and thought, hmm, yummy.
3. A rival theory says the recipe was nicked from an old woman living nearby who made her own sweets.
4. The basic ingredients are sugar, glucose and water (sometimes milk too), boiled in a copper pan. Then peppermint oil is added. The secret is knowing the precise moment to pour it out – at the 'soft ball' stage.
5. The first expedition to carry Kendal mint cake as emergency supplies was the British Imperial Transantarctic Expedition of 1914, commanded by Sir Ernest Shackleton.
6. Almost every Everest expedition has carried Kendal mint cake since 1922, when it was packed in an airtight case weighing 40 lb (18 kg), the maximum a Tibetan porter was allowed to carry up the mountain.
7. After Sir Edmund Hillary and Sherpa Tenzing nibbled mint cake on top of Everest in 1953, Tenzing left some as a gift to his gods. They must have had a sweet tooth.
8. Other expeditions jolly thankful for Kendal mint cake include the *Daily Mail*'s Abominable Snowman expedition of 1952; the Scottish Tierra del Fuego expedition of 1977; most of Chris Bonnington's climbs; plus round-the-world yacht racers.
9. Chocolate-coated mint cake was introduced in the 1970s, increasing sales but appalling mint cake purists.
10. There are three main makers of Kendal mint cake:

Romney's Kendal Mint Cake was carried to the summit of MOUNT EVEREST on 29th May, 1953.
"We set on the snow and looked at the country far below us . . . . we nibbled Kendal Mint Cake."
A member of the successful Everest Expedition wrote—"It was really the most popular item
on our high altitude ration—our only criticism was that we did not have enough of it."

Wilson's, founded in 1913; George Romney's, founded in 1937 and now owner of Wiper's; and Quiggin's, which claims to have been making it since 1880 and is therefore the home of the stuff.

11. George Romney's premises are on the Mintsfeet Trading Estate in Kendal. But there's no connection: the name comes from the River Mint, a tributary of the River Kent, which flows through Kendal.

12. Own-label mint cake is booming. Firms order it specially with their name on – from the Ministry of Defence for ration packs to the folks at Balmoral for their after-dinner mints.

13. Kendal mint cake provides around 380 calories per 3½ oz (100 g). That makes it a better energy boost than any fancy isotonic energy drink. And it makes it very bad for your teeth.

14. When Kendal mint cake was exported to America in the 1950s, the customs people ruled that it wasn't a cake because it didn't have eggs and flour in it. The cargo had to be sunk in the Atlantic.

15. Over 400 tons of Kendal mint cake are produced every year – roughly 4 million bars.

Ten films or TV series set or filmed in the Lakes

1. *Miss Potter* – the life of Beatrix Potter. Hollywood meets the Lake District.

2. *Pandaemonium* – Wordsworth and Coleridge on the big screen.

3. *Withnail and I* – the classic Lakeland film: two London actors come up on holiday 'by mistake'.

4. *Tomorrow La Scala!* – the comedy about a prison opera company was shot at HMP Haverigg near Millom.

5. *The French Lieutenant's Woman* – the final scenes were shot around Windermere.

6. *The Lakes* – the controversial BBC series was shot around Ullswater. It upset lots of locals.

7. *Jane Eyre* – the 1990s TV version was filmed around Dalemain.

8. *Wives and Daughters* – the BBC adaptation of Mrs Gaskell's novel was filmed in and around Levens Hall.

9. *Swallows and Amazons* – shot on Coniston Water.

10. *Brief Encounter* – one of the most famous film scenes was shot at Carnforth station. OK, it's actually in Lancashire, but only just.

Some Lakeland rock climbs

Rock climbing as a sport was invented in the Lake District in the 1880s. Yet another world first. It started around Wasdale, which is still its unofficial HQ. In the early days, when a new climb was made, the climber had the privilege of giving it a name. In the early days, the names were rather boring, like 'North Climb on Pillar Rock'. But after the First

World War something strange happened, and the names of new climbs became weird and rather wonderful.

Sodom and Gomorrah
On Pillar Rock. This was named by C.F. Holland in 1919. On his first ascent he got in a rage when his plimsolls collapsed, his pipe fell down a crag and a small lump of rock hit him in the face.

Joas
On Gimmer Crag. Named by Graham MacPhee in 1928; it stands for 'Just One Awful Sweat'.

Kipling Groove
On Gimmer Crag. Named in 1948 by Arthur Dolphin, who thought it was 'ruddy 'ard'. Geddit?

Cleopatra
On Buckstone Howe. It was named by Bill Peascod, as were Jezebel on Miner's Crag and Delilah on High Crag, between

1949 and 1951. He liked to name his routes after notorious ladies from the past.

Eve
On Shepherd's Crag. Also named by Bill Peascod, in 1951. Eve was the bar maid at the Scafell Hotel climbers' bar. Peascod and his friends got free drinks that evening.

Rigor Mortis
On Castle Rock. It was named by Paul Ross in 1959 'because we thought it rather a stiff problem'.

Incantations
On Great Gable. Like Coroner's Crack and Dead on Arrival, both on Eagle Crag, this was named by Pete Whillance in the 1980s. He just happens to have a morbid taste in names.

Cumbrian names

So you think you might have local connections? If your surname is one of the following, you have Cumbrian or Border ancestors. So feel proud. On the other hand, they were probably Border Reivers, known for their stealing and looting.

Archibold – Armstrong – Beattie – Bell – Burn – Carleton – Carlisle – Carnaby – Carruthers – Chamberlain – Charleton – Charlton – Collingwood – Crisp – Croser – Crozier – Cuthbert – Dacre – Davison – Dixon – Dodd – Douglas – Dunne – Elliot – Fenwick – Foster – Graham – Gray – Hall – Hedley – Henderson – Heron – Hetherington – Hodgson – Hume – Hunter – Huntley – Irvine – Irving – Jameson – Johnstone – Kerr – Laidlaw – Little – Lowther – Maxwell – Milburn – Musgrave – Nixon – Noble – Ogle – Oliver – Potts – Pringle – Radcliffe – Reade – Ridley – Robson – Routledge – Rutherford – Salkeld – Scott – Selby – Shaftoe – Simpson – Tailor – Tait – Taylor – Thompson – Torey – Trotter – Turnbull – Wake – Watson – Wilson – Woodrington – Yarrow – Young.

If you want to do some more work on your family tree, tracking down Cumbrian ancestors by searching through parish records, documents and maps, there are four record offices in Cumbria you can visit. They claim to have 10 miles' (16 km) worth of records. You'll need a County Archive Research Network card, available free from any office in return for proof of identity. Researchers are available to help with your hunt. Open weekdays office hours – though Barrow is also open every third Saturday of the month and Whitehaven every other Saturday morning.

Duke Street, **Barrow** (tel. 01229 894363)
The Castle, **Carlisle** (tel. 01228 607285)
County Offices, **Kendal** (tel. 015397 73540)
Scotch Street, **Whitehaven** (tel. 01946 852920)

Ten fascinating facts

In other words, stuff we haven't been able to work into the book elsewhere.

1. The Lake District has Britain's best view. An ITV series in 2007 asked various celebrities to pick their favourite view before the public voted for the winner. Top of the list was Wastwater. Can't argue with that.

2. Lakeland's biggest tree is thought to be a silver fir near Aira Force around Ullswater. It rises to 164 feet (50 m). It's been there for some time of course; you don't get to that height overnight. There are some big ones round Thirlmere too.

3. The oldest trees in Cumbria are all yew trees – and there are three over 2,000 years old. One is at the 12th-century Martindale Church above Howtown, which, of course, it predates. Another is at Seathwaite in Borrowdale. The most spectacular – and easiest to find, as well as being handy for a drink afterwards – is in the grounds of Armathwaite Hall Hotel near Bassenthwaite Lake. This ancient yew is surrounded by a hedge, which on closer inspection is revealed to be part of the tree itself. Low-lying baby shoots have been trimmed over the centuries to create a hedge that now protects its parent. Lakeland's most famous yew tree – immortalised by Wordsworth as the 'Pride of Lorton Vale' in his poem 'The Yew Trees' – is in the village of High Lorton, near the Yew Tree Village Hall. It's thought to be 1,200 years old.

4. Talking of oldies, Wordsworth always boasted that he had climbed Helvellyn at the age of 70. In July 1999 William Barnes of Brampton, a retired police officer, climbed Great Gable on the day before his 90th birthday.

5. At the other end of the scale, the youngest person to climb all 214 of the fells logged by Wainwright in his *Pictorial Guides to the Lakeland Fells* is Kerry Regan of Caldbeck, who was just seven years and nine months when she bounded up her last one, Scafell Pike, in 2007. Her family obviously likes walking, as her sister Ellen had done the lot by the time she was nine years and ten months. And the girls have a brother, Robin, who was four in 2007 and will doubtless break the record before too long.

6. A first edition of Beatrix Potter's *Peter Rabbit*, the one she privately published in 1901 after it had been turned down by several publishers, was sold at Sotheby's for £55,000. The Armitt Collection in Ambleside has its own copy, but you have to ask nicely and put on white gloves to see it. Prices of the books have partly been

pushed up by collectors in Japan, where they can't get enough of Beatrix Potter, and Japanese visitors flock to Hill Top in their thousands each year. In 2006 a replica of Hill Top was built at Daito Bunka University in Tokyo at a cost of £1 million. Unlike the Sawrey version, it is earthquake proof.

7. The second best drive in England is along the A592 on the shores of Ullswater, according to a recent poll of drivers. The best is somewhere in Cornwall. But then again, another drivers' survey a few years back picked the A686, starting in Penrith and passing through the Eden Valley and the market town of Alston on its way out of Cumbria.

8. Cumbria Tourism has set up a Lake District Escape Line, on which you can listen to some distinctive local sounds to stop you from pining for the Lakes if you're stuck in an office or a traffic jam somewhere. So what seven sounds did they choose? The sound of lake water lapping against a jetty; the crash of Aira Force waterfall; winds on the top of Scafell Pike; birdsong in a valley; the crunch of autumn leaves on a walk; a recital of Wordsworth's daffodils poem; and a Cumberland sausage sizzling in a pan. You can call the line on 0870 224 2856.

9. Jenkyn's Crag by Windermere is the best place to propose marriage in the Lake District. That's according to another not-very-scientific poll by Cumbria Tourism. The next best places are Aira Force and Catbells. Don't forget the ring if you're going up a mountain though. Or you could try Ennerdale Water, where former American president Bill Clinton first proposed to Hillary. She said no.

10. Mountain rescue teams in the Lake District recorded 5,754 incidents between 1991 and 2006. That's about one a day. More than half of them were caused by a slip or fall, but there have been 237 cases of people getting cragfast (stuck on a rock with no way of getting off) and nine avalanche incidents. Team members spent 24,335 man hours on duty in 2006 alone – all of them given for free. So do as Wainwright says, and watch where you put those feet.

A Lakeland quiz

Finally, 20 questions to test your knowledge of the Lakes. If you didn't know the answers before you bought this book, you should do now. Answers are at the back of the book. Except this *is* the back, so they're just below. No cheating.

1. Name the four mountains over 3,000 feet high.

2. Which is the longest lake?
3. And the deepest?
4. How was Mrs William Heelis better known?
5. On which fell are Wainwright's ashes scattered?
6. Which national organisation did Canon Rawnsley help to found?
7. Who is Ulverston's most famous son?
8. What was the connection between Robert Southey and Samuel Taylor Coleridge?
9. Striding Edge is on which mountain?
10. How many people live permanently in the National Park?
11. Who lived at Brantwood?
12. What's the most popular tourist attraction in the Lakes?
13. What's the biggest waterfall?
14. What's a charr?
15. What are Wiper, Quiggin, Romney and Wilson famous for?
16. Which annual Cumbrian show chooses the world's best gurner?
17. What food did Sarah Nelson invent?
18. Where was William Wordsworth born?
19. What's Lakeland's highest pub?
20. Which popular children's TV series was inspired by the Longsleddale Valley?

The answers
Remember, no cheating.

1. Scafell Pike, Scafell, Helvellyn and Skiddaw. 2. Windermere. 3. Wastwater. 4. Beatrix Potter. 5. Haystacks. 6. The National Trust. 7. Stan Laurel. 8. They were brothers-in-law. 9. Helvellyn. 10. 42,000 (you can have from 38,000 to 46,000). 11. John Ruskin. 12. Windermere Lake Cruises. 13. Scale Force. 14. A species of fish unique to the Lakes. 15. Making Kendal mint cake. 16. Egremont Crab Fair. 17. Grasmere gingerbread. 18. Cockermouth. 19. The Kirkstone Pass Inn. 20. Postman Pat.

How did you do?

16–20 Excellent. You're either a local or you've read this book thoroughly. Or you looked at the answers.
11–15 Not bad. You know your Lakeland.
6–10 Could do better. Come here on holiday more often.
0–5 You haven't been paying attention. Go back to the start and read this book again.

Index